PENGUI
THE BU

Frank McDonald is Environment Editor of the *Irish Times* and author of books including *The Destruction of Dublin* and *The Construction of Dublin*.

Kathy Sheridan is an award-winning *Irish Times* staff journalist and feature writer.

The Builders

*How a Small Group of Property
Developers Fuelled the Building Boom
and Transformed Ireland*

FRANK McDONALD AND
KATHY SHERIDAN

PENGUIN BOOKS

*In memory of Uinseann Mac Eoin,
architect, conservationist and
fearless chronicler of events*

PENGUIN BOOKS

Published by the Penguin Group
Penguin Books Ltd, 80 Strand, London WC2R 0RL, England
Penguin Group (USA) Inc., 375 Hudson Street, New York, New York 10014, USA
Penguin Group (Canada), 90 Eglinton Avenue East, Suite 700, Toronto, Ontario, Canada M4P 2Y3
(a division of Pearson Penguin Canada Inc.)
Penguin Ireland, 25 St Stephen's Green, Dublin 2, Ireland (a division of Penguin Books Ltd)
Penguin Group (Australia), 250 Camberwell Road, Camberwell, Victoria 3124, Australia
(a division of Pearson Australia Group Pty Ltd)
Penguin Books India Pvt Ltd, 11 Community Centre, Panchsheel Park,
New Delhi – 110 017, India
Penguin Group (NZ), 67 Apollo Drive, Rosedale, North Shore 0632, New Zealand
(a division of Pearson New Zealand Ltd)
Penguin Books (South Africa) (Pty) Ltd, 24 Sturdee Avenue,
Rosebank, Johannesburg 2196, South Africa

Penguin Books Ltd, Registered Offices: 80 Strand, London WC2R 0RL, England

www.penguin.com

First published by Penguin Ireland 2008
Published with a new Preface in Penguin Books 2009

2

Copyright © Frank McDonald and Kathy Sheridan, 2008, 2009
All rights reserved

The moral right of the authors has been asserted

Typeset by Rowland Phototypesetting Ltd, Bury St Edmunds, Suffolk
Printed in England by Clays Ltd, St Ives plc

Except in the United States of America, this book is sold subject
to the condition that it shall not, by way of trade or otherwise, be lent,
re-sold, hired out, or otherwise circulated without the publisher's
prior consent in any form of binding or cover other than that in
which it is published and without a similar condition including this
condition being imposed on the subsequent purchaser

ISBN: 978-0-141-03780-6

www.greenpenguin.co.uk

Mixed Sources
Product group from well-managed
forests and other controlled sources
www.fsc.org Cert no. SA-COC-1592
© 1996 Forest Stewardship Council

Penguin Books is committed to a sustainable future
for our business, our readers and our planet.
The book in your hands is made from paper
certified by the Forest Stewardship Council.

Contents

Preface to the paperback edition

Shortly before 9.30 p.m. on Friday, 20 February 2009, amid a catastrophic banking crisis that threatened the state's survival, the colossal scale of the Irish political and financial establishments' thirteen-year fling with builders and property developers was finally laid bare. The staggering fact that fifteen customers owed over €500 million each to Anglo Irish Bank jumped out of a PricewaterhouseCoopers report commissioned by the Department of Finance to assess the bank's viability. Almost all of the fifteen were believed to be builders and/or developers.

The first edition of this book went to press late in the summer of 2008 – just before the collapse on 15 September of the giant Wall Street investment bank Lehman Brothers, with debts of more than $600 billion. The Lehman bankruptcy destroyed whatever confidence remained in the capital markets and, by extension, finally smashed the Irish establishment's veneer of complacency, if not its hubris. Two weeks later, as deposits fled Ireland at a rate of billions a week and nervous depositors threatened a run on the banks, Irish bank shares lost a third of their value. Months later, it would emerge that Anglo Irish had lost €5 billion in deposits in a matter of days leading up to 29 September. At a meeting with Minister for Finance Brian Lenihan, the heads of the Bank of Ireland and AIB made it clear that the system's survival depended on a bail-out by the taxpayer. The bankers got off lightly. They left with their jobs and self-esteem intact along with a virtually unconditional two-year guarantee on deposits and bonds for all six Irish banks, which was intended to calm depositors and the stock market.

A few days later, in a bravura performance on RTÉ radio, Seán FitzPatrick, the chairman (and former CEO) of Anglo Irish, revealed a remarkable confidence that the government would act in Anglo's interest. While his bank's fate was being decided at an all-night cabinet meeting, he said, he had gone to bed and slept soundly till morning. He declined to apologize for the catastrophic consequences of the Irish banks' lending practices: 'The cause of our problem was global, so I can't say sorry with any type of confidence, sincerity and decency. But I do say a very genuine "thank you" because that is right.' Had his bank been reckless? 'No, we haven't. We cover all our loans in a belt-and-braces way.'

That tape would be replayed repeatedly in months to come, as revelations came tumbling out of Anglo Irish, each more devastating to the country's international standing than the last. Among them were the Anglo Irish loans to FitzPatrick himself of up to €129 million over eight years and concealed from the end-of-year audit by a temporary placing ('bed and breakfast') in Irish Nationwide. The discovery of this arrangement led to the resignation of FitzPatrick and of Anglo CEO David Drumm.

Soon thereafter we learned some of the details of the unravelling of billionaire Sean Quinn's 25 per cent stake in the bank, as part of which ten wealthy Anglo customers – including, inevitably, some well-known property developers – were bankrolled by Anglo to the tune of €451 million to prop up the bank's share price, leaving an estimated €300 million loss to be met by the taxpayer. We learned, too, about the series of transactions by which Irish Life & Permanent facilitated transfers of €7 billion into and out of Anglo's accounts to flatter the bank's balance sheet.

Despite its renegade behaviour and extremely narrow shareholder and customer base, and despite the ailing economy and public finances, Anglo Irish Bank got a government bail-out to the tune of €1.5 billion in December 2008. Less than a month later, the bail-out having failed to repair its reputation or its balance sheet, the bank was fully nationalized. Soon after, the government also sank €7 billion into AIB and Bank of Ireland. At the time of writing we still had no notion of the full extent of the toxic property debt steaming under these institutions. Nobody knew; not even the banks themselves.

Morgan Kelly, professor of economics at UCD, tried to calculate the likely damage: 'If we suppose that most of the €20 billion lent to builders will not reappear this side of Judgment Day, along with 20 per cent of the €90 billion lent to developers, and 10 per cent of the €120 billion in mortgages, then we are already up to €50 billion. These are only guesses. However, the continuing stream of revelations from Anglo Irish – which bear out the old investment dictum that there is never just one cockroach in a kitchen – suggest that they could be optimistic guesses.' In which case, he concluded, 'we are sunk'.

Although the country's eyes have been trained on the banking sector, the underlying fault in the banks' business model goes back to property: huge loans for residential and commercial developments that were evidently based on the belief that the unprecedently rapid and sustained growth in property values would continue indefinitely. According to the Pricewaterhouse-Coopers report, by late November 2008 a number of large bank customers with interests in shopping centres and land banks in the Dublin area were experiencing cashflow difficulties. The 'large overhang of unsold higher density residential developments in the Dublin area, accounting for a number of years' supply', was also noted, as well as the unsurprising fact that developers were effectively mothballing development sites and landbanks. It would be difficult, said the accountants delicately, to allow interest to roll up on loans where the loan-to-value ratios were so high. In other words, bankers and developers deep in denial would have to be confronted and the painful issue of massive write-offs finally admitted and addressed. The taxpayer, naturally, would absorb the pain.

When the first edition of this book went to press, many of the developers we profiled were struggling with the effects of the bursting property bubble. Since then, for most if not all of them, things have got worse.

One developer who invested heavily at the peak of the boom told us that he has no cash reserves, and is now merely an employee of the bank to which he owes hundreds of millions of euro. 'It was like a ten-year dream,' he said. 'Now it's like a tsunami that just keeps coming.' It suited the bank to put him on the payroll as a kind of project manager of his unfinished sites and landbanks. The upside of this arrangement, for him, is that it allows him to stave off receivership and the threat of personal guarantees being called in. His 'salary', he stressed, is not free money; it is being added to his debt, although in the absence of a sudden, miraculous economic recovery, this is obviously just another banker's illusion. In the meantime, his sumptuous suburban home has gone on the market and the rarely used Mediterranean holiday villa has become the family's principal residence. His attitude is one of wry resignation to his fate: he gambled and lost.

Seán Dunne's scheme for a 37-storey, Dubai-style tower on his 'prime' seven-acre Ballsbridge site, a distillation of Celtic Tiger hubris, was rejected by An Bord Pleanála in January 2009. Although the board – which, according to the *Sunday Times*, voted no by a margin of nine to one – roundly condemned the plan as a 'gross overdevelopment and over-intensification of the site', Dunne chose to blame the decision on 'a snobbish element' in Ballsbridge and the labyrinthine machinations of the planning process. The scheme's opponents demanded an official inquiry into why he had been granted permission by city planners in the first place, for a project that (as we describe in Chapter 8) wildly contravened Dublin City Council's own development plan. According to one leading property expert, the seven-acre site bought by Dunne for a total of €379 million at the height of the boom is probably worth around €100 million now. He predicts that the two hotels on the site, once written off as little more than useless, will be the most valuable part of the asset. After the scheme's rejection Dunne assured Newstalk radio that 'Seán Dunne, as an individual, is 100 per cent solvent'; he couldn't, however, vouch for the solvency of his company.

Ray Grehan, who purchased the former Veterinary College next door to Dunne's Ballsbridge site for a price that trumped even Dunne's €57 million per acre, endured a similar nightmare in progressing his plans for another high-rise cluster; in December 2008, he got permission from the city council to use the €171.5 million site for car parking. Bernard McNamara, who held a 41 per cent stake in the Becbay consortium that bought the Irish Glass Bottle site in 2007 for over €400 million, also saw a catastrophic fall in its value. And Garrett Kelleher, progenitor of the 150-storey Chicago Spire, admitted that construction had stopped for lack of finance in February 2009. The *Architectural Record* was now dubbing it the 'Lien-ing Tower of Chicago', because 'while construction has stopped, the liens keep coming' – including one for $11.3 million in unpaid fees from its illustrious designer, Santiago Calatrava. 'If I'd known in July of 2006 that the world would be where it is today I would have done things differently,' said Kelleher, who had lobbed $140 million of his own money into the pot.

As for Liam Carroll, the king of shoebox apartments profiled in Chapter 3, the auditors of Zelderbridge, his holding company, issued an 'emphasis of matter' on its 2007 accounts stating that the ability of the company to continue as a going concern 'was dependent on the continued support from group companies and their bankers'. In February 2009, Danninger, another of his companies, was hit with five High Court actions, including one from Marks & Spencer and estate agents Savills. Carroll had earlier lost his planning approval for an €83 million office development on North Wall Quay – the putative future headquarters for Anglo Irish Bank – as a result of High Court action taken by Seán Dunne. Sean Mulryan's Ballymore, which (as we describe in Chapter 9) has enormous projects under development in London's Docklands, has had to lay off staff and directors. And the Treasury Holdings duo, Richard Barrett and Johnny Ronan, whom we profile in Chapter 7, had to face the grim task of writing down the value of some of their investments – notably Battersea Power Station in London, acquired so expensively at the height of the boom. Their prospects in China are no longer looking so rosy, either.

But at least the high-fliers were being nursed by their bankers. Also entangled in the unravelling chaos were countless smaller players, buy-to-let 'landlords' who had been lured into the buying frenzy on the delusory premise that valuations would keep on rising and the migrant workers would keep pouring in. Some of these were greedy speculators; others were ordinary young construction workers encouraged by their builder bosses to buy off the plans at 'discount', and even prudent older people taught to trust in the enduring strength of bricks and mortar over equities for their pensions.

Far from rising, the number of migrants fell precipitously, with an estimated 100,000 leaving the country in 2008. The number of Polish workers registering to work in Ireland fell by 53 per cent in the second half of the year and, by December, the number of unemployed non-Irish nationals had more than trebled, from 8,000 to 25,000 in just 12 months. As the Construction Industry Federation predicted a fall in building employment by almost 150,000 from the 2007 peak of 282,000, reports emerged of 'No Irish' signs appearing on building sites in Poland – the result, apparently, of mistreatment of Polish workers on Irish sites. SIPTU official Michael Kilcoyne told the *Irish Times* he believed that Ireland's international reputation as a fair employer had been 'sullied' by the negative experiences of migrants who had come here in search of work.

Still working their way through the system are the trophy-home mortgages taken out by high-flying solicitors, bankers, architects and stockbrokers in their thirties and forties – young professionals suddenly without jobs or prospects. A survey commissioned by the Royal Institute of the Architects of Ireland in January 2009 predicted that 41 per cent of architects would lose their jobs within a couple of months. Many had already been laid off by firms both large and small, but now there was nowhere to go; with economies teetering all over the globe the traditional vent of emigration was no longer an option.

Some 750 solicitors joined the dole queues in December. The value of homes sold at auction in 2008 fell to just 9 per cent of their 2006 peak and the easy, lucrative conveyancing work involved in shifting thousands of identical new houses on large estates had virtually ceased. The Law Society placed advertisements for a career development advisor to help solicitors find careers outside of law. Meanwhile, a quarter of estate agents countrywide had been made redundant by Christmas 2008 with plenty more expected in 2009.

As the dust began to settle on anything between 35,000 and 100,000 unsold or empty homes around the country, Morgan Kelly, whose predictions had thus far been worryingly accurate, estimated that house prices would fall by 80 per cent from peak to trough in real terms. However, it's anyone's guess. Nobody trusts official figures any more.

In November 2008 the Irish Tourist Industry Confederation told an Oireachtas committee that as many as 20,000 of the country's 50,000 hotel beds were now vacant at any one time. This was the consequence of the combination of lax lending practices and state tax breaks for hotels – 'You could nearly build them for free with capital allowances and all that', in the words of one developer – and now the chickens had come home to roost. Because the same phenomena created an explosion in the construction of holiday homes, two thirds of all new homes in the country's most scenic areas are empty for much of the year, according to a study carried out by Donncha Ó hEallaithe of the Galway-Mayo Institute of Technology. Throughout the state, local authorities were facing the fiscal nightmare of housing estates abandoned by broke developers, and the costly task of completing roads, lighting and basic amenities. A 'wholly insufficient' bond system introduced to discourage rogue developers from leaving estates incomplete was to blame, said Labour TD Ciarán Lynch. Even in Dublin, it was estimated that developers owed the city council €142 million in unpaid development levies – mainly because they had abandoned building schemes after first phases failed to sell.

Meanwhile, unemployment rushed towards 10 per cent and the only new jobs being created in Ireland's vaunted 'knowledge economy' seemed to be in fast-food operations. While exchequer returns showed that all tax revenue was down, property-related taxes such as capital gains and stamp duty showed the most dramatic falls, with both down 72 per cent on the previous January. As the government took belated action to fill the gaping deficit, proposing such measures as a pension levy on public-sector workers and a reduction in resources for children with special needs, people took to the streets, mainly to protest that those who had caused the pain were escaping the consequences.

The recrimination game had begun in earnest. In a piece in the *Irish Times* property supplement in February, Isabel Morton – somewhat tongue in cheek – predicted a giddy rush towards the courts, beginning with the fact that hundreds of shareholders were planning to sue certain banks, primarily Anglo Irish. Then, she said, borrowers could sue the banks for lending them more than the recommended guidelines. Property developers, startlingly, could also sue, on the grounds that the banks behaved negligently by breaching the guidelines of sensible lending practices. The banks would then sue the Financial Regulator for failing to regulate. The Financial Regulator could sue the government for failing to ensure that the former were actually regulating. And the government would increase taxes to cover the costs.

In February 2009 the master of the High Court, Edmund Honohan, predicted an 'avalanche' of repossession cases, and warned lenders that their 'behaviour' was a 'relevant factor' that could determine the outcome of a case. Directly beneath that report in the *Irish Times* was another involving contempt of court proceedings over the sale of a family home, where a dogged High Court judge, Mr Justice Richard Johnson, was once again noting that one year on he had still not been given details of bonuses paid to the bank and building society officials who had sanctioned multi-million-euro loans to disgraced solicitors Thomas Byrne and Michael Lynn. An entire era of madness was distilled in a single case on the previous day, when the Circuit Court heard that a Dublin father of three on an Air Corps pilot's salary of around €53,000 a year had managed to build up a twelve-house property portfolio (four of them jointly with Michael Lynn), with loans of €8 million from nine separate financial institutions.

Who could or should have reined them in? The Financial Regulator appears to have been asleep at the wheel and the government that employed him had no wish to puncture the property bubble. Only a small number of courageous economists raised warning flags against a bullying, short-termist establishment. The Economic and Social Research Institute had long been warning that the government's housing policy was highly dangerous and urged that it raise taxes as a brake on demand. But it was addressing itself to a government whose revenues had come to depend disastrously on property froth, in a state where 'light-touch' regulation reigned, proudly headed by Bertie Ahern who – in the words of a major property figure – 'sat at the back of the boat, told the lads to put the spinnaker up and said "Let her off". Then just before the wind changed, he scrambled off the boat.'

Now the boat is in extraordinarily choppy waters – a period of double-digit unemployment, steep tax hikes and savage spending cuts that seems likely to last a long time. Whether one should blame the big developers who spent money foolishly, or the banks that lent them the money, or the government that spurred the process on during the boom and is now spending billions bailing out the banks, is a moot point. What is not debatable is that the story of the men who populate the pages of this book is the story of Ireland's economic boom and of the unfolding economic disaster.

1. Boom

Just as there was no sex in Ireland before television, as the late Oliver J. Flanagan TD once memorably claimed, there weren't any property developers here until the 1960s – at least, not in the modern sense. Before that, there were excellent builders such as Crampton and Strain, whose names are still invoked when the quality houses they built come up for sale, as well as many, many indifferent ones. But there was nobody involved in assembling sites for office developments, arranging loan finance from the banks, overseeing construction and selling on completed schemes as long-term investments for insurance companies or pension funds. Starting in the 1960s, this activity was honed into a fine art; it reached its zenith during the Celtic Tiger boom, when developers made vast profits and increasingly seemed to hold the fate of the national economy in their hands.

You might think that such a sophisticated business would be dominated by urbane Dublin gents, but the truth is that they are few and far between. A disproportionate number of the most successful developers, armed only with national school education and a trade, emerged from the boreens of rural Ireland, often from a large family eking out a living on a farm, where, as one puts it, 'they had to bate the rats out of the barn'. Industry insiders cite the Cosgrave brothers and one half of the old Dwyer Nolan partnership as among the rare Dublin successes. 'They're rare because the Dublin man was cushioned by his mammy,' says a developer, only half jokingly. 'In the country, it was a case of survival. You had to go to ugly places like the bog, snag turnips, tramp hay, spread manure. Fellas who got out of the west always found things easier after that.' Another source says: 'Their ethos is still work, work, work. They've never known anything else.'

'Very few would be rounded personalities, almost by

definition,' says a leading surveyor. 'Getting to the top requires single-minded obsessive behaviour. They wouldn't read a lot. They would be very one-dimensional. Once someone has a certain level of cash in the bank, people assume that he is filled with shards of wisdom, but you wouldn't want to be stuck on a long-haul flight with most of those guys; all the talk is of horses, Mercs, golf and the chopper. People who don't have much money, when they imagine what they would do if they suddenly made a lot, tend to think in terms of freedom – these guys think of money as a score. As a rational human being, when you've broken your back to make a pile of money, do you then go "Bang, I'll hump the lot back on the table"? But that's what they do. Repeatedly. At one level, you have to admire it. But it's compulsive behaviour.'

Most of the top builders are obsessed with privacy. At a lavish charity lunch in a five-star hotel, one wealthy developer explained courteously that his media aversion was about keeping his young children 'ordinary'. 'I don't want them to know what they're worth. I don't want them reading about their money in the papers and I don't want their schoolfriends reading about it either.' But in a functioning democracy, are such people entitled to demand and receive that level of privacy? They have changed the face of Ireland. They deal in the most basic social need – housing – and therefore have a fundamental and continuing power over people's lives – power obtained, to a large degree, with the assistance of the state. Of course, they are less likely to speak gratefully of tax breaks and generously interpreted planning laws than they are to complain about regulations and planning delays.

'Everyone blames the builders for the cost of housing today,' says Ray Grehan of Glenkerrin Homes. 'But housing is a commodity like an Intel chip. If it's scarce, the price goes up. The people I blame are the Department of the Environment and the county managers. The problem was all about not having serviced, zoned land. The only way you'll ever control prices is by having plenty of supply. Yes, landowners got greedy, like everyone else. But had there been enough of zoned land, they wouldn't have got those prices.' Grehan sees 'a lack of trust towards successful people, and it's certainly very much alive in government departments and among civil servants. I won't say that every planning department sees the developer as Public Enemy Number One, but a councillor said recently that on a scale of 1 to 10, Mary Murphy's kitchen is number 1 [in importance] and the developer is number 10. And where you have that attitude, it's very hard to see how things will change.'

Some people think it's easy to be a developer. You buy a site, hire architects to design a scheme for it, secure financing from a bank or banks, get planning permission in the bag and then go ahead with construction. But it isn't so simple, much of the time. There are huge risk factors relating to the money at stake, site conditions, public opposition and the state of the market. 'It's not for the faint-hearted,' one experienced adviser says. 'The planning process is more fraught and high-risk than ever because of Nimby-ism and local councillors who only have their eyes on the next election. It's a high-risk, high-reward business. If it was low-risk, everyone would be doing it.' Property developers were never popular, and even now, in terms of social appreciation, they're right down there with estate agents, lawyers and recruitment consultants. They're perceived as predatory, profit-driven, ruthless and prepared to walk over anyone, or anything, that gets in their way. This perception is coloured by the unscrupulous actions of a few in bribing councillors to rezone land that was never intended for development – with results that we are still living with today. But mostly it's prompted by fear of change being wrought by unseen forces with seemingly unlimited resources. While the 16-storey Alto Vetro apartment block was under construction on the edge of Grand Canal Dock in 2007, a Dublin taxi driver, passing over Ringsend Road bridge, pointed to its towering concrete core. 'D'ye see that? There was only a two-storey house there before,' he exclaimed. 'It just goes to show that in this town they'd build on your big toe if you let them.' Indeed, Alto Vetro's plot ratio (total floorspace divided by site area) was seventeen to one – a record for Dublin – because part of the tower was permitted to encroach on the 'campshire' of the quayside.

What drives them? In some cases, it's pure, unadulterated greed. 'Sometimes it's ego,' one developer admits. 'People do build trophy buildings, going round saying, "I own such-and-such," but it's not so much about individual buildings, more often it's about what you intend to do with a site – the kind of mix you might get, and what value it'll have.' Few are consciously building monuments to themselves. Most developers recognize that buildings are ephemeral: what counts in the end is the value of real estate, and during the dizziest period of the property boom sites were often worth a lot more than the buildings that stood on them. Several Dublin office blocks built in the 1980s have been demolished to make way for newer ones. The better developers have begun to commission top designers and even high-flying 'starchitects' like Norman Foster, Daniel Libeskind and Zaha Hadid to dazzle the planners with their 'signature buildings'. These architects don't come cheap, and neither do the planning consultants whose advice to developers can often prove crucial. In December 2001, even planners were gobsmacked when Bernard McHugh netted €7 million after selling his firm, McHugh Consultants, to Europe's largest environmental consultancy, RPS; the firm had deftly handled such high-profile planning battles as the Spire in O'Connell Street, Luas and the GAA's spectacular redevelopment of Croke Park.

Some of the big builders, such as Sutton-based Gerry Gannon, have become major wholesalers of land, while dabbling in development. These men built up huge 'land banks', buying quite cheaply in the late 1980s and early 1990s and then salivating over the soaring values during the boom that followed – and all because successive governments had failed to implement the 1974 Kenny Report on building land, which recommended that all land designated for urban development should be compulsorily acquired by the local authorities at its existing use value, plus a premium of 25 per cent. As a direct result of this failure, huge profits went into the pockets of everyone who owned land or speculatively acquired it, and the inflated cost was passed on to homebuyers; in Dublin, the site value of most new homes built during the boom amounted to more than half of their purchase price. Between 2000 and 2006, the price of land grew three times faster than the price of houses. Yet in 2006 alone, it was estimated that developers saved €250 million in stamp duty through a loophole in the tax laws – and a promise by Brian Cowen, as Minister for Finance, to close this escape route was never enacted. Developers have also benefited from the cut in the capital gains tax rate from 40 per cent to 20 per cent, which was enacted by Charlie McCreevy as Minister for Finance in 1997.

Tax incentives targeted at the property sector have been behind much of the development frenzy of recent years, and often remain in effect long after they have served their initial stimulatory purpose. The biggest boondoggle of all was Section 23, a tax break first introduced in the 1981 Finance Act with the purpose of reviving the construction industry. Initially the measure could be applied to any qualifying residential property; from 1992 it was applicable only in areas designated for urban renewal under the regime established by the 1986 Urban Renewal Act. Section 23 allowed investors to write off all but the site costs of an apartment or town house against their total rental income in the first year, including rents from other properties owned, with any unused tax relief being carried forward indefinitely. After a slow start, Section 23 eventually became one of the main drivers of development, with investors often snapping up the lion's share of new housing schemes. And, as if this wasn't enough to keep the developers happy, further tax breaks were made available over the years for multi-storey car parks, holiday homes in jaded seaside resorts, hotels anywhere and everywhere, and student accommodation. In most cases, these incentives meant that the capital cost of qualifying new developments could be written off against an investor's tax liability over a 10-year period. What's more, anyone leasing office or retail space in a designated area got tax allowances equivalent to double their annual rent bill *and* didn't have to pay a penny in commercial rates for 10 years.

The incentives – some of which were eliminated or amended following publication of the Bacon Report on residential housing in 1998, and others subsequently by Brian Cowen, who took a more jaundiced view of them than McCreevy – had nothing to do with aiding the frequently invoked 'first-time buyer'. 'The government was quite disingenuous, harping on about the first-time buyer,' says an insider, 'when it was simply aiding and abetting what the builders were doing. Because the legislation they brought in was pitched at the new homes market, it allowed all of that building to go on unchecked.' By making it cheaper to operate as a landlord, the tax incentives actually hurt prospective first-time owner-occupiers by attracting investors into the market; developers could charge a premium of up to €100,000 on apartments in Dublin city centre, for example, compared to similar units that didn't have tax-relief designation.

Although the age of corrupt rezoning seems largely to have given way to the age of the tax incentive during the 1980s and 90s, there may still be cause for concern about how land is rezoned. Green Party TD Ciarán Cuffe estimates that at least 100 of the 800-plus councillors countrywide work as estate agents or auctioneers, 'who one day are rezoning land in one part of the town and the next are selling land'. The advent of pre-planning-application consultations between developers and county planners works against the interests of local residents, Cuffe says. 'It means the door is open to the developers and, often, everything is signed off before the locals even know about it . . . When there are difficulties, they find out how to overcome them. Many developers use the services of private planning consultancies. The attitude is: "Do it – and I don't want no for an answer."'

It's the fact that the developers are now working in a vastly more sophisticated arena involving state-of-the-art technology, demographics data, planning and PR consultants, while sometimes pretending to be 'the fool in the corner in the builder's hat', that makes them so compelling, says one observer. 'A lot have this shambolic country way about them. Put them into a boardroom and they look like muckers, but they'd annihilate you.'

The toughness of some of today's top developers was forged in less favourable times. One developer estimates that 'in the late

1970s and early 1980s, 70 per cent of builders in Ireland went bust. You couldn't sell a house on the northside [of Dublin] in 1985. Builders weren't planting lawns or putting the final top on roads and they got the name of sharks and stroke merchants. A lot of them folded up and went to the UK in 1984–85.' Lenders disdained the land banks offered by builders to settle debts. Some developers had to put their homes on the line, or sell them, to keep going; others returned to their trade on London building sites. Within a decade or so, the same disdained land banks had become gold dust, and those who held them were on the pig's back.

The economic basics of the building boom were pretty simple. Increasing national prosperity and a growing population (fuelled by rising birth rates and positive net immigration) boosted the demand for residential property and office space. During the same period, the supply of credit grew vastly, as Colm Keena has charted in the *Irish Times*: 'In 1996, loans worth £1.3 billion were approved for the purchase of new homes or apartments. By 2000 the equivalent figure was £2.9 billion, by 2004 it was €9.7 billion, and by 2006 it was €13.9 billion.' Interest rates dropped dramatically: against a base value of 100 in 1991, the mortgage rate index fell to 57 by 1996 and to 39 by 2002. It was not until December 2005 that rates started to climb. Meanwhile, mortgage lenders had loosened their criteria, bringing ever more buyers into the marketplace. The result was that in the 10 years to 2007, the average price of a new home in Ireland rose by 153 per cent, while construction costs went up by only 41 per cent.

The boom was even more dramatic in the commercial and retail property sectors. According to the Investment Property Databank, a world-recognized authority on trends, between 1996 and 2006 the capital growth in the value of office investments in Ireland was nearly 160 per cent, while the equivalent figure for retail was over 168 per cent. Tax breaks made the returns even more attractive, benefiting developers to the tune of €3 billion, at the expense of the Exchequer. These schemes also had 'strong negative income distributional effects', according to a Goodbody Report commissioned by the Department of Finance;

in other words, better-off people benefited disproportionately.

The extraordinary inflation of house prices, year after year, created a situation in which developers were not worried about making a profit – that was a given – but simply about how enormous the profit would be. 'Typically, the price of houses in a new development is decided at a meeting on Monday between the agents and the developer,' says one insider. 'There would be much chewing over it, seeing how other sites went, who was selling what for how much, maybe someone would mention that prices were rising at 2 per cent a month. Then they'd chew some more and just pull a figure out of the air. It's all done in such a slipshod way; it's about what they feel they can get away with. Later that week, the houses are duly advertised at that price, go on sale and sell well – and suddenly the builder is roaring at the agent, complaining that they were sold too cheap. What happens then is that you call the next bunch of exact same houses "Phase 2", and the price is hiked maybe 15 per cent. And that could all happen in a few days or in an afternoon. You could have five phases in a development. So you never knew if the prices reported were the prices people were getting the units at. An apartment advertised at €270,000 on a Thursday morning could be €295,000 in a so-called "Phase 2" that afternoon. After houses were advertised at a certain price, you'd have unfortunate buyers ringing up to say they couldn't find one at that price – a bit like Ryanair advertising cheap seats, except that you don't have to live in an airline seat. That was a big feature of the boom, those shifting sands. That's what the word "phase" allowed. Before the boom, it used to be Phase 1 this year and Phase 2 the next; now there was a day between them, if that.'

An agent spreads his hands helplessly: 'But that's the market . . . If it's evident after a few hours or days that buyers are willing to pay that much more for the house, well, do you let them take the profit out of it immediately? Do you [the developer] under-sell it so that someone else can then sell it on immediately for €40,000 more? Do you leave that?'

'That is their biggest nightmare, "leaving money behind" on a site,' says an industry source. 'Their greatest terror is being seen to "sell cheap". There's always that nagging fear. It's always about what you can fit into an estate. They'll say that they are slaves to the planners but when they sit down at the drawing board – apart from the planning process, which *has* given them headaches with the levies they have to pay, getting land serviced, etc. – do they ask themselves, "How would we want to live?"' The answer is obvious. 'You are dealing with a lot of very greedy people, who have made a lot of money. A few are leaving behind them developments that are very close to slums. What was odd in Ireland was that media coverage was confined to the property supplements. If that kind of profiteering was happening in England, it would have made page one in the *Telegraph*.'

Another cause of anxiety for developers is the difficulty posed by third-party objectors seeking substantial sums of money to withdraw appeals to An Bord Pleanála. This type of thing is not unusual, as many developers would testify; indeed, some of them have had to pay out substantial sums to individual objectors or residents' associations in order to eliminate a risk that the appeals board would overturn favourable planning decisions made by local authorities. In January 2001, for example, the Leopards-town Heights Residents' Association withdrew their appeal against Dún Laoghaire-Rathdown County Council's decision to grant permission for a major office development at Glencairn, the former British ambassador's residence – on foot of an agreement specifying that the developers 'shall pay . . . a financial contribution of £200,000 . . . in respect of the enhancement of the association's area' and meet its legal costs and expenses. In December 2004, 22 residents of Morehampton Terrace in Donnybrook shared a pre-Christmas bonanza of €1.1 million – an average of €50,000 apiece – after agreeing to withdraw an appeal against plans by developer Bryan Cullen for 182 apartments and 14 town houses on a site known as Avila, just to the north. A dozen other residents, who had not been so active in pursuing the appeal, received substantially lesser amounts, causing some friction on the road. As with similar arrangements involving third parties withdrawing appeals, the terms were confidential, but news of the deal was leaked to the *Irish Times*, which published a front-page story about it on Christmas Eve.

Soaring prices and cheap credit fuelled the practice of 'flipping' – buying a property and then selling it on almost immediately at a profit – whereby ordinary punters made large amounts of money at the height of the boom. This was sometimes facilitated by developers, who understood that, in a climate of easy credit, flipping could create a new class of property investor that would fuel the growth of the sector even further. For example, in one major development, two close friends of the developer bought a two-bedroom apartment off the plans for €190,000, with a deposit of €5,000. Eighteen months later, when the time came to close, the same apartments were selling for €290,000. 'I then allowed my friends to "assign" it, or sell it on,' says the developer. 'That meant that I got the €190,000 and they got the €100,000. Eighteen months later, in 2005, they used that €100,000 to buy ten units at an average of €270,000 in another development of mine. Fifteen months on from that, those apartments were "flipped" for an average of €340,000. So the initial €5,000 made them €600,000 to €700,000 in the end. They were able to benefit because they were there at the right time, in the right place, knowing the right person.'

Of course, the trick for the flippers was to avoid being stuck with 10 apartments, and no means of paying for them, at the beginning of a downturn. 'One guy is buying 65 units in one of my developments and for that he'll get a 10–15 per cent global discount, meaning he'll be getting €320,000 two-bed apartments for €290,000 each,' the developer said. 'He won't have to close for two years, so his thinking will be that we'll have a year of bad news [in the property market], the market will come back and he'll get between €330,000 and €340,000 for them at that stage. I'll allow him to sell those on before he closes so he'll have three to four months of a window through my agent. If things go well for him, he could make €40,000 to €50,000 a unit, multiplied by 65. If things go badly, he's running the risk of having to take a mortgage out for €15–16 million worth of units. That's the game.' For the developer, the flippers' faith or dumb optimism in the market was crucial. 'For every deposit I got on a contract, the bank would give me the €100,000 to help to make the profit. That's because once you have contracts signed and buyers locked in, the banks know their money is safe.' Someone, of course, pays the price in the end. 'Those €340,000 apartments . . . You'd be lucky to get €290,000 for them now.'

Another developer, desperate to keep a substantial scheme on track, says: 'You have to keep selling . . . I'm giving a bit of value with retail units but making them buy 10. And they are not allowed to sell them on. I'll fit them out and manage them for them. They would be midterm 10-year investors. Retail with rent reviews gives good appreciation. You need to keep reinventing and finding investors. Every developer in town is after them. One investor with a chain of fast-food places and massive cash flow is buying 3 restaurants and 15 residential units.' However, there is a downside: 'It's a lot of work to get investors on board; they're all looking at different tax angles, all have different agendas. They won't go to developers with no name or reputation who've never had to deal with them before. Developers who are waiting for first-time buyers to come to them are going to start hurting because the banks will start calling in interest.'

We know that a number of developers have become extremely wealthy as a result of the sustained boom, but it is difficult to know how wealthy, as Colm Keena has explained:

Limited liability companies are obliged to lodge annual accounts with the Companies Registration Office and some details as to the developers' wealth can be gleaned from these. However, even with audited accounts it is difficult, if not impossible, to establish how much a developer is making. A developer, for instance, can purchase land in his own name, and sell it to his company as it is required, so the true amount of wealth accruing to the developer is not visible from the CRO records. Also, as the years passed, many of the developers amassed significant assets held outside their company structures. In more recent years, as their fame and wealth have grown, many developers have switched their companies to unlimited status. This status means the liabilities of the companies, should they ever get into difficulty, are not limited to the assets of the companies, but can extend to the assets of the owners. Unlimited companies do not have to file accounts with the CRO, and this increased privacy is undoubtedly attractive. Hugely rich people have normal privacy concerns but also have security issues to worry about. Extremely wealthy parents have legitimate concerns regarding how publicity about their wealth affects their children. Wealthy people also fear that publicity about their wealth can have political repercussions, from abusive comment to calls for special taxes. Some worry about what to do with all the money they have accumulated. A few developers are said to be giving large amounts of money in discreet philanthropic donations. The use of unlimited status could also be used to obscure this.

It's nearly always the case that property development is financed by debt rather than equity; very few developers would dream of placing their own nest eggs at risk. And the banks who put up the money behave just like the market itself – 'they over-lend when it's up and close when it's down', as one leading developer says. Seán Dunne has spent a total of about €730 million on the purchase of four properties in Ballsbridge – the Jurys and Berkeley Court hotel sites, Hume House next door and the original AIB Bankcentre, including its landscaped forecourt. The then record prices he agreed to pay in 2005 were gambles, in the classic sense, with no guarantee that he would win. Dunne must have formed the impression that Dublin City Council's planners would go along with the high-rise, high-density scheme he has in mind for the combined hotel sites. But the high prices paid for land in the area by Dunne, soon trumped by Bernard McNamara, Ray Grehan of Glenkerrin Homes and others, assumed a massive increase in density – so it came as something of a shock when city councillors voted down a local area plan that was intended to usher in a high-rise era. Now, all they could do was try their luck with planning applications and see if these would 'fly'.

Although many of the top developers are on friendly terms with each other, they are fiercely competitive – particularly when properties come up for sale by tender. There is a pecking order. A developer can build thousands of homes, but will win acceptance among his peers only when he goes commercial – building office blocks or shopping centres. 'It's about status,' says one. 'Having a varied portfolio also helps to spread the overheads and you get more respect from the banks.' After years of producing high-quality housing schemes such as Mount St Anne's in Milltown, Michael Cotter's Park Developments diversified into commercial property with Fashion City in Ballymount, a retail warehousing park beside the M50 in Carrickmines – sold for €100 million early in 2006 – and a shopping centre in Leopardstown. Castlethorn Construction, run by Joe O'Reilly, also established a first-class reputation for its housing before O'Reilly turned his attention to major commercial schemes such as Dundrum shopping centre, a new retail development on the former Eircom site in South King Street and the mid-2005 purchase (for €125 million) of 50 per cent of the ILAC centre, which runs between Henry Street and Parnell Street. In 2006, Castlethorn bought the Pavilions shopping centre in Swords for a whopping €575 million, with plans to extend it over the site of Ray Burke's house, Briargate. Even more ambitious is O'Reilly's retail-based scheme for the Carlton site in O'Connell Street, which will include two new streets linking it with Moore Street and Henry Street. And cash-rich Liam Carroll, who has built more apartments in Dublin than any other developer – his best-known vehicle, Zoe Developments, became synonymous with shoebox flats – has hit the headlines in recent years as a fearsome corporate raider, building up major stakes in companies such as Greencore and Irish Continental Group.

As political lobbyist Frank Dunlop declared after losing a crucial rezoning vote many years ago, what you need in the property business are 'a spine of steel and balls of iron'. By definition, if you're to be a tycoon, you also need to be driven. 'You can't have "work/life balance". There's a price to be paid and these guys pay it,' says one who knows them well. It's a world of meetings and conference calls, of walking sites and taking flights to discover new opportunities – in your own helicopter, if you have one. There were only 34 helicopters registered in Ireland in 1995, but by June 2007 the number had risen to 146, and many of them are in the hands of developers such as Seán Mulryan. To the insiders, they're known as 'blades'. Lombard, the Royal Bank of Scotland subsidiary that specializes in asset finance, reported a significant surge in the number of Irish people investing in aircraft between 2005 and mid-2007. The *Sunday Business Post* quoted Alan Greene, head of Lombard's aviation division, as saying that most of the 38 aircraft it financed in that period were helicopters bought by property developers. 'Time is money to these guys. They want to be able to travel to different sites as quickly as possible . . . Helicopters start at €180,000 for a two-seater and work their way right up to $10 million. More people are starting to go for high-end models now.'

Sometimes a helicopter isn't quite up to the job. Among the private planes lined up around Dublin and Weston airports – like 'naked willies', in the words of one property guru – is Séamus Ross's Hawker 800 jet, Jim Mansfield's Citation V11, Donal Caulfield's Citation V11 and Niall Mellon's Cessna Citation 550. 'A plane could cost you a million a year sitting on the tarmac,' says a source, 'so you have to use them, and use them for business. You would only buy a jet if you were doing a lot of work abroad. It's a business expense and, if your developments are profitable, it pays for itself.' The convenience and social cachet of a private jet are available at a fraction of the cost from Netjets, which can supply a seven-seater at a few hours' notice. One option is to buy a piece of a plane, called 'fractional ownership', typically for around 50 hours a year at around €4,000 an hour. An even cheaper way is to load up a prepaid debit card to buy chunks of time in 25-hour increments. Seán Dunne is among those believed to use Netjets. Seán Mulryan, who runs Ballymore Properties, often flies to London in his executive chopper to inspect progress on his developments, including the Pan Peninsula towers now under construction near Canary Wharf, or to clinch deals to buy yet more land to add to his huge portfolio; his own private jet is based in London.

For some of these alpha males, among the most desired 'mine is bigger than yours' playthings is a box in the redeveloped Lansdowne Road rugby stadium. Although the asking price for a 24-seater for five years was €475,000 – because there were 'only' 20 of them, said a source close to the action – the competition was fierce. 'The price made no sense but I'm told that no one even asked the price anyway. It's a prestige thing to have.' Seán Dunne, Derek Quinlan and Johnny Ronan were among the winners from the property world, with a few left bristling in the wings. Others, such as Séamus Ross, were prepared to settle for 10-year pairs of tickets, selling for a not inconsiderable €30,000, but still with a waiting list of well over 600.

Trophy houses, naturally, also feature prominently in the successful developer's toy box. Some, like Seán Mulryan, have spent millions restoring beautiful old houses to live in; others have contributed conspicuously to the craze for new-build mini-palazzos. Bernard McNamara set this trend in leafy Dublin 4 when he demolished the old Japanese Embassy to make way for a 15,000-square-feet-plus edifice on Ailesbury Road, complete with swimming pool and private dance hall. Shrewsbury Road, reckoned to be the most expensive road in the country, is home to Seán Dunne and Paddy Kelly. A glimpse into this lifestyle was revealed when Derek Quinlan of Quinlan Private applied for planning permission for a palatial new home on the Irish Monopoly board's equivalent of London's Mayfair. It entailed the demolition of two large semi-detached period properties for which Quinlan paid €25 million in 2006, and, at a size of 1,881 square metres (21,323 square feet) – with seven enormous en suite bedrooms, indoor swimming pool, a gym, massage room and two wine cellars, laid out over four floors – it was destined to be the largest new home in the capital.

It has been estimated by the Bank of Ireland that there are now more than 30,000 Irish euro millionaires, compared to no more than a few hundred 20 years ago, and that at least 300 of them – including many in the property development sector – are worth over €30 million. One (male) observer blames 'the wife with time on her hands' for the most obvious excesses: 'Wheeling out Weddings by Franc, going for the Louis Vuitton handbag, insisting on a "celebrity" rugby player for a scion's 21st, or flying in €150,000 worth of flowers for a teenager's birthday.' But it's not just the wives: builders were prominent among the private jet owners arguing over access to the 66 available slots from Dublin Airport to Roissy-Charles de Gaulle for the France–Ireland rugby match in 2007. One developer notes the 'older guys never knew anything else but work, and they'll never stop no matter how much they make . . . the next generation is going to have the fun.' Heirs taking the reins will be closely watched. They have an intriguing act to follow. Among their fathers, adjectives such as generous, loyal, ruthless, obnoxious, low-key and flamboyant can all feature in one description. But, like any good entrepreneurs, what they all have in common is the ability to sniff out value and churn it into cash, while slashing costs.

Some developers have made so much money during the boom years that they barely know what to do with it all. Ireland is simply too small to absorb billions of euro in private funds, and they've had to find new outlets for investment, often overseas – in Britain, the US, central Europe, Scandinavia, Russia and China, to name some of the places where they've popped up. In general, however, property developers are reluctant to break new ground. 'Nobody wants to be the pioneer in the West who gets shot by the Indians. They want to be second – that's the pole position,' one leading architect observed. 'This is fed by risk-averse consultants, the oracles who've been wrong for so long, but it keeps the banks happy.'

On Planet Developer, extravagant behaviour can be as remarkable for its absence as its presence. Seán Mulryan had Debbie Harry in to sing at his 50th birthday and Bono to stay at the old thatched homestead in the west, but Liam Carroll has lived in the same modest semi for the past 20 years. Many hold tight to their county roots and support the GAA team or local choir; most are philanthropic by inclination, some openly, others discreetly. But even the more visible ones are known for quiet good deeds that might, for instance, involve the loan of a top hotel for a charity function. Among this new Irish aristocracy, where even the most modest of builders has accumulated considerable wealth, some are deeply concerned about the effect on the next generation. A few say, privately, that they plan to give much of it away; one plans to channel a vast chunk of his wealth towards environmental charities but would be horrified if this became public knowledge.

For others, philanthropy and keeping a low profile are not part of the deal. 'You do hear a lot of stuff about developers and drink and it all going badly wrong when they come into a lot of money. There is certainly something different about our lot; they get the oul' horse and go on "the lash" and that seems to be the height of their social ambition,' one source says. 'In other northern European countries, when they make money, they start putting it into art, music, politics, philanthropy. In North America, they would be setting up art galleries and museums and trying to achieve immortality in one way or another.'

A much-anticipated night out on the builders' calendar was Seán Dunne's annual Christmas party, for which the Unicorn restaurant off Merrion Row was taken over and generous hospitality dispensed. Regular guests such as Irish Nationwide boss Michael Fingleton and high-profile solicitor Ivor Fitzpatrick would no doubt feel confident about their status in the eyes of the host. Others, however, rediscover the niggling apprehension that once accompanied an invitation to a slightly unnerving children's party. The problem is the seating arrangements. 'That's how you find out whether you're in or out of favour,' says one. 'One year you might find your place-name tantalizingly close to the host's table, the next you could find yourself in "Siberia".' Some admit to tanking themselves up in Doheny & Nesbitt's, like nervous schoolboys, in preparation for the testosterone-charged, laddish repartee over dinner, or some manly rugby chat with Father Leonard Moloney, headmaster of Clongowes Wood College, all mercifully uninterrupted by silly female chatter: Planet Developer is an almost exclusively male preserve, and only a handful of women are invited along.

December was also the time for the Builders' Ball in the Burlington, an old-fashioned dinner dance, with the crates of drink stashed under the table and a phalanx of estate agents forming a protective shield around their garrulous, red-faced builder clients. 'Then the big guys got so big they wouldn't go,' says one mournfully. In a regrettable sign of the times, the Builders' Ball has been rebranded as the rather more sophisticated Irish Homebuilders' Ball.

One occasion recalled with particular fondness is the Sherry FitzGerald blowout in May 2006, when the estate agent flew 200 builders and agents to London for the Chelsea Flower Show. Obviously, for Sherry Fitz and group chairman Mark FitzGerald ('My fascination with property began as a 10-year-old'), corporate confidence was in the stratosphere. The company had booked out the five-star Kempinski Hotel in Great Marlborough Street, formerly England's second-oldest magistrates' court, now a gleaming edifice that 'oozes flamboyant sophistication' according to its own publicity, complete with two glass-floored 'treatment rooms', one suspended over the large swimming pool. The lavish lunch in Chelsea came studded with added attractions such as a talk from the celebrity gardener Diarmuid Gavin. After lunch, all of the liggers were ferried back to the Kempinski for what one guest recalls as 'the most hilarious and wildest party in property history'. Parties in five different locations around the hotel, fuelled with unlimited champagne, full open bar and chocolate fountain, helped to maintain the feeling that, as the guest put it, 'They're gonna queue for ever.' At 5.30 a.m., 'destroyed by drink', the revellers finally retired.

Even the legendary Fianna Fáil fundraising tent at the Galway

Races had pretensions beyond its station. A 2005 report by mutinous FF activists in the Galway West constituency expressed concern about a 'sense of elitism' being created by the tent at Ballybrit and advised the boys back at party HQ to find ways 'to make it more open and inclusive'. Bertie Ahern made it clear that the party depended on Galway race week as one of five key annual fund-raising events. With tables of 10 costing €4,000 in 2006, the tent cleared around €250,000 for the week. Among those spotted under the chandeliers that year were Bovale's Mick Bailey (fresh from his €22 million tax settlement), Séamus Ross, Bernard McNamara (who was a Fianna Fáil councillor before he became a property mogul), Seán Dunne, Seán Mulryan and Johnny Ronan.

The annual gathering, organized by Fianna Fáil fund-raiser Des Richardson, came to symbolize 'a peculiarly Irish ethos of power-mongering', wrote Justine McCarthy in *Village* magazine. Over time it became a PR fiasco for host and guests. In his inimitable way, Socialist Party leader Joe Higgins wondered if government tax breaks managed to trickle down to those 'multimillionaires who jet and helicopter their way from tax exile to tug the Taoiseach's sleeve, when, like an Arabian prince, he sets up his tent at the Galway Races each year'. But during the Ahern era Fianna Fáil was quite unable to run the party without it, apparently, and for the property boys, a dose of derision plus a rehash of their little tribunal/tax/property difficulties by the silly-season media was probably fair exchange for befriending a government minister to the point of playing golf with him or maybe getting his mobile phone number.

The tent, and all it stood for, could not be sustained. Just two weeks after Bertie Ahern stepped down as Taoiseach, his successor Brian Cowen confirmed that this scandalous shindig had finally come to an end. Officially, it was being 'suspended' pending the outcome of a 'strategic review' of the Fianna Fáil organization, including how funds were to be raised. In that context, the tent had 'served its purpose'. The move was widely welcomed. European Commissioner and former Minister for

2. The Bad Old Days

The building boom that got under way in the 1990s was unprecedented in its scope, but it was not the first time Irish developers had gone on a spree that altered the look and feel of the country. Dublin, in particular, was transformed by development in the 1960s and 1970s, rip-roaring decades for the destruction of the city's Georgian fabric. On 31 December 1959, the *Irish Times'* anonymous architecture correspondent wrote: 'It is well known that, as far as the central city is concerned, the days of Dublin's Georgian heritage are numbered.' That correspondent was Paddy Delaney, an architect, town planner and partner in Delaney McVeigh and Pike Architects; and he did not write in sorrow. 'When these decayed and obsolete monuments of a past age come to be demolished, many of their sites will be redeveloped with buildings much larger in bulk and greater in height than the present ones.' The city, in other words, was to be transformed, its drab streets and squares, the products of a bygone age of horse-drawn carriages, made bright and sparkling by a new generation of architects and their property-developer clients.

The assault on Dublin's fabric was led not by rapacious property speculators but by the state and its agencies. The starting gun had been fired in 1957 by the Office of Public Works' demolition of two impressive mid-18th-century houses in Kildare Place, a stone's throw from Leinster House. According to Patrick Beegan, Parliamentary Secretary in charge of the OPW, the houses had 'reached the end of their useful life', with 'poor and rambling' accommodation that was 'quite unsuited to modern requirements'. Another government minister said: 'I was glad to see them go. They stood for everything I hate.' A reference, apparently, not to substandard housing but to the legacy of British rule. In the following year, a new Office Premises Act laid down minimum standards – covering toilets, washing facilities, lighting, heating and ventilation – for all office buildings employing more than five clerks.

This was the context in which the ESB sought to replace 16 late-18th-century houses on Lower Fitzwilliam Street – part of the longest Georgian streetscape in the world – with a modern office block. The architects, Sam Stephenson and Arthur Gibney, were still in their twenties when they won the ESB competition; both were Dubliners through and through, gregarious, likeable men about town. The more cerebral Gibney shunned the limelight while Stephenson revelled in controversy, making provocative statements about the future of Georgian Dublin even though the Old Dublin Society was chaired by his father.

Their ESB plan for Lower Fitzwilliam Street caused a public outcry that was led by the Irish Georgian Society, which had been formed in 1958 by Desmond and Mariga Guinness following the demolition at Kildare Place and Dublin Corporation's decision to pull down much of Dominick Street. Its first committee included Lord Talbot de Malahide, Lady Dunsany, Sir Alfred Beit, Sir George Mahon and Desmond FitzGerald, Knight of Glin. They were perceived as the remnants of the Ascendancy seeking to preserve an outmoded heritage, and they did not succeed in saving Lower Fitzwilliam Street, but the Georgian lobby had a number of successes, one of which was entirely unintentional: its campaigning to save the threatened 18th-century terraces in the city centre helped in no small way to spawn the mutant fake-Georgian semis in the suburbs.

One boon to the developers was the collapse in June 1963 of tenement buildings in Bolton Street and Fenian Street, with lives lost in both cases. These unfortunate events caused panic in Dublin Corporation. In the succeeding 12 months, its dangerous buildings section condemned 900 old houses, compared to an average of just 30 in previous years. By early 1965, some 2,000 houses had been condemned, and over 1,200 of these were actually demolished. 'Property owners were suddenly able to de-tenant premises which formerly they could not get tenants out of,' according to a lengthy exposé in *Build* magazine. 'Moreover, they could grab the property of others by a simple phone call to the corporation [saying] that they thought a wall or a chimney looked dangerous.'

The flight to the suburbs of Dublin's middle class since the mid-19th century had left the inner city as a preserve of the poor, who were more concerned about putting bread on the table than about the city's architectural heritage; thus there were few articulate indigenous defenders of the urban fabric. But office blocks didn't just deface the city; they also helped to kill it. Once-thriving streets, where people used to live above the shops, were ruthlessly denuded and the inhabitants forced to move to the suburbs or, worse still, to 'new towns' on the perimeter of the city. Major institutions moved out, notably UCD from Earlsfort Terrace to Belfield, St Vincent's Hospital from St Stephen's Green to Elm Park and RTÉ from the GPO in O'Connell Street to Donnybrook. Many schools were also lost to the suburbs, with St Andrew's College relocating to Booterstown, Wesley College to Ballinteer, the High School to Rathgar and Alexandra College to Milltown. In most cases, the property they left behind was snapped up by voracious speculators for new office developments.

Anyone with a stash of spare cash was putting it into property, and St Stephen's Green was the nexus of much of the development activity – and the movers and shakers behind it. Colm McDonnell, a medical consultant practising in Ely Place, got together with a London-based financial institution to buy five Georgian houses on the south side of the Green in 1963, demolishing the lot for an office block designed by Desmond FitzGerald, then professor of architecture at UCD. FitzGerald's speciality was seeking out sites with development potential, getting planning permission for office blocks that he designed, and then hawking these permissions to likely developers. (It was not until 1977 that the Supreme Court ruled that applicants must have a 'beneficial interest' in a property in order to make a valid planning application.) Though the professor was a noted collector of Georgian silver, it didn't seem to concern him that his schemes would bring about the loss of Georgian houses, including one on the Green with an elaborate stucco ceiling depicting the Four Seasons; it had to be salvaged by the OPW and is now in Dublin Castle. And while the five houses were being demolished for an office block pre-let to the Department of Justice, the developers were good enough to allow Fianna Fáil to put up a large 'Let Lemass Lead On' billboard on the site in time for the 1965 general election.

Right next door, three more Georgian houses were demolished by Bernard Fitzpatrick, a wholesale jeweller with a premises off Grafton Street, for another office block designed by Stephenson Gibney. In 1967, then Minister for Finance Charles J. Haughey performed the official opening of Citibank's new premises on the ground floor, declaring: 'I for one have never believed that all architectural taste and building excellence ceased automatically with the passing of the 18th century.' Two years later, he acquired Abbeville in Kinsealy, one of Dublin's finest 18th-century country houses, and its 250-acre estate for £204,000. Haughey had done very well as an accountant and partner with Harry Boland in Haughey Boland and Company, which represented many of the companies investing in the 'new Ireland' his father-in-law Seán Lemass was helping to create. Indeed, he did so well that the Haughey family was able to move in 1959 from a semi-detached house in Santry to Grangemore, a 19th-century mansion on 45 acres, north of Raheny, which was bought for just £13,000. Ten years later, with this land rezoned for suburban expansion, he sold it to the Gallagher Group for £260,000 and was easily able to purchase Abbeville with the proceeds. It was a controversial deal because Haughey had availed himself of a device he had personally introduced in the 1968 Finance Act, to avoid paying any tax on his windfall gain.

Matt Gallagher of the Gallagher Group, who hailed from Tubbercurry, Co. Sligo, was one of Haughey's cronies and had tipped him off to buy Grangemore in the first place. He was also, according to his son Patrick, one of a number of business figures who had agreed to provide funding to the then rising-star minister so that he could concentrate on his political career. They would frequent the bar in Groome's Hotel on Cavendish Row, opposite the Gate Theatre, where Haughey would often hold court. At the time, Matt Gallagher had become one of the largest builders in Dublin, with a rolling programme of up to 4,000 houses in planning or under construction. Like many others of his ilk, he had made a small fortune in the building trade in England after the Second World War, returning home to set up a factory in the local parish hall making doors and windows before diversifying into system-building and later conventional housing. He was also quite ruthless. On one occasion, another developer sought his advice about a problem he was having in Monte Carlo with sitting tenants on a site where he was planning to build a block of luxury flats. 'The thing to do,' Matt helpfully advised, 'is to get two bags full of starving rats and let them loose in the attic. Your problems will be gone inside a week.'

Gallagher was one of the key figures in Taca (literally 'support' in Irish), the Fianna Fáil fund-raising operation. Taca's secretary was Harry Boland and one of its most prominent supporters was Charlie Haughey. It was all about forging close links between the government party and the business community, relieving them of money in return for direct access to ministers. 'Fianna Fáil was good for builders and builders were good for Fianna Fáil, and there was nothing wrong with that,' according to Patrick Gallagher, who inherited his father's business in 1974 at the age of 22. As the *Sunday Tribune* noted in its obituary on the former Taoiseach, it was Haughey who had organized the first Taca dinner at the Gresham Hotel in 1965. Kevin Boland, who had just become Minister for Local Government, recalled that it was attended by the whole Cabinet, including traditionalists (such as Boland himself) who were very dubious about men in mohair suits. 'We were all organized by Haughey and sent to different tables around the room,' he said. 'The extraordinary thing about my table was that everybody at it was in some way or other connected with the construction industry.'

Haughey, of course, was one of the men who wore mohair

suits in the 1960s. Donough O'Malley, who went on to achieve immortality as the man who introduced free secondary education in 1966, was another. Before he became Minister for Education, he occupied the pivotal position of Parliamentary Secretary at the Department of Finance, in charge of the Office of Public Works, handling state contracts for the construction or leasing of office accommodation for a growing army of civil servants. For the developers, a 'pre-let' to the state removed much of the risk element in what they were doing by guaranteeing a stable supply of 'blue chip' tenants. O'Malley actually saw it as his role to encourage property development, because it meant instant jobs for construction workers and healthy profits for Fianna Fáil's core supporters.

When the Green Property Company sought to demolish several Georgian houses on both sides of the junction of St Stephen's Green and Hume Street in the late 1960s, to replace them with a pair of office blocks designed by Stephenson Gibney, Donough O'Malley backed its plans. In a deal arranged by Sam Stephenson, he gave an assurance that two houses owned by the state would be given up to facilitate the proposed development. John Corcoran, the debonair ex-bookie who ran Green Property, lost no time. Almost as soon as he had planning permission in the bag for the first phase of the scheme, with no appeal by An Taisce or anyone else, a crew began demolishing three of the target houses. *Build* magazine, then edited by the fiery Uinseann Mac Eoin, commented: 'When certain people are prepared to make a quarry out of the best parts of St Stephen's Green for a couple of greenbacks shared around their friends and are obviously able to get away with it, Foras Forbartha, the Arts Council, Bord Fáilte, An Taisce and all the rest of them might as well close their doors.' In a revealing interview with Mac Eoin, Stephenson said: 'A city must live. It must evolve and keep changing.'

But why start with the best parts of it? he was asked.

'Because developers are primarily interested in a return for their money,' the bold Sam replied.

'But this is chequebook planning!' Mac Eoin exclaimed.

'That is so, but it is inevitable in a democratic society,' Sam responded.

With the surviving Hume Street buildings proposed to be listed for preservation, Dublin Corporation refused permission for the second phase of Green Property's development – though this decision was controversially overturned by Kevin Boland on appeal. Conservationists occupied the threatened houses in protest. Boland denounced the lot of them in a famously venomous speech in the Dáil, fulminating against a 'consortium of belted earls and their ladies and left-wing intellectuals . . . a group of pampered students [who could] afford the time to stand and contemplate in ecstasy this eighth wonder of the world, the twin architectural masterpieces at the corner of Hume Street and St Stephen's Green.' The occupation went on for six months, with over 1,000 people attending a protest meeting at the Wolfe Tone statue and significant political support from Opposition politicians such as Garret FitzGerald and Declan Costello; in an ironic gesture, Charlie Haughey sent round a Christmas hamper. It came to a climax in June 1970, when Green Property hired a 50-strong goon squad, armed with pickaxe handles and a battering ram, to smash the hall door of 45 St Stephen's Green and evict the occupiers. After they were dragged down the stairs and kicked out of the door, one of them managed to find a working telephone kiosk to summon supporters and, within an hour, they had managed to regain possession of the house by sheer force of numbers.

It took a political cataclysm – the Arms Crisis – to bring about a resolution of the Hume Street conflict. George Colley had taken over from Haughey as Minister for Finance, and he was anxious to reach a compromise. After calling in all sides for talks, he announced that Green Property would seek planning permission for a revised scheme of office blocks with façades 'in a style that will maintain as far as possible the existing quality and character of the streetscape'. The era of Georgian pastiche had been well and truly inaugurated: the original houses were demolished and replaced with fakes. As one visiting English architecture critic remarked at the time: 'The only reason why Dublin remained for so long the beautiful 18th-century city the English built is that the Irish were too poor to pull it down. This, unfortunately, is no longer the case.' He was quite wrong about the provenance, of course – Georgian Dublin was built by the Irish, not the English – but bang on about the money.

Though Charlie Haughey was now in the political wilderness, close friends and associates did not desert him. Des Traynor was the first articled clerk to be taken on by Haughey Boland and Company; Haughey came to rely on his friend's acumen as an accountant and, more importantly, his discretion. Traynor became Haughey's bagman, a 'walking bank' for The Boss. As Colm Keena reported in the *Irish Times*, 'People would literally meet him in public places and hand him envelopes and briefcases stuffed with money and bank drafts. He then lodged these to his secret accounts.' Equally, when they wanted money, even substantial sums like £75,000 in Haughey's case, all they needed to do was to phone Traynor and he would arrange to have it sent round. Among those who had secret Ansbacher accounts in the Cayman Islands for many years – far removed from the Revenue's prying eyes – were John Byrne, Liam McGonagle, the estate agent John Finnegan, Arthur Gibney, Sam Stephenson, Charlie Haughey and his son-in-law John Mulhern, Cement Roadstone Holdings chief executive Jim Culliton (from whose headquarters Des Traynor was running his highly unorthodox 'bank' after he became CRH's chairman in 1986) and, of course, Traynor himself. By 2005, the Revenue had collected £53 million in back taxes, interest and penalties from those who used this scam to hide their money offshore. In December 2007, Traynor's estate made a tax settlement of just over €4 million.

Even in the 1960s, it was widely believed that Haughey was a 'sleeping partner' in John Byrne's burgeoning property business. Des Traynor was a director of Byrne's principal vehicles, Carlisle Trust and Dublin City Estates, as well as being deputy chairman of merchant bankers Guinness and Mahon – and it was he who arranged for the controlling interest in Byrne's empire to be transferred offshore to the Guinness and Mahon Cayman Trust, in the Cayman Islands. Byrne's lavishly appointed home in Ballsbridge – Simmonscourt Lodge, on four acres – where he and his wife Ciara, a one-time Rose of Tralee, have lived for many years, is reportedly full of photographs of Haughey, who was a regular visitor in the good old days.

Born on a small farm near Lixnaw, Co. Kerry, the eldest of 12 children, Byrne showed his early entrepreneurial flair by cutting turf during the Emergency and selling it house-to-house from a donkey cart. Like so many others who found their way into the property world, he went to London after the war was over, making his first fortune in the ballroom business. On returning to Ireland he built up a string of dance halls, and he was among the first to spot the significance of the 1958 Office Premises Act: as he correctly foresaw, it would create demand for functional, modern office space. In April 1959 he commissioned Desmond FitzGerald to design a 12-storey office block for the site of the Carlisle Building, overlooking O'Connell Bridge. A roof restaurant offering splendid views over O'Connell Street and the Liffey Quays closed down after just 18 months and Byrne converted the space it occupied into an office for himself. The remainder of the building, except for the ground floor and basement, was let to the state, as were an extension finished a few years later and D'Olier House, another of FitzGerald's utilitarian office blocks further along the street.

One of the few cases where Byrne encountered difficulties in securing state tenants involved Seán Lemass House, an office development incorporating the former St Vincent's Hospital on St Stephen's Green, completed in 1976. The Carlisle Trust bought the 78,000-square-feet building a year later for £4 million, and Byrne immediately set about signing up a state tenant. Fianna Fáil had returned to power in a landslide victory in the June 1977 general election, so this should have been a relatively easy proposition. He thought he had netted the Department of Fisheries, but the deal fell through in mysterious circumstances. The same happened with the Department of Posts and

Telegraphs. Wherever he turned, he found himself facing a brick wall. It transpired that the wall was the Minister for Finance, George Colley, who personally vetoed any and all proposals to lease Seán Lemass House because he was convinced that his arch-rival, Haughey, had a stake in Byrne's property empire. (At the time, Haughey was serving in the same Cabinet as Minister for Health and Social Welfare.) Realizing that he was beaten, he sold out for £5.4 million to young Patrick Gallagher, for whom Byrne had become a surrogate father since the death of his own dad in 1974. The man from Lixnaw had been one of Matt Gallagher's closest friends and it was only natural that he should take Matt's son under his wing.

Patrick Gallagher's sentimental attachment to John Byrne didn't get in the way of his biggest ever property coup. In June 1979, a month after closing the deal to purchase Sean Lemass House, the young tycoon resold it to the Irish Permanent Building Society for £7.5 million, netting a profit of £2.1 million. (The building was promptly renamed Edmund Farrell House, in honour of the building society's late founder.) It came as a shock to ordinary people that property speculation could produce such staggering rewards, but the money men around town were ecstatic. For them, this coup underlined the value of property investment and confirmed Matt Gallagher's son as the man with the Midas touch. He also had all the trappings – a string of racehorses, a stud farm, friends in high places and a chauffeur-driven Rolls-Royce. Though still in his twenties, he was surrounded by an eager host of accountants, architects, auctioneers, bankers and lawyers. Everything he said, no matter how banal, was listened to atten-tively. On one occasion, he told a stuffy bank board meeting: 'The three most exciting things in life are sex for the second time (you never get it right the first time), your first winner at Royal Ascot and a flight on Concorde.'

Patrick Gallagher was heir to the fortune amassed by his father, who had died suddenly in January 1974, leaving an estate tech-nically valued at 'nil' as a result of the timely transfer of assets to several trusts; the Revenue received not a single penny. Groomed to step into his father's shoes, Patrick had become a company director at the tender age of 12 and, as time went on, he played an increasingly active role in the family business. The Gallagher Group was its main component, but there was a fringe bank, Merchant Banking Ltd, as well as a complex maze of associated companies – all of which were subsidiaries of Bering Estates, a holding company with its 'headquarters' in the Cayman Islands. One of the directors of the Gallagher Group for many years was Des Traynor.

After winning a fierce battle to build a ghastly office block in Molesworth Street – a scheme that entailed the demolition of two of Dublin's most distinguished Victorian buildings, St Ann's School and Molesworth Hall – Gallagher seemed unstoppable. Banks were prepared to advance any sum for whatever project he had in mind simply on the basis of his extraordinary record as a moneymaker. The Northern Bank Finance Corporation lent him £1 million to acquire Straffan House, a palatial mansion in Co. Kildare where he intended to live in style, and another £1 million to buy No. 16 St Stephen's Green, the largest semi-detached house in Ireland, on to which he tacked an ugly office block in order to make the sums stack up. Gallagher boasted that his company had grown twenty-fold since he took over from his father and predicted that its annual turnover would soon top £160 million – a stupendous figure in 1980. There were sites to be acquired, much bigger than before, and he was going to get them.

Since the mid-1960s, the Slazengers of Powerscourt, in Enniskerry, Co. Wicklow, had bought out the interests of more than 150 individual property owners and drawn up plans for a massive office and shopping development on the west side of St Stephen's Green, bankrolled by the Northern Bank Finance Corporation and the First National Bank of Chicago. But nothing came of these plans and there wasn't much happening on the site apart from the funky stalls of the Dandelion Market. After the entire four-acre holding was put up for sale in 1981, Gallagher agreed to purchase it for £10.5 million – using the artful dodge of acquiring shares in the Slazengers' Isle of Man-registered company, Lambert Jones Estates. Not long after this he was negotiating with his uncles – James (a long-time Fianna Fáil TD), Hubert and Patrick – to purchase a four-acre site on Earlsfort Terrace, which had been derelict since the trio demolished Alexandra College in 1972. The Gallagher brothers, who were known as The Three Stooges because of their constant bickering, agreed to sell it to their nephew for £9.5 million.

Soon it emerged that Gallagher was bidding for the H. Williams supermarket chain. *Business and Finance* magazine scented the truth – that the great tycoon was strapped for cash and his sole purpose in bidding for H. Williams was to get his hands on its turnover of £50 million a year. The problem was that Gallagher had taken on too much debt: interest rates were rising and, whereas it was his standard practice to put down small cash deposits on the acquisition of sites, his down-the-line exposure was enormous. Two days later, on 30 April 1982, Gallagher's bankers put his group into receivership. It transpired that the banks were owed £30 million – a spectacular level of indebtedness unmatched by any other company in Ireland at the time. The Bank of Ireland and Allied Irish Investment Bank were owed £7 million each, while the Northern Bank Finance Corporation was exposed to the tune of £11 million.

Gallagher's own 'bank', Merchant Banking Ltd, collapsed with the rest of his property empire, having provided a handy source of cheap credit for the group over many years. When the crash came, it emerged that there was a shortfall of £4 million, with hundreds of depositors left high and dry, including many who had lost their life savings. It also emerged that a 'loan' of £30,000 had been made to Charlie Haughey, and no interest was ever charged on it. The liquidator's report to the High Court said bluntly that the bank had been 'operated and run by the directors with scandalous disregard not only for the Companies Act but also for the Central Bank Act'. According to liquidator Paddy Shortall, possible offences included bribery, conspiracy, corrupt trans-actions, falsifying or destroying books, publishing fraudulent statements, making false returns to the Central Bank, concealment of property and obtaining credit by false pretences. On foot of his report, the Garda Fraud Squad was called in, but no further action was taken against Gallagher in this jurisdiction. However, he was prosecuted for fraud in Northern Ireland, where Merchant Banking had a subsidiary, and served two years in Crumlin Road jail, Belfast. After his release in 1992, he made a new career in South Africa. In a 1998 interview with Frank Connolly of the *Sunday Business Post*, he revealed that Haughey had approached him two days after becoming Taoiseach in December 1979 to request help in clearing a £1 million debt he had with AIB. Gallagher gave him £300,000 out of his own pocket – and out of 'a sense of duty', just as his father had done before. But since the money was coming from the group's funds, rather than his own, it was dressed up as a 'deposit' on the purchase of Abbeville – though this transaction never came to pass.

In 1988, the year Dublin celebrated its 'millennium', the St Stephen's Green shopping centre was built by British Land on the former Slazenger site. Designed by James Toomey, its façade was meant to evoke the great Palm House in the National Botanic Gardens. But the fussy wrought-iron and glass treatment was likened to a Mississippi riverboat that somehow got stranded on St Stephen's Green, minus its paddle-wheel, while the rolled-out brick wallpaper along South King Street crudely mimics the Gaiety Theatre.

By then, the focus was starting to shift to a new El Dorado in Docklands. The first step towards achieving renewal of its redundant riverscape was taken in 1986 by the Fine Gael–Labour coalition with the establishment of a statutory authority to take charge of the Custom House Docks site. It was chaired by former Dublin Corporation planner Frank Benson, who had later worked for the developer Robin Power before going back to the public sector to become chairman of An Bord Pleanála after it was reconstituted in 1984. The Custom House Docks Development Authority (CHDDA) lost no time in producing a master plan for the 27-acre site and then invited tenders from developers to undertake the project, which was underwritten by lucrative tax incentives. Fianna Fáil had returned to power when the competition reached its climax, and there was much lobbying behind the scenes; one of the competitors (not from the winning consortium) allegedly turned up to meet a well-placed contact in the Shelbourne Hotel with 'a suitcase full of banknotes', saying 'Who do I give this to?'

The minority Fianna Fáil government had decided that the centrepiece of the whole Docklands project would be an International Financial Services Centre – a bright idea suggested to Haughey by another of his benefactors, billionaire financier Dermot Desmond. His agenda – and the government's – was to 'have men in suits on the site', one bemused chartered surveyor was told. Desmond was the quintessential northside boy made good, with a net worth of more than a billion euro and a nickname, The Kaiser, to go with his distinctive fin de siècle moustache. He founded National City Brokers in 1981, turning it into one of the most successful stockbroking firms in Ireland, and masterminded such mega-deals as the 1988 takeover of Irish Distillers by Pernod Ricard. During a titanic struggle over a share deal with Fyffes, which ended up in the High Court, Desmond boasted of his access to the corridors of power while Charlie Haughey was Taoiseach, though he said he 'did not head out to Kinsealy' to arrange tax clearance for the takeover; NCB also won a number of state commissions, including the flotation of Irish Sugar as Greencore plc. The IFSC was intended to provide an in-town tax haven for internationally traded financial services, including banking, asset financing, fund management, corporate treasury and investment management, and even 'captive re-insurance' – all subject to a very low corporation tax rate of only 10 per cent at the time; no wonder it attracted at least half of the world's top 50 banks and half of the top 20 insurance companies. Within 10 years, it was netting the Exchequer more than £400 million a year. The first phase was developed under the direction of Frank Benson and his team, working with the winning consortium headed by Mark Kavanagh, a cool, unsentimental ex-hippie who inherited control of the building firm Hardwicke after his father's death in 1978. On the day of the 1989 general election, Kavanagh called out to see Charlie Haughey in Abbeville and gave him £100,000, of which £25,000 was intended for the Brian Lenihan fund (to finance a liver operation for the then Tánaiste) and £75,000 for Fianna Fáil. The money was contained in one cheque made out to the party and three bank drafts for cash, and Kavanagh complained later that he had never been given a receipt. As the Moriarty Tribunal subsequently found, Haughey passed on the cheque for £25,000 to Fianna Fáil and lodged the rest to his Ansbacher account.

Dermot Desmond was one of the key figures involved in the Byzantine transactions involving the Johnston, Mooney and O'Brien site, which had been purchased by UPH in November 1988 for £4 million and then sold on nine months later at a profit of £2 million to a complex consortium of offshore companies, which, in turn, resold it to Telecom Eireann for £9.4 million in 1991. Desmond's close friend, businessman Michael Smurfit, had an interest in UPH and was also Telecom's chairman at the time. Also involved in this extraordinary deal was one of his buddies, estate agent John Finnegan, who billed Telecom for a 'finder's fee' of £120,000 for pointing out the derelict bakery to Smurfit after lunch one day; he was eventually paid £39,000. When details of the transactions were first exposed, Desmond maintained that he had provided only 'mezzanine finance', but a government-appointed inspector, John Glackin, concluded later that the Isle of Man company involved, Freezone Ltd, was owned by the financier. Desmond hotly disputed this finding, though it later emerged through the Moriarty Tribunal that he had used this offshore vehicle to pick up an 'insignificant' bill of £75,000 in 1990 for the refurbishment of Haughey's yacht, *Celtic Mist*.

The disclosures resulted in Desmond having to step down as chairman of both NCB and Aer Rianta, while Smurfit resigned as chairman of Telecom. Desmond became a tax exile domiciled in Monaco, following in Smurfit's footsteps, though he retained his appetite for high-risk deals, often netting millions of pounds in the process. When in Dublin, he operates from a Master of the Universe suite on the top floor of the IFSC South Block, which he purchased in 1990 for £25 million, with glass walls that can be made opaque at the flick of a switch and a small gym with a lancet window and breathtaking view westwards over the Liffey Quays. Just in front, as if to remind us where we had come from, socialite and charity fund-raiser Norma Smurfit commissioned Rowan Gillespie's Famine memorial featuring gaunt, wraithlike figures carrying their few pathetic possessions towards an unseen coffin ship.

Meanwhile, the suburbs continued to expand, and the process was almost entirely led by developers. Corruption flourished in an environment where a speculator could make a fortune if a piece of land he owned could be rezoned for residential, commercial or industrial development: councillors accepted bribes, and governments of various political hues ignored the problem.

Fianna Fáil's Ray Burke was one of the few politicians to be directly implicated at an early stage. As far back as 1974, when he was a member of Dublin County Council, the *Sunday Independent* and *Hibernia* reported that he had received a payment of £15,000 from a company controlled by house-builders Brennan and McGowan. There was a Garda investigation, but no action was taken.

In July 1993 the *Irish Times* ran a week-long series of articles on the rezoning blitz; one story, headed 'Cash in Brown Paper Bags for Councillors', quoted a developer's agent as saying: 'There is a certain number of people in that council chamber who put a value on their votes. They are the power brokers who can bring five votes with you, or five votes against you, depending on how they're looked after.' Again, the Garda investigation got nowhere, mainly because it could not guarantee immunity from prosecution for informants with first-hand evidence.

In July 1995, a Newry firm of solicitors, Donnelly, Neary and Donnelly, placed an advertisement in the *Irish Times*. It offered a £10,000 reward for information leading to the conviction of anyone involved in land rezoning corruption. The Newry solicitors were acting for anonymous clients – later revealed as barristers Michael Smith and Colm MacEochaidh – who were convinced that the rezoning of amenity and agricultural land was being corruptly arranged. The individuals who contacted Donnelly, Neary and Donnelly on foot of the advertisement included James Gogarty, the elderly former managing director of Joseph Murphy Structural Engineering (JMSE) Ltd. Gogarty alleged that in June 1989 he had witnessed the handing over of brown envelopes containing a total of £80,000 to Ray Burke, who by this time held two ministerial portfolios – Justice and Communications – in the Fianna Fáil–PD government. The money came from JMSE and Bovale Developments, and was in return for helping to iron out planning difficulties on a range of sites around north Co. Dublin.

Bovale, run by Roscommon-born brothers Mick and Tom Bailey, was one of the most active firms of house-builders in Dublin at the time, with numerous housing estates already built – often with the benefit of 'material contraventions' of the county plan, pushed through by its loyal supporters on the council – and a substantial land bank assembled for future development. Burke's other major 'clients' were Tom Brennan and Joe McGowan, who were for a time the biggest house-builders in Ireland. As a county councillor, Burke sponsored rezoning motions for lands they had speculatively acquired, particularly in the Swords area; as an auctioneer, he would later sell the houses they built on these lands. A Brennan and McGowan company built his house, Briargate, on an acre of land east of the village. Detective Superintendent Brendan Burns suspected in 1989 that Burke could probably produce a fake mortgage for the house, but he couldn't even do that; it had been supplied to him by Brennan and McGowan free of charge. Burke had no concept of the public interest, and some of the land rezoning he promoted cost the public dearly.

Two months after advertising their £10,000 reward offer, Michael Smith and Colm MacEochaidh issued a lengthy statement condemning 'official inertia' with regard to planning corruption and calling for a public inquiry. 'This is not blackmail,' they said. 'It is the resort of persons forced to take action in an arena which, outside of a banana republic, should be the realm of government.' But Labour's Brendan Howlin, then Minister for the Environment, declined even to meet them, while his Fianna Fáil shadow, Noel Dempsey, said it was 'very difficult to accept' their bona fides. The then Minister for Justice, Fine Gael's Nora Owen – herself a former Dublin county councillor – was also unenthusiastic about establishing a public inquiry. And with the media hamstrung by libel laws, Gogarty's allegation about Ray Burke took a long time to surface in print, even though journalists had been aware of it from an early stage. Bertie Ahern was also well aware of it when he appointed Burke as Minister for Foreign Affairs after the June 1997 general election. He later memorably declared that he had been 'up every tree in north Dublin' to see if there was any truth in Gogarty's claims and had asked the then party whip, Dermot Ahern, to undertake a pro-forma 'investigation'; extraordinarily, Dermot Ahern did not interview Gogarty.

After the *Sunday Tribune* finally broke the media silence in July 1997, claiming that Burke had received £30,000 from Bovale Developments, it was clear that his position was becoming untenable. Three weeks later, Burke issued a statement saying he had 'done nothing illegal, unethical or improper' and accusing Gogarty of conducting a vendetta against him. It was not until *Magill* published a 1989 letter from Bovale's Mick Bailey telling Gogarty that he could 'procure' a majority of Dublin County Council to support the rezoning of lands owned by JMSE that the government finally agreed to establish a tribunal of inquiry into allegations of planning corruption. That same month, October 1997, Burke resigned from the Dáil, still insisting that he had done nothing wrong. The Taoiseach also leapt to his defence: Bertie Ahern complained in the Dáil about 'the persistent hounding of an honourable man', saying Burke had been driven from office 'on the basis of innuendo and unproven allegations [in] a sustained campaign of incremental intensity'. After being nailed by the Planning Tribunal for being repeatedly evasive in his evidence, Burke was targeted by the Criminal Assets Bureau and pleaded guilty in 2004 to persistent tax evasion over a nine-year period while he held accounts in London, the Channel Islands and the Isle of Man, including one in the name of Caviar Ltd. He was sentenced to six months in jail, but was let out of Mountjoy Prison after four months for 'good behaviour'.

Ahern's willingness to reappoint such a tarnished figure to the Cabinet in 1997 was queried by Socialist Party leader Joe Higgins in the Dáil in February 2005, after Burke was sent to jail:

The Taoiseach must explain because when Fianna Fáil was mired in corruption and sleaze in the 1980s, nobody believes he did not know what was going on. He was the party fixer and the runner for party leader Mr Haughey. It is simply not credible that he did not know what Mr Burke and his team of cronies were up to regarding rezonings and land corruption. The Taoiseach may have kept his own face out of the feeding frenzy at the speculators' trough but he knew it was there, he knew who was bucketing the swill into it and he knew the biggest snouts who were slurping from it, but, unlike when I was a young fellow on a farm in Kerry when we had to take a stick to the greediest pigs, he simply left them at it . . .

In response, Ahern said his decision to appoint Burke as Minister for Foreign Affairs 'was based on what my bona fide view was then. If I knew then what I know now years later after all of the investigations, I would not have appointed him.'

The floodgates had well and truly opened five years earlier. On 19 April 2000, after being warned that he could end up in jail if he didn't cooperate, Frank Dunlop told the Planning Tribunal in Dublin Castle how he had paid a total of £112,000 to 15 councillors, on behalf of the developer Owen O'Callaghan, to secure their votes in favour of the rezoning of 180 acres of land at Quarryvale, in west Dublin, in May 1991. The biggest pay-off, of

£48,000, went to a 'powerful individual', later identified as the council member and local TD Liam Lawlor.

Dunlop's revelations rocked the political establishment. The can of worms suspected by many close observers had turned into a truckload. And it was not just Quarryvale. At least a dozen other landowners, speculators or developers had contributed large sums of money to the 'war chest' into which Dunlop dipped when confronted by demands or requests for money. Altogether, according to Dunlop, more than 25 councillors – a third of Dublin County Council's total membership – were on the take, though most of them insisted that any monies they received were 'political donations' rather than bribes. One Fine Gael councillor, the late Tom Hand, had sought £250,000 for his support in rezoning Quarryvale because it would be worth so much to the developers; he brazenly provided the address of a bank and an account number in Australia, to facilitate this proposed transaction. Dunlop was so astonished by the scale of Hand's demand that he mentioned it to other Fine Gael councillors on his payroll and later to the then party leader, John Bruton, who first denied he had ever been told about this, but later admitted he had – although he found it quite incredible. Hand eventually settled for £20,000 as the price of his vote, while Fianna Fáil whip Pat Dunne got £15,000 and party colleague Seán Gilbride £12,000. Colm McGrath, then a Fianna Fáil councillor and later an independent, got £2,540 at the time. Dunlop testified that he made cash payments of £1,000 or £2,000 to other councillors at their homes, in the county council's car park, in the nearby Royal Dublin Hotel or in Conway's pub, round the corner on Parnell Street. Some were paid to turn up for a crucial vote, others to stay away.

Over £1.8 million was paid to Frank Dunlop for his services in relation to the Quarryvale project, mostly for his consultancy work. But it also included more than £364,000 in reimbursed legal fees, which Dunlop ran up in dealing with the tribunal. He told the tribunal that O'Callaghan had said he would 'look after' the legal fees, but stopped picking up the tab after Dunlop admitted giving money to councillors, as this had come as a 'total surprise' to him. Indeed, O'Callaghan told the tribunal in June 2008 that he had never discussed bribery and corruption on Dublin County Council with Dunlop. Yet the Cork developer saw nothing wrong with acceding to Colm McGrath's request to help him out by discharging a debt of £10,700 (equivalent to €40,000 today) or giving a £30,000 contract to McGrath's company, Essential Services Ltd, to provide security at Quarryvale. Two other councillors, Colm Tyndall (PD) and John O'Halloran (Ind.), earned revenue from insurance premiums and catering contracts, respectively, on the shopping centre site; these were simply 'business relationships' in O'Callaghan's book. And when Seán Gilbride gave up his teaching job in 1991 to devote himself full time to 'politics', complaining to Dunlop that this would leave him short, he was paid £1,750 a month in lieu of his salary, amounting to a total of £15,500 in 'political donations', as O'Callaghan characterized them; the money was paid out during the period that coincided with the county council's crucial votes on Quarryvale – a project Gilbride said he was 'proud' to support. Needless to say, none of these payments or arrangements were declared at the time by any of those involved.

The originator of the plan to build a shopping centre at Quarryvale was not O'Callaghan but the Sligo-born developer Tom Gilmartin, who had spent most of his life in England and was based in Luton. Even though the first phase of the M50 was still under construction, it was clear to Gilmartin that this new orbital motorway would open up opportunities for business parks, retail warehouses and shopping centres. He recognized the strategic significance of Quarryvale, at the M50's midpoint, and set about assembling a 180-acre site on which to build a massive motorway shopping centre. In order to complete his acquisition programme, Gilmartin had to get his hands on a 69-acre holding owned by Dublin Corporation and zoned at the time for industrial development. At first, it seemed that this could be done by private treaty, without any need for a public tender. But Green Property's John Corcoran, who had got planning permission to develop a shopping centre in Blanchardstown, was tipped off about the proposed sale by George Redmond and quickly indicated his interest in acquiring the corporation's Quarryvale site: he was understandably concerned that a rival shopping centre, more than twice the size of the one he was planning for Blanchardstown, might be developed just a few miles down the road. When the site was advertised for sale by tender in January 1989, Green offered £4.4 million and said it would be prepared to pay £7 million if the site was rezoned for retail – something that the corporation couldn't possibly guarantee, as this was a matter for Dublin County Council. As a result, Gilmartin's unconditional offer of £5.1 million was accepted, even though senior corporation officials were well aware by then that what he had in mind was a huge out-of-town mall, with a potentially damaging impact both on the city centre and on its own commercial rates base. However, they took some comfort from the fact that he was also planning another major shopping centre, twice the size of the one in St Stephen's Green, for Bachelors Walk and Ormond Quay, with basement parking for 1,400 cars and, more improbably, a city bus station on the roof.

Gilmartin had grown up on a small farm in Lislarry, near the Atlantic coast. After failing to get a civil service job in Dublin, he left Ireland in the bleak 1950s and worked on assembly lines in the British motor industry before setting up in business on his own – making his first fortune by supplying equipment for automation to Vauxhall and other car manufacturers. He branched out into property development in the late 1970s, investing in the new town of Milton Keynes and later in Northern Ireland, where he redeveloped a tired shopping centre in Bangor, Co. Down; when it was destroyed by fire in 1987, he was compensated by his insurance company and then sold the site to another developer. By the time he arrived in Dublin in 1988 and set his sights on Bachelors Walk and Quarryvale, Gilmartin was cash rich and in a good position to buy what he wanted in a depressed market. His plans were of great interest to the government because of their sheer scale – a million square feet of retail space in the city centre and another million and a half square feet on the outskirts – and ministers were more than willing to lend their support, at least at the outset. Senior Dublin city and county officials, led by then city manager Frank Feely, were summoned to Government Buildings in September 1988 by Charlie Haughey and told in no uncertain terms that they should be much more proactive in facilitating development, including Gilmartin's plans. Haughey was accompanied at that meeting by three key ministers – Ray MacSharry (Finance), Pádraig Flynn (Environment) and Ray Burke (Justice). Flynn met Gilmartin on a number of other occasions in 1989, as did Bertie Ahern, then Minister for Labour. Gilmartin would later tell the Planning Tribunal that Joe Burke suggested he should make a contribution of £500,000 in return for the support he was receiving – an allegation which the former Dublin city councillor denied, describing it as outrageous.

After Liam Lawlor brought him to a meeting with Haughey and a number of ministers in February 1989, Gilmartin was approached by a man he didn't recognize who said he'd make a lot of money from development in Ireland and asked him to deposit £5 million in an Isle of Man bank account. Gilmartin retained Lawlor, at a fee of £3,500 per month, to try to iron out the problems. Three months later, in an attempt to fend off fellows looking for money from him, Gilmartin decided to make a substantial donation to Fianna Fáil. He gave Pádraig Flynn a cheque for £50,000, which Flynn asked him to make out to 'cash' and then lodged in a bogus non-resident account he and his wife Dorothy had at the AIB branch in Castlebar; the party got none of it. (Flynn told the Planning Tribunal in April 2008 that he had paid almost £23,000 in gift tax on this donation in 1998, after it first became public, and denied that he had discussed tax designation for Quarryvale with Gilmartin.) 'He had cast-iron evidence of three senior members of the Fianna Fáil government taking money,' one of Gilmartin's former associates told the *Irish Times* in 1999. 'All they're good for is thieving and robbing and running to Brussels with the begging bowl,' Gilmartin would say. His own motives, by contrast, were patriotically altruistic, according to himself; he had seen too many Irish emigrants 'roaming the streets of London' and wanted to 'end this human cargo' by creating jobs for people at home.

The underlying problem with Quarryvale was that it had never been intended for this type of development. Since 1972, successive Dublin county plans had zoned another site in Balgaddy, adjoining the Dublin–Cork railway line, as a 'town centre' for Lucan/Clondalkin. Owen O'Callaghan had acquired an option on the Balgaddy site in 1988, but soon became aware that government ministers favoured Quarryvale instead. Eddie Kay, former manager at AIB's corporate divison, had been told by O'Callaghan (one of the bank's long-standing clients) in December 1989 that it had 'strong government support', while Tom Gilmartin himself informed him that it was likely to get the benefit of tax incentives – at least, that's what he had gleaned from Pádraig Flynn. Like Gilmartin, O'Callaghan could see that Quarryvale's location at the midpoint of the M50 could not be beaten. It was for this reason that he concluded Balgaddy was not viable and decided to throw in his lot with Gilmartin.

Unlike Gilmartin, O'Callaghan had lots of experience of working in Ireland. Having started out as a builder in Cork, turning out some 6,000 houses and half a dozen industrial estates over the years, O'Callaghan Properties diversified into retail development with the lacklustre Paul Street shopping centre in the early, very unpromising 1980s. O'Callaghan moved on to much larger shopping centres at Merchants Quay in Cork and at Arthur's Quay in Limerick. But it was clear that he would have to break into the Dublin market if he was to make it really big, and the foothold he gained in Balgaddy was his springboard.

He was still on the sidelines, however, when Gilmartin unveiled his plans for Quarryvale at the Berkeley Court Hotel in July 1990, flanked by a team of architects, engineers, surveyors and estate agents, all of them more sharply dressed than he was. The model that formed the centrepiece of this public launch showed a gargantuan shopping centre stretching to 1.5 million square feet, surrounded by acres of surface parking for up to

10,000 cars with direct access via slip roads to and from the M50. Called Westpark, the scheme would also have provided 400,000 square feet of retail warehousing – big boxes for B&Q and its ilk – as well as a high-tech business park, 'executive housing' and a leisure and conference centre. Nothing quite so grandiose had been proposed in Ireland previously, and there were questions about whether Gilmartin and his newly formed Irish company, Barkhill, would be able to fund it. In fact, the various costs associated with assembling the Quarryvale site had caused Gilmartin to move quickly into serious debt, and he had to borrow £8.5 million from AIB in February 1990 to keep Barkhill afloat. Eventually AIB gave Gilmartin an ultimatum: either he agreed to pool resources with O'Callaghan, who was itching to get involved, or it would put his venture into liquidation. In his evidence to the Planning Tribunal in April 2008, AIB's Eddie Kay denied that the bank was 'colluding' with O'Callaghan, but he did concede that the bank had put pressure on Gilmartin to sign a deal with the Cork-based developer as the deadline to lodge a motion to rezone Quarryvale approached. Gilmartin reluctantly agreed; under the divvy-up, each of the two developers got 40 per cent of Barkhill and the remaining 20 per cent went to AIB.

The bank's confidence in O'Callaghan's ability to make Quarryvale pay was confirmed when he moved quickly to ensure that the site was rezoned. Working closely with him on this project were two of the most experienced hands in the business – Frank Dunlop and the well-connected architect Ambrose Kelly. The trio held regular strategy meetings at Dunlop's offices in Upper Mount Street, often attended by key councillors, as well as meetings with local community groups and an endless round of drinks and meals with individual councillors. Their game plan was to sell the scheme as a much-needed amenity and source of jobs for the deprived communities of north Clondalkin. 'In the early 1990s, when Frank Dunlop was acting as an ATM for some county councillors, 60 per cent of the heads of household in Quarryvale were unemployed,' wrote Fintan O'Toole in the *Irish*

Times. 'While one councillor was allegedly receiving £40,000 in a single payment, the average gross income in Quarryvale was £131.72 a week, much less than half the average industrial earnings.'

As Brendan Bartley noted in his book *Poor People, Poor Places*:

What one sees if one ventures into north Clondalkin are littered and unkempt approach roads, run-down neighbourhood centres, public buildings which are invariably surrounded by large palisade fencing and shuttering, poorly kept open spaces, a skyline dominated by large electricity pylons and housing estates which face inwards and turn their back on the public areas. The neighbourhood centres which were to be at the heart of each neighbourhood have failed.

Now, suddenly, they were to have a huge shopping centre on their doorsteps and a promise from O'Callaghan himself that he would fund training courses aimed at getting local people 'job ready'. Thus, it was no wonder that almost every significant community group rallied to his cause, as well as the area's four councillors – Colm McGrath, John O'Halloran, Colm Tyndall (PD) and Fine Gael's Therese Ridge, who became known as 'Mother Therese'. In May 1991, just a month before that year's local elections, Dublin County Council voted by 29 to 13 to relocate the 'town centre' zoning from Balgaddy to Quarryvale, like Birnam Wood come to Dunsinane. It didn't matter one whit that it was located at the north-eastern extremity of the 'new town' it was meant to serve, or that the planners warned this would be 'seriously detrimental' to the realization of the long-established county development plan. Every Fianna Fáil councillor – with the exception of Anne Brady – voted in favour of the rezoning.

They didn't expect all hell to break loose, which it did when John Corcoran held a dramatic press conference in the middle of the local election campaign to denounce the council's 'irresponsible' decision and warn that it could result in Green Property's long-standing plans for Blanchardstown being cancelled. A huge political storm blew up, with the result that 12 of the most prominent rezoners, including Liam Lawlor, lost their seats. It became obvious then that Barkhill would need to scale down its scheme if it was to have any chance of the rezoning decision being confirmed when a politically chastened council got around to adopting its county development plan in 1992. O'Callaghan offered to 'cap' the retail space at a relatively modest 250,000 square feet, in the expectation that this could be increased over time – which indeed it was. He also came up with the brilliant wheeze of offering to build a 40,000-seat football stadium, with a retractable roof, on the Balgaddy site, just to show that it could be used for something. Needless to say, although full planning permission was granted for this project in 1993, nothing ever came of it. According to Dunlop, the £35 million project was merely 'a ruse' designed to ensure that the rezoning of Quarryvale was not reversed. It was also fiendishly clever, because this sham scheme effectively froze Balgaddy for five years while work got under way on the Liffey Valley shopping centre at Quarryvale.

Meanwhile, Tom Gilmartin was being frozen out of the scheme he had originated. Both AIB and O'Callaghan came to regard him as a 'loose cannon', according to former Bank of Ireland official Paul Sheeran, who had known Gilmartin since 1972 and regarded him as honourable, truthful and highly respected in London Irish business circles. Sheeran told the Planning Tribunal that Gilmartin had not been aware of the payments made to Dunlop by O'Callaghan through a company called Shefran Ltd or the bank account it had in Rathfarnham, from which Dunlop drew money to pay bribes. Multimillionaire tycoon lawyer Noel Smyth, who acted as Gilmartin's solicitor, described him to the tribunal as a 'very good guy . . . an honest man [who had been] naive or stupid or maybe a combination of both' in the way he handled Quarryvale. Smyth, with his own long and wide experience of property deals, said he believed Gilmartin had lost 60 per cent of Barkhill because 'he didn't know the system or the system betrayed him'. Gilmartin himself believed he was 'held to ransom' by O'Callaghan and that the bank was also 'thwarting' him.

Meetings at the AIB headquarters in Ballsbridge were often very heated, according to Michael O'Farrell, senior manager of the bank's corporate division. In his evidence to the Planning Tribunal, O'Farrell said he could not recall Gilmartin calling AIB and O'Callaghan a 'shower of gangsters', but he was aware that the Luton-based developer had often complained that he was being 'coerced' out of the Quarryvale project.

Eventually, after Gilmartin took legal action against O'Callaghan and AIB, a settlement was reached in 1996 and he was paid £7.6 million for his 40 per cent stake in the company, plus £1 million in damages and a £150,000 allowance for 'political contributions'; Noel Smyth negotiated on his behalf, earning a cool £1 million for himself. Deeply disillusioned by what he had encountered in Dublin, Gilmartin returned to England to face a massive tax bill from the Inland Revenue that would have absorbed much of the settlement money. It was only when he came back to give evidence at public sessions of the Planning Tribunal that the tables were turned. In 2005, his string of allegations that O'Callaghan had 'bragged' about making payments to leading Fianna Fáil politicians prompted the Cork developer to initiate High Court proceedings to have the inquiry halted, claiming it was 'biased' against him. He lost the case, appealed to the Supreme Court and lost again; the court also directed that he should pay the tribunal's legal costs, estimated at more than €2 million.

There is no doubt that O'Callaghan was politically well connected. He contributed significant sums to Cork TDs Micheál Martin and Batt O'Keeffe, and also responded positively to an appeal for funds to replenish Fianna Fáil's empty coffers in the early 1990s, when the party had an accumulated debt of more than £3 million. The scale of this debt was a matter of serious concern to Bertie Ahern, an accountant by training, honorary treasurer of the party and Minister for Finance at the time. Golf classics and vastly overpriced meals in the Fianna Fáil tent at the Galway Races generated handy revenue, but nowhere near as much as the party needed. So in September 1993, 10 businessmen were targeted to receive letters, jointly signed by Ahern and then Taoiseach Albert Reynolds, asking them to consider donating £100,000 each. 'This is an exceptional situation and we ask you to consider this request favourably in the context of these strained [*sic*] circumstances,' the letter said. 'A senior representative of the national treasurers' committee will be in touch with you personally in this regard in the near future.' Owen O'Callaghan got one of these letters and had a follow-up meeting with Ray MacSharry, then Ireland's EU Commissioner. O'Callaghan told the Planning Tribunal that he had been positive about the request for £100,000, but said he would have to think about it because of its size; at the time, you could have bought a decent house for £100,000. In the end he donated £10,000 at a Cork fund-raising dinner in March 1994, another £10,000 towards Brian Crowley's campaign to represent Munster in the European Parliament, and then paid the balance of £80,000 to Fianna Fáil party head-quarters in June 1994.

That kind of money buys goodwill, and Owen O'Callaghan needed it. Along with Michael Tiernan, his partner on Arthur's Quay in Limerick, he had been pursuing a shopping centre scheme for Athlone – and getting nowhere fast. Golden Island conjures up images of sun-drenched beaches, but in Athlone it was part of the Shannon floodplain, on the east bank of the river where the town dump used to be located. The 30-acre site near a new sewage pumping station was owned by local businessman Tom Diskin, and he had joined forces with O'Callaghan and Tiernan in a battle to have it developed as a regional shopping centre. It was not the ideal location for such a scheme, being relatively remote from the main street; indeed, the chamber of commerce feared that it would 'suck the heart out of Athlone'. But Diskin was undeterred, and laid the groundwork well. Miraculously, he managed to get the council's plan amended to drop an earlier warning about the 'detrimental' impact of edge-of-town superstores and substitute it with a specific objective 'to encourage the development of a commercial core in Golden Island'. The developers argued that the lack of a good shopping centre in Athlone was resulting in an annual 'leakage' of £40 million in consumer spending to Galway, Mullingar, Tullamore and other towns.

But they needed urban renewal designation to make Golden Island a runner, and Athlone Urban District Council by the narrowest of margins – the casting vote of its then chairman, John Butler – backed their application for tax incentives in June 1994. That same month, however, when then Minister for the Environment Michael Smith announced the latest package of urban renewal designations, Golden Island was not included; indeed, Smith pointedly described Athlone as 'an unmitigated disaster' because no urban renewal had taken place on foot of the designation of 17 acres on the west bank of the Shannon in 1987. Clearly, more work needed to be done by the Diskin–O'Callaghan–Tiernan consortium if their scheme was to get off the ground.

Whatever they did, it worked. After the Fianna Fáil–Labour coalition collapsed in November 1994, Bertie Ahern and Michael Smith signed off on the designation of Golden Island on their last morning in office, just hours before John Bruton's Rainbow Coalition took over. According to Tom Gilmartin's evidence to the Planning Tribunal, O'Callaghan 'had to go to Albert [Reynolds] and Albert had to intervene to get the designation through before the government fell, which culminated in a meeting with Owen O'Callaghan and Bertie Ahern the night – or night or two – before the government actually fell.' Gilmartin claimed O'Callaghan told him he had given Reynolds £150,000 in relation to the Golden Island development in March 1994 – an allegation vehemently rejected by Reynolds as 'spurious, unfounded, defamatory and untrue'. He also claimed that O'Callaghan had told him in October 1989 that Ahern was 'on his payroll' and had later 'bragged' about giving him payments totalling £80,000 between 1989 and 1993. Ahern vehemently denied receiving any payments from O'Callaghan, and characterized Gilmartin's allegations as 'ridiculous and fanciful'. In a detailed statement issued during the 2007 general election campaign, Ahern declared: 'I simply did not receive any money from Mr O'Callaghan nor did I do any favours for him.'

The alleged use, or rather abuse, of state benefits – specifically, urban renewal designation – to raise funds for Fianna Fáil was one of the matters examined by the Planning Tribunal. In late 1998, a year after it was established, the tribunal requisitioned several files from the Department of the Environment, including documents relating to a 1988 decision by Pádraig Flynn to designate land in the centre of Tallaght for urban renewal incentives. It was this decision that led to the construction of The Square shopping centre by Monarch Properties, after the site had lain fallow for several years. The tribunal also examined files relating to decisions made by Flynn in another round of urban renewal designations in 1988 and 1990. Among those to benefit was veteran property developer John Byrne, whose land around the Brandon Hotel in Tralee was designated in 1988, while another of his sites, the former Tara Street baths in Dublin, got the same benefits in 1990. Other files related to a major extension of the urban renewal scheme in 1994, while Michael Smith was Minister for the Environment and Bertie Ahern was Minister for Finance. One of the major beneficiaries then (though this instance was not examined by the tribunal) was Ken Rohan, another donor to Fianna Fáil; his site at the edge of the Grand Canal Docks, then occupied by the derelict IMP meat factory, was included within a new tax-incentive zone. This enabled him to sell half of the site to Cosgrave Brothers for a major residential development while developing the rest of it for offices, known as Grand Canal Plaza, which are still owned by his highly profitable Airspace Investments group. In the same year, Bertie Ahern amended the Finance Act to give a tax break on art collections in historic houses which are open to the public; the sole beneficiary of the incentive (which was not scrutinized by the Planning Tribunal) turned out to be Ken Rohan, who used it to avoid a tax bill of £1.5 million.

The Planning Tribunal was seeking to establish whether there were links between the decisions made on urban renewal designation and contributions to Fianna Fáil, which reduced its debt from more than £3 million to just £500,000 over a two-year period when Bertie Ahern was party treasurer and Minister for Finance. Certainly, during 1993 and in the early part of 1994, several property developers reported receiving phone calls from associates of Ahern, who were aware that they had sites in particular areas and told them that if they wanted to 'end up on the right side of the line', they should drop out to the Berkeley Court Hotel to see Fianna Fáil fund-raiser Des Richardson. The tribunal also investigated an allegation that files relating to the 1994 urban renewal scheme – including draft maps of the proposed designated areas – had 'gone missing' from the office of Emmet Stagg, the Labour Minister of State for Housing and Urban Renewal, having been requisitioned by the Department of Finance, and then turned up in Richardson's office at the Berkeley Court. Stagg was so alarmed by this development that he travelled to Roscrea one Monday morning in April 1994 to report it directly to Michael Smith. A month later, responding to questions posed by the *Irish Times*, Smith denied that Fianna Fáil was conducting a 'Dutch auction' for urban renewal designation, citing golf classics as the explanation for the party's stupendous achievement in slashing its debt. 'If I found out that anyone, anywhere, was contributing on the basis of expecting designation of their property, that area would be ruled out of contention altogether,' he said.

Meanwhile back in west Dublin, the Liffey Valley shopping centre established itself as a money-spinner almost as soon as it opened in October 1998, with Marks & Spencer as the anchor store. Work on its construction had got under way two years earlier, in May 1996 – the same month that O'Callaghan finally parted company with Tom Gilmartin and replaced him with the Duke of Westminster, who took a 50 per cent stake in Barkhill. (It must have been a very black day in Mayfair when the duke and his highly respectable property holding company, Grosvenor Estates, learned of Frank Dunlop's testimony before the Planning Tribunal.) Although the size of the shopping centre was capped at 250,000 square feet, other commercial facilities were being planned for the Quarryvale site, including a multiplex cinema, retail warehousing, offices, a hotel, leisure centre and 'motor mall'. Even before the first shoppers streamed in, the promoters were campaigning to have the cap lifted so that they could include a large supermarket (oddly, the first phase didn't have one) and a wider range of other outlets in order to compete head-to-head with The Square in Tallaght and Green Property's shopping centre in Blanchardstown.

Following the break-up of Dublin County Council into three separate local authorities, South Dublin County Council lifted the cap in 1998 and planning permission was granted to Barkhill to double the size of Liffey Valley. Even after this was overturned by An Bord Pleanála in March 2000, on the grounds that it would cause serious congestion on the M50 and undermine local shops, the planners carried on regardless, conferring 'town centre' zoning on the site, and de-designating Balgaddy.

Residents of north Clondalkin, particularly in the Quarryvale housing estate, felt sidelined by the whole saga, as Kitty Holland reported in the *Irish Times* in June 2007; they still had no library, no medical centre and no sports facilities. 'On the green fields opposite Liffey Valley's retail parks, two O'Callaghan Properties signs are erected by the road. "Future Bus Terminal", reads one. "Site for Offices, Civic Buildings and Medical Centre", announces another. Almost a decade after they were erected, they are faded and even a little battered. The site remains vacant.' Holland quoted one local resident, Phyllis Forte, who had represented residents at numerous meetings with Owen O'Callaghan. 'People did feel very let down, especially after all the time and effort that had been put into the meetings and consultations . . . There had been such hope that things were going to change.' She produced a letter from the developer, dated 2 November 1999, in which he told of plans for a 'community block' on Coldcut Road, where the faded signs were located. This was to include 'a restaurant, FÁS training centre, a medical centre, library and small offices', as well as 'an oratory, as we discussed on Thursday night last, [and a] historical trail around the perimeter of the site depicting the historical events in the Lucan/Clondalkin area'.

A spokesman for O'Callaghan Properties was quoted as saying that the commitment to build civic amenities had been genuine, but blamed An Bord Pleanála for overturning the plans. 'Currently a local area plan is being put together in consultation with residents. Liffey Valley is now a designated town centre and the facilities will be incorporated into that,' he said.

As it was, most of the shops were out of the price range of local residents.

'It's for people in their big cars on the M50,' as Phyllis Forte said.

It was a different matter entirely when developers ran into determined opposition from well-heeled residents of west Dublin's more affluent suburbs, notably Castleknock. That's what happened when the US-owned Ogden Group put forward a £300 million scheme for the disused Phoenix Park racecourse in the mid-1990s. One of the largest and most controversial development proposals to come before the planning system, it was marketed as the Sonas Centre (*sonas* being the Irish word for happiness or well-being) and was to include a 65,000-seat stadium, an indoor arena, national conference centre and a 349-bedroom Sheraton Hotel. But the most contentious element by far was a casino which would have been the largest in Europe; it was to be the 'financial engine' for the whole scheme, according to Norman Turner, the stocky Englishman who was driving the Sonas project.

Ogden Group had been trying to advance it since 1993, when it bought the 105-acre racecourse, and Turner had every reason to believe that the project was a real runner. At the time, Bord Fáilte regarded a casino as an 'attractive addition' to Ireland's tourism facilities, Fingal county manager Davy Byrne warmly welcomed it, and the promoters were also encouraged in their endeavours by then Taoiseach Albert Reynolds. The legendary former government press secretary P.J. Mara, who had set up as a public affairs consultant, was actively working as a lobbyist for the project. Turner's associate Robert White had gone to school in Drumcondra with Bertie Ahern, then Minister for Finance in the Fianna Fáil–Labour Coalition and later leader of his party in opposition after that government collapsed in disarray in December 1994. And Fianna Fáil heavyweight Brian Cowen had attended Ogden's celebration party at the Conrad Hotel in May 1996, after An Bord Pleanála granted full planning permission for the project, largely on the grounds of its 'macro-economic impact'. Thus, when it was put to Robert White that Ogden still needed to obtain a casino licence and the Rainbow Coalition government had shown no willingness to grant one, he smiled, saying: 'But what about the next government?'

All of this was known at the time. What wasn't known and only emerged much later was that Turner gave an envelope containing $10,000 in cash as a secret donation to Fianna Fáil fund-raiser Des Richardson at a 'liquid lunch' in Manchester in the spring of 1994. Or that Ahern, during his time as Minister for Finance, had arranged to get an Irish passport for Turner. Or that the National Lottery had opened confidential talks with the Manchester businessman on the possibility of getting involved in the casino project, while Ahern was the minister with political responsibility for the Lottery. Or that Ahern, as leader of the Opposition, had accepted 'corporate hospitality' from Turner, who paid for several trips so that this politically powerful Manchester United fan could watch his favourite football team playing at Old Trafford. Against that backdrop, it's no wonder Ahern was unwilling for so long to pledge that Fianna Fáil would not grant a casino licence if the party was returned to power in 1997, which it was; his only reservation related to the huge number of 'one-armed bandits' – several thousand slot and poker machines – planned by Ogden because of the potential social ills of this form of gambling. It seemed to escape his attention that 20,000 people had objected to the company's planning application, as a result of a very well-organized campaign by a coalition of residents' associations, the West Dublin Action Group.

Local politicians Brian Lenihan and Liam Lawlor were feeling the heat, however. Unusually for Lawlor, the Sonas Centre was one of the few development projects he 'resolutely' opposed; heck, he had even turned down a very tempting £100,000 offer from Ogden to lobby for the scheme. Harry Shiels, chairman of the West Dublin Action Group, recalls that he had 'no trouble' persuading the then Taoiseach, John Bruton, to give a commitment that the Gaming and Lotteries Act would not be amended to allow a casino. But Bertie Ahern was a different matter. 'We got no support from Mr Ahern on the issue, and I would be worried that, if Fianna Fáil were in power, it may have been a different story,' he said at the time. It was only when it became evident that the campaign against the Sonas Centre was so strong that it threatened Fianna Fáil's prospects of winning two seats in Dublin West did Bertie Ahern give in on the issue. In April 1997, just before the general election was called, he made it clear that 'there will be no casino, as proposed, for the Phoenix Park racecourse site'. Both Lenihan and Lawlor breathed sighs of relief and went on to win their seats.

After the truth about what went on behind the scenes began to emerge via the Planning Tribunal, Ahern had this to say: 'I was broadly in favour of the development, as most people were, because it was providing 2,500 jobs and lots of construction jobs, but I was totally opposed to the gambling end of it, because all through my political career I had opposed one-armed bandits.' But this statement was disingenuous, because he was well aware that the 'gambling end of it' was inseparable from the rest; Turner himself was on record as saying that the scheme would go ahead only if a casino licence were issued. Ahern's spokesman also suggested that, while he knew Turner, it was a 'matter of public record' that he had objected to the casino proposal when planning approval was sought. This was simply untrue; his April 1997 statement in the Dáil as leader of the Opposition came three years *after* Ogden made its application.

Ahern denied that there was 'anything improper' about him attending Manchester United matches at Ogden's expense or arranging an Irish passport for Turner, as he would have been entitled to one anyway because his mother came from Cork. He also denied that he had given 'implicit approval' for the casino project by permitting An Post, which runs the National Lottery, to enter into negotiations with Ogden with a view to becoming involved in the casino. But John Hynes, former chief executive of An Post, said he was 'fully satisfied' from his contacts with civil servants in the Department of Finance that Ahern 'did not demur' when Hynes entered talks with the casino promoters. 'There is no question whatever in my mind as chairman of the company that my lines were clear with the minister,' Hynes said. 'Had I not known that, I would not have gone one inch down the road.' Turner had also made it clear to Hynes that Ahern 'was known to him, was aware of all aspects of the project, and was not opposed to the casino'.

Their meetings were attended by Robert White, whom he understood to be an associate of Ahern, 'keeping an eye' on the political dimension to the project. 'I was now comfortable that the National Lottery Company was not operating outside an envelope of departmental and ministerial approval. The minister had two open channels providing feedback on the discussions, one official and one party political.' Ahern responded by saying, 'To be frank, if I had been asked to give approval to that, I am sure that I would have, but I was not asked ...' Fine Gael environment spokesman Phil Hogan, who revealed the passport aspect of the affair, obtained a Department of Finance file which noted Norman Turner as saying he had received assurances from government ministers that there would be no problem 'about the promotion of amending legislation' to facilitate a casino. In one briefing, Ahern is noted as having misgivings about the extent of gaming machines. 'But other than that issue there is no indication that he expressed opposition to the concept of the casino project,' Hogan said. 'When the issue became hot with local residents, he decided to switch tack in order to gain votes in the 1997 general election.'

Bertie Ahern's change of tune meant that the Sonas Centre was doomed, leaving Norman Turner and Robert White with no option but to cash in their chips. In July 1998, Ogden sold the old racecourse to developers Flynn and O'Flaherty for £37 million – nearly three times as much as it had paid for the property five years earlier. Emboldened by the government's 1999 Residential Density Guidelines, which promoted higher density housing in locations close to good public transport, Flynn and O'Flaherty set about having the racecourse rezoned for residential development. The 2001 demolition of one of its most memorable features, the timber-framed gate house and turnstiles, was brushed off by Fingal County Council as a 'stupid mistake'; these buildings were meant to be retained. By mid-August 2003, Flynn and O'Flaherty had secured full planning permission from An Bord Pleanála to roll out more than 2,300 new homes across the racecourse, along with an 18-acre public park and other community facilities, including bars, restaurants, shops, crèches and a primary school, all designed by OMS Architects. In May 2004, when the first phase was launched, Flynn and O'Flaherty grossed €110 million in one day and stood to 'make vastly more money from the Phoenix Park racecourse than the bookies ever did in 90 years of racing', as Jack Fagan put it in the *Irish Times*.

Ahern's close links with the Sonas Centre promoters would not have come to light without the work done by the Planning Tribunal. The tribunal also – more dramatically – brought about his political downfall. Investigating Tom Gilmartin's allegation that Ahern had received £80,000 from Owen O'Callaghan in relation to the Quarryvale project – which the Cork developer dismissed as 'absolute and total rubbish' – the tribunal trawled through Ahern's bank accounts and uncovered a bewildering array of transactions, including several in sterling. Many of these transactions – amounting to a value of nearly €900,000 in 2008 terms, by the calculation of Colm Keena – could not be easily explained; by the time his former secretary Gráinne Carruth broke down in the witness box while attempting to do so, the Taoiseach's credibility had suffered irreparable harm. Ahern announced his resignation on 2 April 2008, declaring that he had 'never received a corrupt payment'.

3. The Boxes

It sounds completely absurd, but it's true: a picture of the Statoil filling station on Usher's Quay graced the cover of Dublin Corporation's first urban renewal brochure in 1986. The photograph was cleverly taken, with the balustrade of Father Matthew Bridge in the foreground, but it was still a decidedly odd image of 'urban renewal'. It was, in fact, a sign of desperation: there was so little happening at the time in the inner city that even a petrol station was seen as 'progress'. The Liffey Quays were in dire straits, pockmarked by derelict sites and dilapidated buildings, as a result of long-term road-widening plans and a marked reluctance among developers to invest in the inner city. Within Dublin's canal ring, it was estimated that 150 acres of land were lying derelict – roughly six times the size of St Stephen's Green.

This state of affairs was the stimulus for the 1986 Urban Renewal Act brought in by the Fine Gael–Labour coalition government, under which generous tax incentives and rates rebates were provided for qualifying commercial or residential developments in designated areas. But it is a remarkable fact that, apart from flats that had to be provided as the 'residential content' of much larger office developments, there wasn't a single freestanding, purpose-built apartment block developed on the quays – or anywhere else in the inner city – until the autumn of 1991. That first block on Wolfe Tone Quay, designed by BKD, was a real breakthrough. Despite the juicy tax incentives available through Section 23 and the Urban Renewal Act, developers were mainly interested in building more offices – and the odd petrol station – and the city planners were more than prepared to facilitate them. In a crude form of urban dentistry, they sought to fill the holes in Dublin's fabric with whatever the developers wanted to build – and anything, even a petrol station with pretensions, was better than nothing. The planners were also under the government's cosh to produce development, in a generic sense; 'never mind the quality, feel the width' was the mantra of successive ministers as they reeled out onward and upward figures on square footage and investment levels.

Neither the planners nor the developers anticipated that there would be a market for residential space in the inner city, let alone a thriving one. But there was one man who could see that there was money to be made from developing flats in town, and that man was Liam Carroll. A Dundalk-born mechanical engineer who worked for Jacobs International, he was bitten by the property bug in his early thirties when he bought a site, had a house built by subcontractors and reckoned that there was no great mystery to this property game. The really surprising thing is that he went on to become the main engine of urban renewal in Dublin, building more apartments in the inner city than all other developers combined.

Carroll started out on the fringes of the inner city, building humdrum apartments and town houses in Beaver Row, Donnybrook and 'Fisherman's Wharf' in Ringsend – not a real place, of course, but a marketing name invented by Carroll's trusty estate agents, Hooke and MacDonald. They had also handled the sale in 1990 of 'Portobello Harbour', on the Grand Canal, a scheme of back-to-back 'town houses' built on a site once occupied by Brittain Motors. Designed in mock-Palladian style by Carroll and his own team of architectural technicians, the houses on the canal frontage are four storeys high, with one room per floor and staircases so constricted that residents found it difficult to get double beds in.

Carroll completed the scheme by building an office block near the corner of Lower Rathmines Road, which provided a basic working environment for the technicians to churn out a seemingly endless series of architect-free apartment schemes in such locations as Arran Quay, Usher's Quay, Bridge Street, Brunswick Street, Francis Street, Werburgh Street, Cornmarket,

Newmarket, Abbey Street, Dorset Street, Great Strand Street, Gardiner Street, Ringsend Road and Bachelors Walk.

Purchasers got only the bare minimum – usually shoebox-sized single-bedroom apartments laid out by the dozen on long, narrow, artificially lit corridors redolent of a budget hotel, with just one tiny lift to serve them, or no lift at all in many cases. Balconies, where they were provided, were of the clip-on variety with just about enough room for a few pot plants. Storage space was non-existent, with even the upper level of a hot press fully taken up by a heavy-duty PVC cold-water tank. Kitchens usually consisted of small windowless galleys in 'alcoves' tacked on to the end of living rooms, while nearly every apartment was 'single aspect' – in other words, windows faced only one direction. And what the estate agents described as 'landscaped courtyards' were merely surface car parks with some trees planted to take the bare look off the concrete cobblelock paving. Show flats were generally decorated in chintzy suburban style, often using scaled-down furniture to give the impression that there was more space, but bedrooms were still so small that one had to walk sideways to get past the end of the bed. Many of these shoeboxes were purchased by young first-timers seeking a tax-efficient foothold on the housing ladder and by people from the country looking for somewhere to stash the kids when they went to college in Dublin. But most of them were snapped up by an army of investors availing themselves of the Section 23 tax incentive, which allowed them to write off the capital cost against all rental income.

Month after month, Hooke and MacDonald were able to claim another 'sales coup' as scheme after scheme sold like hot cakes to a public largely uneducated in what to expect of apartment living in a European capital city. Liam Carroll, their principal client, was making money hand over fist. He had a genius for site assembly. Every site he developed, usually in run-down areas where property could be acquired cheaply, was assembled by him personally, rather than at arm's length through agents, and he would often go back again and again to reluctant vendors until he clinched a deal. He knocked on doors himself, cut the deals himself, wrote the cheques himself. His administration, like everything else about him and his business, was and is famously sparse. His defence of the shoeboxes he produced was that he was building flats that people such as nurses, gardaí and teachers could afford.

At a professional level, to paraphrase the football chant, no one likes him and he doesn't care. Commonly described as 'abrupt' and 'direct', he has an extreme aversion to media attention of any kind – except when he needs it to launch a development. Asked to characterize Carroll, one leading architect said, 'in a word, miserable . . . He thinks people are always looking for something off him.' Another disaffected observer said, 'I saw him outside the Four Courts recently in his anorak with a bagel and Coke for his lunch. He'd prefer that to going into a café.' Whether any or all of this is down to his legendary thriftiness, solitary nature or general aversion to men in sharp suits and fast cars is moot. Few know him well enough to be definitive. People who have been in the business for 20 years and are active in the Construction Industry Federation and the Irish Home Builders' Association have never clapped eyes on him. The hearty dislike for him in some quarters may be attributable to his refusal to play the social game or to explain his actions. 'He's a complete loner. He's not into paying big corporate fees, or hanging around the Dáil bar. There is no inner circle. He's not beholden to Irish banks: he'll use international ones if it suits him.'

It was only when other developers entered the Dublin apartment market with more sophisticated schemes that Carroll finally engaged architects, commissioning O'Mahony Pike to design the 16-storey Millennium Tower and its flanking blocks at Charlotte Quay; previously he had complained that architects were 'only interested in designing penthouses for fellows with Mercs'. This move paid off handsomely, with Zoe Developments winning permission from An Bord Pleanála to retain four floors that the city planners had wanted to lop off. Carroll knew that this victory was won on design grounds; had he stuck to his old ways of doing things, the tower would probably never have risen above 12 storeys.

It was not long before Carroll started to work through a new vehicle, Danninger, which largely eclipsed Zoe. Zoe's earlier output had already prompted the Department of the Environment to take action by issuing new apartment design guidelines that set minimum standards for the size of flats as well as specifying a more varied mix of unit types in every scheme. The guidelines, issued in 1995, were a long time coming; apparently, some senior officials were afraid that the bubble would burst if higher standards were applied. Ken MacDonald – managing director of Hooke and MacDonald, which sold more inner-city apartments than any of its competitors – wrote an article for the *Irish Times* in which he railed against the notion that apartments should be more commodious, arguing that this would make them unaffordable. The idea of banning single-aspect flats with corridor access was 'an extraordinary design limitation which would push up the cost of apartment construction' he said. 'To place unnecessary obstacles on architects, builders and ultimately homebuyers would be very damaging to the entire urban renewal process.' Fortunately, the then Minister of State for Urban Renewal, Liz McManus, was a qualified architect, and she could see for herself that standards needed to be improved. But the new guidelines came too late to prevent Bachelors Walk falling victim to the standard Zoe treatment – 335 apartments, of which 293 are single-bedroom units, laid out along narrow corridors behind a mock-Georgian façade. It was schemes like this that consultants (commissioned by McManus to carry out a root-and-branch review of the urban renewal programme) had in mind when they criticized 'small and spatially repetitive' apartments, with tiny bathrooms and kitchenettes, 'many of them internalized with little natural light or ventilation'. Such apartment blocks seemed destined even then to become the tenements of the 21st century.

Given his own aversion to architects at the time, it is an extraordinary fact that Liam Carroll found himself sitting on the jury for an architectural competition in 1997. He had bought a site on the corner of Bow Street and North King Street, but couldn't get his hands on the site next door because it was owned by Dublin Corporation – and the corporation, at city architect Jim Barrett's instigation, wouldn't sell it to him unless he agreed to co-sponsor the competition and build the winning scheme. This led to an unusual collaboration with Grafton Architects, the highly respected practice run by Yvonne Farrell and Shelley McNamara; Carroll used to refer to them as 'the girls'. What they produced was a complex of six town houses and sixty apartments, rising to five and six storeys on the street frontages, with tall workshop units on the ground floor, sharply defined corners and sliding cedarwood shutters at every level of the framed brick façades. Though its interior spaces were compromised by Zoe's standardized approach, the contrast between this project and most of its other schemes could not be more marked. Curiously, however, the apartments were first let rather than sold and only years later marketed for sale, mainly to investors, as 'Smithfield Lofts', while most of the workshop and retail units at street level remain stubbornly vacant.

Carroll's development activity had intensified in 1996 after his purchase for a then record £8 million of the Gasworks site off Barrow Street, where the mix Danninger proposed was to include 17,565 square metres of office space, 600 apartments and local shopping facilities; Carroll let one of the office blocks to Google, undercutting offers from his rivals. Over 200 of the apartments, also designed by O'Mahony Pike, were built within the iron framework of a Victorian gasholder – a greedy nine storeys rather than a more generous eight – laid out around a circular landscaped courtyard, open to the sky. Curiously, though all of the other apartments in the Gasworks scheme were profitably sold, these uniquely different units failed to find ready buyers at the prices sought in June 2006 (ranging from €675,000 to just over €1 million), and Carroll subsequently decided that the gasholder would be more profitable if it was turned into a 500-bedroom hotel.

Needless to say, those who had bought apartments in the scheme were horrified by this change of plan. As the *Irish Times* reported, their objections 'focused on the issues of noise, risks to safety and security, loss of privacy, access to parking, general disruption and the presence of smokers'. Among the objectors was fashion designer Mariad Whisker, who complained that the proposed hotel could attract stag and hen parties, not to mention rugby supporters wishing to stay close to the redeveloped Lansdowne Road, and the entire complex, which had been marketed as a 'prestigious residential development', would be at risk from 'unsociable behaviour'. Local Labour councillor and former Lord Mayor Dermot Lacey characterized the plan as 'an ill-conceived, ill-thought-out, cheap attempt to make a big profit'; at the time of writing it was still before An Bord Pleanála.

Equally remarkable was Liam Carroll's success in letting a second office block at Cherrywood to Dell in 2004 at a time when the vacancy rate for suburban offices was nearly 30 per cent. But he was slow to see the benefit of extending the Luas tram system southwards from Sandyford and was the last developer in the area to contribute towards its capital cost; other developers operating in the area that would be served by Luas, notably Treasury Holdings and Park Developments, had to bring in economist Peter Bacon to lobby for the development levy. Carroll didn't always get his way. In 2004, he lost an appeal to An Bord Pleanála against South Dublin County Council's decision to impose a development levy of €5.5 million towards the provision of public infrastructure to serve a mixed scheme of 537 apartments, 15 retail units and a 140-bedroom hotel at Belgard Square, Tallaght. A year later, he lost another appeal to An Bord Pleanála over revised plans by Danninger to convert the former convent buildings at Loreto Abbey, Rathfarnham, into offices. After buying the 12-acre site in 2000 for £14 million, his original plan was to convert the buildings into a nursing home and build 10 apartment blocks in the wooded grounds. Danninger also lost two High Court actions claiming that it had contracts to purchase two sites in the city centre. In a case involving Walden Motors in 2003, Mr Justice Kelly expressed surprise that it had ever been brought. And in February 2007, Carroll's claim that he had a contract to develop a Dublin Bus site on Abbey Street was also dismissed. He suffered another setback a month later when

Dublin City Council rejected his plans for a major office development on the former Brooks Thomas timber yard at North Wall Quay, because of its 'excessive bulk'. A revised scheme was later agreed with the Dublin Docklands Development Authority; it is intended to house Anglo Irish Bank's new headquarters.

Much more ambitious is Carroll's plan for a huge mixed-use development of offices, shops and nearly 800 apartments in 10 blocks on South Bank Road in Ringsend – a 12-acre site he bought from AIB for more than £20 million in 2000; among the local objectors was John Gormley TD, now Minister for the Environment and Green Party leader. In late 2006, Carroll managed to persuade Bohemians soccer club to sign over the title to Dalymount Park in a deal worth €65 million – €40 million in cash, to be paid in instalments, plus a new 10,000-seat stadium at Harristown, near Dublin Airport. Carroll will attempt to have the five-acre Bohemians' site in Phibsborough rezoned for development.

His first major venture outside Dublin was in Tralee, Co. Kerry, where he has developed an extensive site along the south side of Dan Spring Road. Formerly a swamp, it is now lined by apartment blocks terminating with the Fels Point Hotel, which Carroll owns and operates. He is also developing the €120 million Parkway shopping centre in Limerick, which will have a lettable floor area of 23,225 square metres (250,000 square feet). It is being built alongside an existing retail park developed by Dunloe Ewart, and will reinforce the unfortunate pattern of out-of-town shopping that is squeezing retail in the city centre.

Nobody knows what Liam Carroll is going to do next – apart from himself and a tight circle of henchmen. Certainly, it would have been difficult to imagine that the man behind Zoe Developments and all the shoebox apartments it built in the early 1990s would go on to become one of Ireland's leading corporate raiders. His most recent target was Irish Continental Group, which owns Irish Ferries. In the midst of a take-over battle between two consortiums for control of the company, cash-rich Carroll built up a stake of 10 per cent – possibly to become kingmaker (a role he also sought to play in Jurys Doyle and Greencore), or with his sharp eye on the 33 acres of land ICG owns in Dublin Port. Carroll first entered the Greencore lists in summer 2006, when he paid €170 million for the 22 per cent stake in the food company held for years by Dermot Desmond. He bought more shares to bring his stake to 29.5 per cent – just below the level at which he would have to make a formal bid for the company. By the end of 2007, Carroll's personal stake was valued at nearly €300 million, but he was clearly not in the game to make ready-to-go sandwiches. Although he never publicly said so, what appears to engage his interest is Greencore's land bank of 900 acres, mainly in Carlow and Mallow, where sites occupied by sugar factories once owned by the state are likely to be redeveloped.

Carroll showed his mettle in a titanic struggle to wrest control of property company Dunloe Ewart from the wily solicitor-developer Noel Smyth in 2002. What seemed like a simple revenge attack on Smyth for besting him over a site on Sir John Rogerson's Quay proved to be infinitely more sophisticated. Famously, Carroll sustained his two-year campaign without a single phone call to Smyth, who said: 'If you can imagine somebody spending fifty million to buy into your company and won't spend 10 cents on a phone call . . .' Smyth wasn't accustomed to getting the cold shoulder. He was a trusted adviser at various times to such movers and shakers as Dermot Desmond, Ben Dunne, Phil Monahan and Paschal Taggart, although some of these relationships turned sour. Often, this had to do with his practice of waiving his fees as a solicitor in exchange for a percentage of the action; as Pat Doherty once said, he was the sort of solicitor 'to whom you went for advice only to come away with a business partner'. Few could reconcile Smyth's aggressive pursuit of property deals with his devout Catholicism, which included attendance at Mass every morning in St Mary's Church, Haddington Road, keeping a holy water font beside the door of his office in Fitzwilliam Square, breaking business meetings for the Angelus and bankrolling a countrywide tour in 2001 of the relics of St Thérèse of Lisieux, after whom his Sandyford home is named. In public, he is chiefly remembered for his dramatic appearance at the McCracken Tribunal in 1997 with documentary evidence of his meetings with Charlie Haughey in relation to the £1.3 million in payments Haughey had received from Smyth's client, Ben Dunne.

Carroll added to his stake in Dunloe Ewart month by month. To raise money to buy back shares and stave off a hostile takeover, the company had to sell such assets as the Bloomfields shopping centre in Dún Laoghaire, the Mill shopping centre in Clondalkin and its entire property portfolio in Belfast, which Smyth had spent 12 years building up. But Carroll prevailed in the end. In November 2002, his vehicle – appropriately named Rambridge – made a successful bid for Dunloe Ewart, in a transaction that valued the company at €197 million. Noel Smyth did quite well out of it, netting an estimated €30 million in profit on his initial investment. Thus, Carroll took over Dunloe Ewart and its valuable four-acre site on Sir John Rogerson's Quay, in Docklands, on which Smyth had secured planning permission for a major mixed-use scheme of offices and apartments, as well as 412 acres at Cherrywood, in south Co. Dublin, which Dunloe was to develop in a joint venture with British Land; this land bank alone, its true extent almost buried in the portfolio, could have been worth up to €1 billion. It is said that Carroll's first request after taking over Dunloe was for the keys to the company's S-class Mercedes. Among the many unverifiable tales about his frugality is one about his trip to London to buy out British Land's stake in the Cherrywood development: the story goes that he turned down the smoked salmon lunch on offer, saying it was a bit rich for him and that he'd already had a Ryanair sandwich, thank you.

Colm Keena of the *Irish Times* estimated in October 2007 that Liam Carroll's wealth is probably in excess of €1 billion. Surprisingly, given his own desire for privacy, Carroll's major holding companies filed substantial amounts of financial information with the Companies Registration Office. The largest, Zelderbridge, had net assets of €779 million at the end of

December 2005. Although not obliged to file accounts, figures showed that the 66 companies it owned had made operating profits totalling €28.2 million that year. A Zelderbridge company, Andinka, which makes loans to other companies in the group, increased its issued share capital by nearly €200 million during 2005, the new shares being paid for in cash. It is an indication of the level of Carroll's development activity that these loans were worth €425 million in the same year. Records show that he and his wife became directors of Zoe Developments in the late 1980s. The company's first mortgage was taken out with Arlington Securities, the British vendors of a number of buildings on Bachelors Walk, rather than with a bank. By 2000, Zoe had accumulated profits of £21 million. After Danninger had become the main apartment development company in the group, its 2000 and 2001 accounts gave an insight into how profitable the business had become, showing a very healthy operating profit of 32 per cent on sales. It also receives €3.76 million annually in rent from the state for properties in Dublin.

One of the secrets of Carroll's success as a corporate raider is that he has accumulated a war chest by turning his rental income, both present and future, into valuable securities. 'The process works through bundling the rental income from several properties together,' the *Irish Daily Mail* explained in March 2008. 'The client's bank then places this income into a rental conduit which is subsequently sold on to other banks.' Renting apartments rather than selling them off also leaves open the possibility of replacing whole blocks with more lucrative schemes, and in March 2008 Carroll sought planning permission to demolish a 47-unit apartment block on Watling Street, built just 10 years earlier, with the intention of building offices on the site; we can expect to see more of that in the future.

In an industry where stables of thoroughbreds, €18 million choppers and private Girls Aloud gigs are standard kit for even the minnows, Carroll is a maverick, a puzzle wrapped in an enigma, a soft-spoken billionaire in blue jeans, woolly geansaí and ageing Toyota saloon, trucking home to Mount Merrion every evening to the same ordinary, four-bed semi he moved into more than 20 years ago with his wife, Róisín, a former maths teacher, and their family of three. No sign of glass-covered swimming pools chez Carroll, then?

'They might have done a kitchen extension,' muses a long-time neighbour. 'We'd see him going out in the morning in his jeans and jumper and six-year-old Corolla and for a good while we thought he was a carpenter. Then he turns out to be the biggest developer in Dublin. I think he's been seen in a suit once, at his daughter's school debs.' The glitz of the charity-ball circuit and councillor-schmoozing race meetings are not his thing. His life revolves around his wife and children. Outings might involve Sunday lunch in the old Berkeley Court, weekends in Kilkenny, GAA matches at Croke Park, a stroll up to Kiely's of Mount Merrion for a pint or a cup of tea. Family holidays used to be in a mobile home in Louth; later they graduated to Italy and Portugal, always with an eye to child compatibility. The grown-up children, in turn, are equally modest, lacking either flashiness or a sense of entitlement. At a personal level, there are some people who describe him as a 'decent' man. 'Liam Carroll was way ahead of his time; he built in the inner city when no one else would touch it,' says another big developer wryly. He craves neither publicity nor possessions.

The last thing he would have wanted was a front-page piece in the *Irish Times* highlighting his loss of some €20 million on the sale of shares in Aer Lingus – especially when it was described by anonymous stockbrokers as a 'fire sale'. As Ciarán Hancock reported, Carroll had bought the 31 million shares at close to €2 apiece, but sold them for only €1.15. It was more complicated than that, however, because the reclusive developer had acquired his Aer Lingus shares through 'contracts for difference'. CFDs give an investor the benefits of trading in shares at a percentage of what they would cost to buy, without actually having to own them or declare his interests. But there is a downside: if the shares fall in value, the investor is exposed to 'margin calls', which can prove very costly. What Liam Carroll was doing in selling his

Aer Lingus shares was 'crystallizing his losses', as one market watcher pithily put it. When he was asked to comment by the *Irish Times*, all the man himself said was: 'I never comment to newspapers.'

At the end of it all, the mystery remains. What continues to drive a man like Liam Carroll? With more land than he can possibly develop in his lifetime, he continues to prowl for more. While other successful developers of his generation start to ponder their legacy, there is little sign of this from Carroll. Is there a grand gesture lurking in the great enigma? The answer is, probably not.

The Cosgrave brothers, by contrast, like to make their mark. Their early housing schemes feature roundel plaques inscribed, in Kilroy Was Here style, 'Cosgrave Bros'. And some of those schemes made a mark by going where other developers feared to tread. Custom Hall, in Gardiner Street on the north side of Dublin, is a humdrum piece of neoclassical pastiche, with five-storey blocks of smallish flats standing on stilts above basement car parking; but it took a lot of courage to build in Gardiner Street in the early 1990s. The junction with Sean MacDermott Street was known as 'Handbag Corner' because of the dexterity of local thieves in snatching bags from cars while women drivers were stopped at the traffic lights. Custom Hall pioneered the regeneration of Gardiner Street, changing the image of the area.

By the mid-1990s, the Cosgraves had a proven track record in building houses and apartments in the Dublin area. Schemes designed for them by Ambrose Kelly's Project Architects included Ha'penny Bridge House on Ormond Quay, with its kitsch reference to the bridge over its entrance and just one lift to serve the 60-plus apartments, and the fussy-looking Pembroke Square in Upper Grand Canal Street, on a site once occupied by Irish Meat Packers. They built a remarkably similar apartment block at Charlemont Street, on a site which had been derelict for years while in the hands of Albert Holdings, a company controlled by civil engineering group Murphy International. Now within a stone's throw of the Sandyford Luas line, it also adjoins the headquarters of ACC Bank and the Hilton Hotel. Other schemes from the 1980s and early 1990s include the Noddyland-style Sweepstakes, in Ballsbridge, and the disappointingly under-scaled Donnybrook Manor on Morehampton Road, as well as Shrewsbury, in Ballsbridge; The Orchard, in Ranelagh; Temple Manor, in Celbridge; Chesterfield, in Castleknock; and Christchurch Hall, in High Street.

The three brothers – Michael, Peter and Joe – must have stepped on someone's toes during their long involvement in the Dublin property scene but, if so, no one seems to remember. Unlike other developers, who leave human debris and dismay in their explosive wake, the Cosgraves scatter pixie dust. Throughout the industry, there is the same definitive, single-word response to queries about them: 'Gentlemen.' Or even: 'Absolute gentlemen.' Their drive for quality is widely admired: 'Some of the others might do just about what's necessary on a site, but the Cosgraves actually care. If [named developer] didn't have to put heavy-gauge railing around an open space, he wouldn't. The Cosgraves would, simply because they'd see it as the right thing to do,' says an industry source. But the goodwill is not simply down to quality buildings. Another source not known for his warm feelings towards developers says: 'It would restore your faith in human nature that good guys could make a few quid in a tough business . . . They are genuinely nice, decent guys and they're not stupid, just sound.' A professional who has worked on complex Cosgrave projects is equally effusive: 'I couldn't say enough good things about Joe Cosgrave. He's just a really nice guy . . . Of all of them, I would single him out as being very good and generous. And he's willing to take advice.'

The original three Cosgrave brothers are all still in their forties. A fourth brother, Willie, in his early thirties, is now also involved, and their sister, Helen, is involved at the accountancy end of the business. 'There is no leader, which is most unusual in a successful company,' says one who knows them well. 'Peter tends to look after the commercial side, while Michael and Joe are more hands-on-site. Some people suggest that Peter is the brains, more of the intellect behind it, and he has developed the commercial side, but he couldn't have done that without the finance generated from the thriving residential end.' None of the three had a third-level education. 'If there is an academic-type deep-thinker among them,' says a friend, 'it would probably be Peter. He's a bit different, quieter, and can be seen as hard work to talk to, where Joe is more jovial and loves the craic.' All three were tradesmen to begin with – Joe and Peter were carpenters, Michael drove machines – which may surprise some who believe that the brothers were born with silver spoons in their mouths. They were reared in Churchtown, Dublin, where their father, Jack, ran the animal pound and bred turkeys and pigs for sale. His money-making instinct was passed on to his sons, along with a shrewd brain, motivation and a code of ethics, but he was by no means a wealthy man in those years. He would tell stories about the time the cats got at the turkeys they needed to sell for Christmas, for example, leaving them with little to celebrate. But he had also been a man about town in the 1960s, his drinking buddies including fellow Churchtown man P. V. Doyle, the late hotelier, and he combined a lifelong interest in snooker with the ownership of Jason's snooker hall in Ranelagh.

Joe, Peter and Michael were still in their early twenties when they began their foray into house-building as Cosgrave Brothers, starting with a handful of houses in Bluebell and the purchase in 1979 of five housing sites in Stillorgan from Patrick Gallagher. 'They're tough – but not with the same extreme, eh, cute hoorness, that you'd see in other fellas in the business,' says an acquaintance. 'They're always ready to give a handout and they have great connections. You'd never hear a word of jealousy out of them about others. Ego doesn't come into it.' But that should not be mistaken for a lack of shrewdness. For example, when they built an eighty-apartment scheme on a prime four-acre site in Simmonscourt, Ballsbridge, in the mid-1990s, they chose to rent rather than sell them. 'If those eighty-odd apartments had been sold then, they'd have gone for around €100,000 each. Now they're worth about three-quarters of a million to €1 million each, a big advance on the €10 million total it would have cost for the site and the apartments in the first place. But look at the land they're on – based on Seán Dunne values, that four acres is worth around €200 million now. If you demolished all the apartments, you'd get even more for the site. Cute move.' In recent years, it is estimated that they have spent more than half a billion euro investing in England, and the same again in New York.

In the early 1990s, Jack Cosgrave went into partnership with his son-in-law, Bryan Cullen, with a company called Jackson Properties, into which the brothers may have had some initial input. When Jack died in 2004, at the age of 73, he left almost €54 million in his will. The old animal pound registration book was one of the mementoes of his life presented at the huge funeral. His wife Patricia – 'she was the original Irish mammy; to her the boys were "The Men" and none of them left the family home till they got married' – still lives in the house where Jack was born. The couple's legacy is a bunch of united siblings who choose to work and play together. They live low-key lives, in lovely houses in desirable areas, such as Sandycove, Mount Anville and overlooking the Castle Golf Club in Rathfarnham. They all have mobile homes at the rather affluent end of Brittas Bay, in Ballincarrig. Joe was the last of them to move in to Brittas about four years ago, 'and he clearly wouldn't have moved in at that stage if they were just putting on a united front', adds a friend. He also has a villa in Marbella that was 'good value' 10 years ago. 'They're not at all flamboyant or into trophy purchases, such as racing cars or speedboats,' says an acquaintance. They share a helicopter with others and avail themselves of private jets, says the friend – which, on Planet Developer, is rather restrained behaviour. Joe's is the Cosgrave face at the charity balls – 'bidding quietly but generously' – and the main networker by all accounts. In 2006 he hosted a €10,000 table for Bill Clinton's Leadership for the Future address in the Burlington Hotel, where his guests included Albert Reynolds.

The Cosgraves' unlimited holding company, Borg Developments, is owned by an Isle of Man company, Waterpool Ltd, which is in turn owned by another Irish-registered unlimited company, Genstar. As Colm Keena reported, Borg had 39 mortgages registered for the period since 1985, the majority for plots of land and buildings in Dublin. Most of these mortgages are taken out with AIB, and some are with Lombard and Ulster. The brothers are also in receipt of substantial rental income.

In 1996, the Cosgraves bought St Helen's House in Booterstown for £2 million, taking it off the hands of Seán Dunne, who had toyed with turning the listed 18th-century building into a hotel and then offices. With the addition of a bedroom block to the north-east, it has been trading as the four-star Radisson Hotel since 1998 and is still owned by the brothers. The accounts for one of the Genstar group companies, St Helen's Hotel Ltd, show that they were paid €1.65 million in rent by the company in 2005, as part of a 35-year lease arrangement.

A bigger coup was their acquisition in 1996 of a 22-acre site in the middle of Blanchardstown and its subsequent development as the West End Retail Park; it enabled them to poach such prime tenants as Next, Burton and Wallis from Green Property's nearby shopping centre by offering them much more trading space for roughly the same rent. But their most talked-about scheme was Ardilea Wood, a gated enclave of 10 luxury faux-Edwardian detached houses off Roebuck Road in Clonskeagh, finished in 2000. It didn't seem to matter that the houses faced a massive concrete retaining wall; they were perfectly pitched to nouveau riche aspirations.

In 1998, the Cosgraves paid £8 million for the Howth Lodge Hotel on Claremont Road in Sutton, with the intention of replacing it with over 130 apartments. But this scheme was strongly opposed by local residents and An Bord Pleanála refused permission in March 2000, citing the height, scale, bulk and 'monolithic form' of what had been proposed. A revised plan for a less dense development of 54 apartments was later approved, and these trophy flats – many with superb sea views – sold like hot cakes in 2004 at prices ranging from €695,000 to €2.5 million.

The proceeds went towards funding the purchase of a prime residential site on Thormanby Road for €15 million – €1 million per acre.

At George's Quay in the city centre, the brothers astonished competitors and conservationists alike by engaging big-league architects Skidmore Owings and Merrill to produce a sculpted glass office tower, more than 100 metres high, flanked by two tall apartment blocks with a covered shopping mall that would have brought some street life into the area. But although Dublin City Council decided to approve this scheme, it was shot down on appeal in 1999 – largely because of its visual impact on the Custom House and Trinity College. In the end, the Cosgraves had to revert to building an improved version of Keane Murphy Duff's 1990 plan for Irish Life, which consists solely of offices.

The Cosgraves are about to make a much bigger mark in the middle of Dún Laoghaire. In mid-2001, they agreed to purchase the old borough's golf club on a 78-acre site straddling Upper Glenageary Road in exchange for a new 300-acre course in Ballyman, near Enniskerry, and a *douceur* of €20 million to clinch the deal. Though this was highly controversial locally, 80 per cent of the club's members voted to accept the offer at an emergency general meeting in June 2002. Work later proceeded on laying out the expansive 27-hole course around Carrigollan Hill as well as building a new 2,500-square-metre clubhouse, fitness centre and 12-bay driving range. The developers' only setback was that they had to concede a public right of way through the site. They also had to pay the ESB to divert a power line through nearby Carrigollan Woods, cutting a swathe through its forestry.

Meanwhile, the Cosgraves had to ensure that the old golf club in Dún Laoghaire was rezoned for development – a step that the county council initially refused to make. This led former county manager Derek Brady to issue a 'health warning' on the county development plan, saying that insufficient land had been zoned for housing. It was only after then Minister for the Environment Martin Cullen intervened to direct the council to amend its plan in March 2004 that councillors – at the end of a marathon meeting which went on until 4 a.m. – voted to rezone the golf club site, designating 60 acres for development, with 18 acres set aside for public open space. In February 2007, when Cosgraves finally lodged a planning application for the first phase of the scheme – 626 apartments and 230 houses, including 171 'social and affordable' homes – the county council received more than 400 objections, mainly on the grounds of density, traffic, 'ghettoiza-tion' and the loss of so much green space. The master plan, by architects McCrossan O'Rourke Manning, includes a 5.5-acre public park with a lake as its centrepiece, as well as new pedestrian and cycle paths – and even a shuttle bus to the DART station in Dún Laoghaire. After requesting further information on issues regarding water, waste, site planning and traffic management, council officials approved the planning application in September 2007. Although councillors had decided that a local area plan should be drawn up to guide the development of this part of Dún Laoghaire – something that should have been done at the outset – the view taken by senior officials was that they were legally obliged to deal with the application. But the absence of an area plan was cited by many of the 16 residents' associations and individuals, who listed it among their main grounds for appealing the decision to An Bord Pleanála.

In 2001, the Cosgraves suffered a major setback when the appeals board flatly rejected plans for a major business park on a 193-acre site at Fassaroe, outside Bray, because it would have been heavily car dependent. It was clear then that the provision of public transport would be critical to unlocking the development potential of a land bank that embraces 600 acres in Ballyman and Fassaroe; otherwise, as Wicklow TD Dick Roche warned, the consequences of building up to 7,000 new homes as well as a business park generating 6,000 jobs would be 'truly horrific'. Luas offered the solution – but only if it could be diverted. The original plan was to extend the Sandyford line from Cherrywood to Bray, where it would link up with DART and rail services on the Dublin–Rosslare line. But the Railway Procurement Agency decided to change this plan, opting to terminate the Luas line at

Fassaroe rather than at Daly Station in Bray, after the Cosgraves agreed to part-finance the capital cost. Although the government's Transport 21 investment programme, launched in November 2005, showed a direct connection between the Luas and rail lines in Bray, all three route options put forward by the RPA for public consultation in 2007 terminated at Fassaroe, way out west of the town; all that was offered in terms of the 'seamless integration' promised by Transport 21 was a bus link between the proposed terminus and either Bray station or a new Luas stop at Woodbrook. Bray-based architect Adrian Buckley was right on the button when he complained that the diversion of Luas away from Ireland's eighth largest town was 'developer-led', to underpin future residential development in and around Fassaroe.

But the Cosgrave brothers also have plans for Bray, having spent €30 million in 2004 on the purchase of 20 acres of land from St Gerard's, the exclusive fee-paying private school, with the aim of building more houses there. They're also developing a 50-acre site at Santry Demesne – bought several years ago from IDA Ireland – for 12 logistics and retail warehousing units, four five-storey office blocks, 35 enterprise 'starter units' and three motor showrooms. All told, this scheme will provide 77,000 square metres of space with on-site parking for over 1,900 cars. In Drimnagh, they had to fight off local opposition to plans for eight blocks of apartments and 'live-work units' on a clapped-out industrial estate. Residents said the scheme would have a 'huge impact' visually and environmentally on Drimnagh Castle and the low-rise housing in the neighbourhood, but An Bord Pleanála decided that it could go ahead. And when 'Lansdowne Gate' was completed in early 2008, instead of following the example of other builders by slashing prices in a more difficult market, the brothers decided to lease the 280 apartments at rents of up to €1,700 per month – mainly to medical staff in the nearby Coombe and Crumlin hospitals – until it became more profitable to sell them. The Cosgraves also snapped up the redundant Dublin Exchange Facility, behind Jurys Inn on Custom House Quay, for €42 million – partly to avail themselves of some €6.5

million in unused tax allowances accrued from the original development under the incentives available for approved schemes in the IFSC.

Like other cash-rich developers, the Cosgraves have been investing some of their profits in Britain. Their first deal, in January 2006, involved two retail buildings at Caxtongate in Birmingham (bought for £80 million). This was followed by two blocks near Oxford Circus in London (£136 million) and the Liberty shopping centre in Romford, Essex (£281 million), plus the adjoining Littlewoods store (£30 million). It will be interesting to see if these investments pay off, given the downturn in consumer confidence and retail spending in the UK. In any case, it's a long way from shoebox flats in Gardiner Street.

4. From the Back of Beyond

In September 1999, the *Longford Leader* named four local boys made good – Jimmy Flynn, of Flynn and O'Flaherty; Joe O'Reilly and Liam Maye, of Castlethorn Construction; and Michael Whelan, of Maplewood Homes – as being among the dozen or so builders who controlled 7,000 acres of zoned housing land in the Dublin area that had yet to be developed. According to the paper, one of the aims of new planning legislation introduced by Noel Dempsey as Minister for the Environment was 'to push these builders into developing their zoned land rather than limiting development and keeping house prices up' by hoarding it. But the 2000 Planning Act didn't put an end to developers with huge land banks choosing when and where they would be brought into play. In any case, the Longford men fingered by the *Leader* were among the busiest builders in Dublin. Sure, they had accumulated land banks by buying sites as cheaply as possible – something that became more and more difficult as the economic boom continued – but there was no hard evidence that they had deliberately hoarded land to cash in on expected rises in house prices. Others did, and that's one of the main reasons why some of Dublin's new suburbs ended up in Longford. And Louth, Westmeath, Laois, Offaly, Carlow, Kilkenny and Wexford, as well as all over Meath, Kildare and Wicklow. There simply wasn't half enough housing being built in Dublin itself, which meant prices were high and many first-time buyers sought out more affordable homes in the ever-widening commuter belt.

Jimmy Flynn and his business partner Noel O'Flaherty weren't just interested in building houses. By the mid-1990s, they had built an office park at Richview in Clonskeagh and profitably sold on the blocks to financial institutions such as Scottish Provident, as well as Wainsfort Manor, a well-designed low-rise housing scheme on land acquired from the Holy Ghost Fathers in Kimmage; a later phase of this scheme gave the purchasers of smallish ground-floor apartments a large rear garden complete with Barna shed. In 1994 they laid the groundwork for one of their most ambitious projects by paying £3.2 million for a 20-acre site in Swords, located on the pivot between the main street and the bypass. Two years later, Fingal County Council designated the one-time village as its 'capital' and was developing plans to build a fine new headquarters for itself at the other end of Main Street, near Swords Castle. But what the burgeoning town really needed was a strong commercial core, and there was no better location than Flynn and O'Flaherty's newly acquired site, which had previously been used for horse grazing. In September 1996, they unveiled plans for a major shopping centre with more than 23,000 square metres of retail space, a bar, restaurants, offices, multiplex cinema and car park, in a scheme said to be worth £100 million. Designed by OMS Architects in close collaboration with council planners, the Pavilions was to be different from run-of-the-mill shopping centres, with a range of facilities as well as open streets and courts to make Swords more vibrant during the day and at night.

In 1999, Flynn and O'Flaherty did a deal with the Eircom pension fund to purchase the Pavilions by putting up the money for its construction. With success already guaranteed by high-profile pre-lets of two anchor stores and 52 shops, the developers set about acquiring adjoining land for future extensions. In 2000, they paid almost £3 million to disgraced former Fianna Fáil minister Ray Burke for his family home, Briargate, where he had received bribes from Bovale Developments and JMSE in June 1989. Land to the rear of the house was used to create a temporary access route for the Pavilions to alleviate weekend traffic chaos in the area after it was officially opened by Bertie Ahern in May 2001. A second phase, including the 11-screen Movies@Swords multiplex, a glazed atrium and 15 additional retail units, was added in September 2005. Costing €40 million, it was also 'forward funded' by Eircom Superannuation. The Pavilions was such a runaway success that Flynn and O'Flaherty sought planning permission for a third phase, with a further 7,400 square metres of retail space, a leisure centre, medical consulting units and 300 apartments. By then, the Eircom pension fund had decided to 'rebalance' its investment portfolio, shedding some of the property elements; the obvious candidate to realize a handsome profit from healthy capital appreciation was the Pavilions.

There was intense competition for the prize, involving several developers, financial instutions and private equity funds. In a dramatic illustration of what retailing machines are worth, it was snatched by Joe O'Reilly's Chartered Land for a record €575 million in July 2006 – a deal described by the *Irish Times* as 'the largest and most significant property investment ever to have been completed in Ireland'. The purchase included the adjoining five-acre site assembled by Flynn and O'Flaherty for another extension that would more than double its retail space from 44,000 to 94,000 square metres, turning the Pavilions into a major regional shopping centre for the whole of north Dublin and further afield. Cleverly, O'Reilly offloaded 50 per cent of the existing centre to two financial institutions, Irish Life and Irish Pension Fund Property Unit Trust, for €240 million, but kept the development site for himself. And with the benefit of his experience in developing Dundrum shopping centre, O'Reilly lined up both Marks & Spencer and House of Fraser as anchor tenants for the extended Pavilions.

Joe O'Reilly was a site foreman with Manor Park Homes when he got together with fellow Longfordman Liam Maye and builder John Fitzsimons to set up Castlethorn Construction, giving up his wellington boots for business suits. O'Reilly and Maye (who died in May 2008) each had a 40 per cent stake in the company, with the remaining 20 per cent held by Fitzsimons; the industry view is that O'Reilly acquired his stake in Castlethorn without having to put up any equity himself. Having made millions from Castlethorn, he went on to set up Chartered Land on his own account, to pursue major commercial developments such as its shopping centre scheme for the Carlton site in Upper O'Connell Street.

Now in his mid-forties, O'Reilly was of the generation that began to benefit from third-level education, emerging with qualifications in buildings management from Athlone Regional Technical College and DIT Bolton Street. Like fellow Longford developer Séamus Ross, he spent a year or two in Frankie Mulleady's construction business, riding his bicycle to work as a quantity surveyor for the Longford-based builder, whose vision was to try to keep young Longford lads employed at home throughout the tough years of the 1970s and 80s. The adjectives most used to describe O'Reilly are 'shy' and 'private'. 'He was a bashful, light, little fellow, very straight, but with nothing out-standing about him,' says an acquaintance from the old days. Not much has changed in one respect. He is still the man who famously shuns publicity, the unseen presence at his own launches. His Chartered Land website features photographs of all 'our people', with the single exception of the chairman, O'Reilly him-self. The Castlethorn website features no people or photographs at all. Industry sources describe him as 'the small guy who goes out of his way to be a face in the crowd', or 'the fella playing the role of the "fool" in the building-hat in the corner'. But he was way ahead of the pack in terms of timing, says one: 'He was selling off land to others in addition to building in his own right. He was very clever, buying land before it was rezoned.'

Known as 'Mr Shopping Centre', he works long hours and keeps the people around him on high alert. Staff phones are apt to ring at weekends and late evenings but it is said that he inspires huge loyalty in employees and expects nothing from them that he is not willing to give himself. Industry figures describe him as 'the biggest single player in the Dublin retail market', 'a man in a big hurry', 'a flamboyant, bullish character', 'a most driven individual', 'on the ball . . . the kind whose right hand doesn't know what the left hand is doing'. 'He worked the planners, using proper first principles,' says an admiring fellow developer. 'He's probably the Number One in town when you mix in what he's done, what he's doing and what he's going to do.' They talk of a very bright, down-to-earth, dynamic, understated, cautious individual with a keen interest in quality and who makes excellent use of architects.

He is said to have made little or no use of borrowings, unlike other high-profile developers such as Ray Grehan and Seán Dunne. O'Reilly is believed to be a Fianna Fáil supporter and to have donated money to Seán Ardagh, a Dublin South Central TD for the party, in 2000. A devoted husband to Deirdre, a former nurse from Monaghan, and father of four young children, he lives in a beautifully renovated house in Foxrock. The trappings of wealth include a mid-range helicopter, a Mercedes and a five-bedroom holiday home in the Denis O'Brien-owned Portuguese resort of Quinta do Lago, bought about 10 years ago for the modest (at least on Planet Developer) sum of around £600,000. But he has held on to his north Longford accent, is regularly seen at mass in Aughnacliffe with the family and continues to be a generous supporter of his own Dromard parish GAA club, Páirc na nGael. He prefers a pint to a Michelin-starred meal, and when he takes a table at Punchestown races in aid of Longford GAA he invariably surrounds himself with his many siblings rather than useful contacts. 'He likes golf and skiing,' says an acquaintance, 'but there's not much else to say about Joe O'Reilly. He's a pleasant guy, very low-key; you'd never see him on a bender. To chat to him, he's an ordinary joe, not remotely interesting, boring, shrewd, serious . . .'

From the outset, Castlethorn Construction put an emphasis on quality. Its name was always up front on planning applications and marketing material for new homes from the time it built its first housing scheme in Palmerstown, west Dublin; unlike many other developers, O'Reilly didn't use a different vehicle for each scheme. The company's biggest break in its early years was the purchase in 1991, for around £5 million, of a development site at Carysfort College in Blackrock. It was here that O'Reilly became one of the first Irish developers to recognize the power of marketing. Having obtained planning permission for an upmarket development of detached and semi-detached family homes, Castlethorn engaged advertising agencies and PR companies in a huge campaign for the scheme, called Carysfort Park, and it sold like hot cakes. Later, when Castlethorn built Avoca Park, also in Blackrock, a unique selling point was the involvement of four design teams in fitting out the houses using only quality Irish materials, in an 'Irish by Design' initiative inspired by the patriotic streak in Joe O'Reilly's personality. It was a radical step for its time, and its main purpose was to pull in viewers to the show houses. 'Up to then, the approach had been to discourage time-wasters or what the motor industry calls the tyre-kickers,' says an industry figure. 'But Joe encouraged the tyre-kickers. They paid a pound for the exhibition brochure, which went to charity, and the publicity spin-off was phenomenal.' There was also a pay-off: one of the show houses sold for almost £3 million, a staggering sum then.

Castlethorn's Riverwood scheme of 450 houses on Carpenterstown Road, Castleknock, was probably the first in Ireland to use the Surrey Design Guide's winding cul-de-sac layout and variety of house types, rather than the endless repetition of standardized low-density semi-detached dwellings, boxed in by the strait-jacket of wide 'distributor roads'. The Surrey model was a cut above this bleak formula, making internal estate roads much safer places for kids to play. Hot on the heels of the 1999 Residential Density Guidelines, which were introduced by Noel Dempsey to make better use of urban land by building housing at higher densities, Castlethorn developed The Courtyard in Clonsilla, not far from Blanchardstown shopping centre and Coolmine rail station, with three-storey apartment blocks and town houses in a courtyard setting aimed at young professional first-time buyers or older people 'trading down'. O'Reilly was also quick to appreciate the impact Luas was likely to have on property values in Dundrum. In 1997, long before construction of the Sandyford line got under way, Castlethorn was planning 57 apartments in three blocks adjacent to Dundrum Castle on Ballinteer Road, within walking distance of the line.

The company also added some gloss to its portfolio by acquiring Killeen Castle in Co. Meath, ancestral home of Saint Oliver Plunkett, and 440 acres of wooded parkland in 1995 for what now seems like a snip at £2 million. After a long hiatus, during which O'Reilly and his partners toyed with the possibilities, it is being developed as a luxury resort hotel with more than 200 rooms, a leisure and conference centre and championship golf course designed by Jack Nicklaus. The €200 million project includes 100 houses in woodland settings that will, according to its promoters, offer 'the epitome of elegant country living ... removed from the stress and bustle of city life'.

This was in marked contrast to most of Castlethorn's output in the burgeoning suburbs of Dublin – places like Pelletstown, where the last remaining tract of farmland within the city boundary was rezoned for intensive residential development; or Stepaside in the foothills of the Dublin Mountains, where apartment blocks with names like Bellarmine began rising up along the road to Enniskerry. Pelletstown, sandwiched between the River Tolka and the Royal Canal, was seen by city planners as a demonstration project for higher-density housing in a suburban setting, and was kick-started in 2001 by Castlethorn and Ballymore Properties with plans for more than 1,000 apartments.

Five years on, with much of Pelletstown already built, O'Reilly raised €70 million by selling a 'ready-to-go' 12-acre site with planning permission for another 500 apartments to Capel Developments. He had just bought a 52-acre site on the Woodbrook Estate in Shankill for €160 million and needed the money to finance plans to build some 1,400 new homes there and another 600 at nearby Shanganagh Castle. O'Reilly was also seeking to concentrate resources on Adamstown in west Dublin, where Castlethorn had bought 300 acres of land in the mid-1990s, confidently expecting that it would be zoned for housing because of its proximity to the Dublin–Cork railway line. In fact, he got more than he bargained for. Adamstown was designated in June 2001 as the state's first strategic development zone (SDZ), with a fast-track planning regime designed to facilitate the early delivery of new homes. The other developers involved in this experiment to show the value of master planning are Mick Whelan's Maplewood Homes and Tierra, run by the McGreevy brothers. Castlethorn was also the beneficiary of another SDZ designation for Hansfield, between Clonsilla and the Meath county boundary, having bought land there too when the time was right – along with Manor Park and Menolly Homes.

The Adamstown vision was certainly compelling – landmark modern buildings, roads designed as streets rather than traffic conduits, urban parks instead of formless prairies and essential facilities such as schools being delivered in tandem with new housing for up to 30,000 people. What the master plan sought to do, as South Dublin County Council senior planner Paul Hogan said at the time, was to present a realistic high-density, mixed-use, public-transport-based alternative to the conventional low-density, mono-use, roads-based development of the suburbs. Its objective was to provide a lively, interconnecting network of streets, squares and public spaces and interesting buildings mixing residential, commercial, public and community uses to encourage human interaction, pedestrian movement and the sense of being in a town or village. People living in Adamstown, in other words, would be within easy walking or cycling distance of all amenities, as well as a rail station for commuting to work. And An Bord Pleanála's approval of the master plan was conditional on these facilities being provided in phases as development progressed. 'The country is watching and probably wondering can it be done, will it be done right, will it deliver on the promise,' Joe O'Reilly told the *Irish Times* when the first sod was turned in February 2005. 'We are confident Adamstown will deliver on the vision [and] that the entwined streams of infra[structure] and housing will be delivered on time, on budget and according to plan.'

A long queue formed when the first phase, Adamstown Castle, was launched in February 2006, with 330 spacious apartments and town houses priced between €280,000 and €520,000. Fourteen months later, with some 1,300 new homes approved and 900 under construction, Taoiseach Bertie Ahern officially opened the new rail station serving Adamstown, years ahead of the completion of most of the housing planned for the area. The station and its 300-space park-and-ride site – currently surrounded by fields – was funded entirely by the development consortium led by Castlethorn; this was one example of a public-private partnership (PPP) scheme that actually worked. And in a reversal of the traditional time lag of facilities taking ages to materialize, two primary schools opened in September 2007, the first playground was in place and the first crèche under construction.

Just north of the station, a 20-acre site has been earmarked for a town centre with a full range of community, civic, residential, retail and commercial facilities. In January 2008, what was billed by Castlethorn as 'one of the largest ever mixed-use planning applications in the history of the state' was lodged with South Dublin County Council. It sought approval for a primary healthcare centre, an inter-church place of worship, a leisure centre and swimming pool, a library ('Ideas Store'), enterprise centre, 60 shops, cafés and restaurants, a multiplex cinema, 900 apartments, underground car parking, intimate traffic-free streets and several civic squares. It was clear that a huge amount of work had been invested in preparing this plan, involving seven architectural practices (Duffy Mitchell O'Donoghue, Grafton Architects, HKR, Henry J. Lyons, Metropolitan Workshop, O'Donnell and Tuomey, and OMP) as well as engineers, landscape architects, movement and wind consultants and even colourists. Indeed, the diversity of the design team should ensure that Adamstown's new heart will have its own unique and memorable sense of place.

Joe O'Reilly's most strategic move was the 1996 acquisition of a 22-acre site near the heart of Dundrum, formerly occupied by Pye Ireland's television factory, for £8 million. The price was way above what others were offering; although the site had 'district centre' zoning, nobody else had O'Reilly's vision of developing it for what would become Ireland's largest shopping centre when it opened in March 2005. It didn't sail through the planning system, however. Dún Laoghaire-Rathdown County Council, with its eye firmly focused on commercial rates revenue, bumped up the zoning of the Pye site to 'major town centre' status and granted planning permission for Castlethorn's scheme. But in October 1999 An Bord Pleanála overturned this decision, citing the 'monolithic' nature of the development, particularly its main block, and the 'undesirable' impact on an old mill house and pond. Architects Burke-Kennedy Doyle (BKD) went back to their drawing boards and produced a revised version, which broke up the monolith and preserved both the old mill house and pond as part of a new 'civic square', and this got the green light in July 2000.

Building it was even more of a challenge, as the shopping centre had to be cut into rising ground and its six-level underground car park required the excavation of some 300,000 cubic metres of granite. But the investment paid off, producing 150,000 metres of retail space occupied by the likes of Tesco, House of Fraser, H&M and Harvey Nichols. Dundrum became a shopping mecca for the most affluent parts of Dublin, attracting 15 million shoppers in 2007 and grossing €700 million in retail sales. Castlethorn intends to make it an even bigger draw. In 1999, it paid £14 million for Dundrum's clapped-out 1970s shopping centre at the other end of the old village and got planning permission to redevelop it in February 2004, a year before the first phase of the village's transformation into a town was finished. None of this would have been possible without the Dundrum bypass, which had opened in 2002 at a cost of €44.4 million, most of which (€33 million) ended up in the pockets of landowners on the 1.2 km route.

Always on the lookout for new opportunities, O'Reilly paid €32.5 million in late 2002 for the so-called Gaiety Centre on South King Street – a grim office block from the early 1980s owned and occupied by Eircom next door to the Gaiety Theatre. Seeking something stylishly angular, he commissioned Andrzej Wejchert – the Polish-born architect who designed the UCD campus in Belfield – to produce a 'transparent' seven-storey retail and residential complex for the site. But in May 2004, just three months after approving plans for the second phase of Dundrum town centre, An Bord Pleanála rejected the scheme on the grounds that its height, scale and bulk would have a negative impact on the relatively narrow street and 'seriously injure' the residential amenity of apartments to the rear. Some 12 months later, O'Reilly won approval for a scaled-down version of the €100 million scheme and lined up Zara and H&M as anchor tenants for its 3,700 square metres of large-floorplate retail space on three levels, topped by 'luxury office suites'. High-turnover retailers love large expanses of floor space, if they can get their hands on them; one of the many problems afflicting Grafton Street is that most of the buildings in the area are relatively small.

With all the money Castlethorn was making from selling new homes at the height of the boom, O'Reilly was able to embark on a buying spree – though the sheer scale of it must have needed to be underwritten by his main bankers, AIB. In mid-2005 he paid €50 million for Merrion House in Booterstown, a three-storey office block where each floor is as big as a football pitch, which regrettably replaced the graceful Imco building in the late 1970s. Clearly, this high-profile site has significant development potential. A month earlier, O'Reilly forked out €125 million for a 50 per cent stake in the ILAC shopping centre, the once-tawdry mall tacked on to Dublin's northside retail core.

He was also buying up or acquiring options in and around the Carlton site on Upper O'Connell Street and had it 'half bought up before anyone even knew about it', according to one official source. His aim was to position himself to take over the abortive Millennium Mall project, centred on the former Carlton cinema, from putative developers Richard Quirke and Paul Clinton, and it would obviously make sense to link this with a comprehensively refurbished ILAC centre. But it turned into a long struggle, complicated by endless legal actions initiated by Clinton in an effort to quash the city council's compulsory purchase order for the pivotally located site; it was uncertainty over the outcome of these proceedings that scuppered the great prospect of relocating the Abbey Theatre in O'Connell Street.

O'Reilly stuck with it, however, and consolidated his holding in the area by buying the Royal Dublin Hotel in December 2006 for an undisclosed sum, with an eye to demolishing the building. But few could have imagined the radical intervention which his architects – a consortium comprising BKD, Donnelly Turpin and McGarry Ní Éanaigh – would propose. Not only would there be a new shopping street running east–west to connect a dead stretch of Upper O'Connell Street with Moore Street, but also another street running on a diagonal to the corner of Henry Street, all covered by a glazed 'rainscreen' roof. What's more, the €1.2 billion development would involve physically moving the Carlton's art deco façade further up the street as well as creating a cascade-like high-rise apartment block in the middle of the development site, with views over the city towards the mountains beyond. One of the development's selling points was a 'park in the sky', improbably inclined at an angle of 20 degrees and orientated towards the north-east, which meant that it would get little sun. Questions were raised about the demolition of several historic buildings on the O'Connell Street frontage as well as the creation of such a wide opening – more than 30 metres – to draw in the shoppers. And it is an open question whether another shopping centre would be viable in the north inner city, given the economic downturn as well as competition from Arnotts' big plans to redevelop a whole quarter further south, centred on Prince's Street and Independent House on Middle Abbey Street, as an extended shopping precinct.

The sheer ambition of the Carlton scheme led Joe O'Reilly to set up his own development vehicle, Chartered Land, in mid-2006. It describes itself as 'Ireland's most dynamic property company . . . committed to creating a portfolio of innovative landmark commercial developments that define town and city-scapes'. In 2007, O'Reilly appointed northerner Dominic Deeny, who had long experience of shopping centres in Britain and Ireland, as chief executive and hired a team of project and asset managers, including Australian architect Gary Cooper, who had worked for Treasury Holdings. But he was invisible, other than to those who know him, at the glitzy launch of a revised master plan for Grand Canal Square in September 2007 when the great hall of the Royal College of Physicians in Ireland was transformed by bordello lighting, a backing track of nightclub music and big screens showing off Daniel Libeskind's architecture. With a diamond-like 2,000-seat theatre as its centrepiece, this Docklands square would provide 'an architectural expression of the vitality of Dublin', according to the perky international starchitect. Hosted by Chartered Land, the launch was attended by members of the city's business community and its real purpose was to persuade them to lease space in two of the three office blocks that will form elements of the overall master plan. The third block had already been taken by solicitors BCM Hanby Wallace, one of whose partners – Brian Wallace – is a long-time director of Castlethorn. According to Libeskind, who made his name with the jagged Jewish Museum in Berlin and always seeks local references for his projects, the colours in the façades of the three office blocks were 'inspired by the Book of Kells'. He also predicted that Grand Canal Square would become 'almost a paradigm for bringing everyday life together with culture and commerce'. However, there was nothing to enliven the office blocks at street level – no shops, cafés or restaurants. O'Reilly's share in the overall scheme is estimated to be worth €350 million. If he hadn't got involved, it might not have happened; the Grand Canal Theatre was first unveiled in May 2004 by Devey Properties, but it didn't start moving until Chartered Land took over in November 2006 and Harry Crosbie was lined up to own and operate it.

Through Castlethorn, O'Reilly was slated to get involved in the redevelopment of at least one run-down local authority housing estate – O'Devaney Gardens, near the Phoenix Park – for a more socially mixed housing scheme. All 276 flats on the 16-acre site were to be demolished and, in line with a 'charter' negotiated with the existing council tenants, replaced by 280 social housing units, 250 'affordable' homes and 292 apartments for private sale.

But when it came to developing a 12-acre site on Brighton Road in Foxrock, Castlethorn sought to create an exclusively private development of 49 detached houses, most with five or six bedrooms and some with double garages big enough for a pair of SUVs. In order to comply with the watered-down 'social and affordable' housing requirement of Part V of the 2000 Planning Act, O'Reilly proposed that lower-class units would be provided at the company's Bellarmine scheme in Stepaside on the basis that it would be difficult to provide social and affordable housing on a high-value site in Foxrock.

Although Dún Laoghaire-Rathdown councillors voted unanimously in March 2007 to recommend rejection of this swap offer, it was later accepted by housing officials as the best deal they could get for people on the council's waiting list. What else could the officials do, especially after Martin Cullen, as Minister for the Environment in 2002, had cravenly capitulated to lobbying from builders to amend Part V so that social and affordable housing would no longer have to be provided on the site of any new residential scheme? Instead, Cullen ordained that they could provide it anywhere in a council's administrative area or make an equivalent financial contribution towards the shrunken public housing programme. Meanwhile, out in Stepaside, Castlethorn planned to demolish Old Wesley Rugby Club in Kilgobbin Lane and remove its pitches to make way for 52 houses and 229 apartments in five blocks, ranging from three to six storeys in height, as well as surface parking for 228 cars. Inevitably, there has been local opposition to these schemes from people who wanted to preserve Stepaside as a village, but the march of apartment blocks across the landscape could not be halted.

If there is a template for the kind of man who emerged from the bogs and drumlins of rural Ireland and, with minimal education, a gambler's instinct, hard labour and ruthlessness, rose to the top, it is Séamus Ross. A native of Drumlish in north Longford, he was one of four children of Jimmy Ross and Mary Ann Mulleady. With a tiny house and about 15 acres, times were hard and the contribution of the family's hog to their income was significant: neighbours from miles around walked their pigs to the hog for insemination at half a crown a time. After national school and a few years at the vocational school in Ballinamuck, Séamus was 15 when he went to serve his time as a carpenter at Frankie Mulleady's construction business. After about 18 months, he migrated to Dublin with his fellow north Longfordman Mick Whelan, and they set to work as roofers. It was common to share bedsits, four and five men to a room. A bath was rare and wonderful. Those who knew them back then recall 'nothing particularly outstanding' about them. One source remembers, 'Séamus was not remarkable for his intelligence but he was a bigger gambler and would have been a huge worker. He'd do hard, physical work around the clock.' A combination of luck and sweat left the two well poised to take advantage of the rising tide. They set up a company called Drumlish Homes, built on good sites in Castleknock and Newlands Cross and took big risks. 'Make no mistake, those guys took serious chances,' says an old acquaintance. 'Ross's own home would have been on the line in the early days.'

When the slump came after the oil crisis in the early 1970s, the banks backed off, refusing to take what appeared to be worthless land banks in lieu of loan repayments – a decision they must have regretted deeply later. Mick Whelan went back to carpentry in London for a time, while Ross, according to a friend, experienced 'rough' times in Ireland. In the end, the joke was on the bankers. By the mid-1980s, the land banks they had disdained were turning into gold dust. Ross had married Whelan's sister, Moira, and he was dropping into Sunday Mass in Drumlish in a shiny Mercedes and honing his ambition on small estates of 20 to 30 houses at a time. Now in his mid-fifties, the devoted family man lives with Moira in a glorious house on 60 prime acres beside Luttrellstown demesne in west Dublin. His mode of transport is a helicopter and Hawker private jet, believed to be undergoing an upgrade to transatlantic capability. His joint 50th birthday and 25th wedding anniversary bash, held in a marquee at his home, included the renewal of his marriage vows before the same priest who married him and Moira, with entertainment provided by a ceilidh band and a showband. One friend says, 'He is home for his tea every day.' He invites his friends in for set dancing lessons (complete with teacher) in his ballroom, sponsors the Meath football team, and has adopted for his horse-racing colours the maroon and saffron of Father Manning Gaels, the GAA club of his native parish in north Longford. His county pride goes deep. His circle of friends, successful entrepreneurs like himself, who include Jimmy Flynn, John Mahon and Oliver Bardon, have been dubbed the 'Longford Mafia'. His political friends include the Lenihan brothers – he can pick up the phone to Brian, his local TD, and Conor – and his Fianna Fáil leanings are overt.

With a company building up to 1,000 houses a year, aiming for high-density sales at relatively small margins, Ross is said to rely heavily on Brendan Byrne of Sherry FitzGerald New Homes for advice. He is widely regarded as a 'gentleman', honest, straight-talking, no-nonsense. 'He can have a slight inferiority complex about his lack of education,' says an acquaintance, 'but watch him with lawyers and he can tear their arguments apart, see ways around things that they never would.' Those he has singed in business deals, however, are less enamoured, saying he 'lacks depth' and is 'a cute hoor ... the kind who'd get the better end of a 50–50 deal'. The ruthless streak common to all such men emerges in predictable ways. 'He takes defeat badly and can simmer for days. Personally, he's unbelievably generous, but in business, he'd fight over tuppence,' says one industry source. 'He's tough, tough, tough ...' When the construction boom began to tail off in 2006, cutbacks meant men being laid off. 'The attitude would be "if men have to go, they have to go", even some who've been here for years.' But they all concede that Séamus Ross at least has walked the walk.

He and Moira became the sole owners of Menolly Properties in 1996. Between 2000 and 2002 its turnover jumped from £66.7 million to €157.4 million, with an even more dramatic rise in pre-tax profits from £6.3 million to €27.5 million in 2002 in the same period. Bank loans stood at €41 million, down from €78 million in the previous year, with Anglo Irish Bank as the group's principal lender. Colm Keena, who scrutinized Menolly's company accounts, reported in the *Irish Times* on a transaction whereby, in 2001, 'the group put £4.99 million into a family trust, and the trust loaned the money back to the group as an interest-free loan'. It was only after that transaction and the payment of £904,000 to the two directors that the pre-tax profit of £3.3 million for the year was calculated; this entirely legitimate ruse would have cut the company's tax bill for the year quite substantially. There were also land sales to the group by one of its directors (who else but Séamus Ross?) with £7.9 million showed as being owed to him at the end of 2000. But the accounts suggest that Ross and his wife weren't particularly ravenous; profits made by the group were reinvested in the business, rather than paid out in big dividends. Whether this restraint has continued is impossible to say because ownership of Menolly was transferred in 2003 to an unlimited holding company, CPS (Ireland), which is no longer under a legal obligation to file accounts – and Ross, no more than other property developers, is reluctant to talk about money.

In 1999, Menolly set a new record by building and selling 840 houses on the Manorfields estate near Clonee, Co. Meath, in a matter of months – mainly to first-time house-buyers. It did even better at Wolstan Haven, near Celbridge, Co. Kildare, where three-bedroom semis were snapped up for just £125,000. Thornberry, also on the Dublin side of Clonee, marked a move towards building apartments, but the more typical Menolly development at the time was a mix of houses and apartments, such as nearby Linnetfields, where the company continued with its policy of pitching prices below those of other developers to achieve high-volume sales. Then, just a year after the government paid more than £23 million for Farmleigh, the Guinness family home on 78 acres of wooded grounds at the edge of Phoenix Park, Menolly forked out over £25 million for a further 28 acres of Guinness land nearby. Miranda Iveagh, charming and vivacious widow of the late Earl, could not have been more pleased, re-investing much of her share of the proceeds in the restoration of Wilbury Park, an early 18th-century neo-Palladian mansion in Wiltshire. Given the proximity of such superb amenities as Farmleigh and Phoenix Park, Menolly built a suitably upmarket estate of 450 homes on its expensively acquired site.

Menolly's scheme to rezone and develop 42 acres of land around Dunboyne Castle in Co. Meath proved controversial. Ross hoped to build a hotel and spa, as well as a large housing estate, and Meath County Council voted in favour of the re-zoning over the strong opposition of local residents. Four years later, Menolly successfully overcame local objections to win planning permission from An Bord Pleanála for 344 houses and 10 blocks containing 208 apartments in the grounds of the castle – though its plans to build a neighbourhood centre to cater for new residents were turned down by the appeals board. The only problem with this development is that the 145-bedroom hotel and leisure centre, which extend outwards from the 18th-century mansion built for Lord Dunboyne, now look out over a large suburban housing estate to the rear, designed by architects and planning consultants Fenton Simons; it is not a happy marriage. Menolly also built commuter housing at Riverbank and High-lands, in Drogheda, as well as at Lakepoint, in Mullingar. But it has concentrated its activity in the greater Dublin area, build-ing such schemes as Rosedale, off Navan Road; Ravenswood in Ongar, near Clonsilla; Rockbridge, in Celbridge; and the Headlands, in Bray.

Séamus Ross successfully fought a claim by the late Liam Lawlor that he had a 20 per cent stake in a joint venture with Menolly in developing lands at Phibblestown, Castaheany and Allendale, in west Dublin. The case went all the way to the Supreme Court, which found that there was no basis for Lawlor's claim. Ross came to regard Lawlor as 'a plague', according to his evidence to the Mahon Tribunal in October 2003. He said he had paid the former Fianna Fáil TD more than £40,000 in two instalments in 1996 to have the postal address of the 550-unit

Earlsfort housing estate in west Dublin changed from Clondalkin to Lucan, to make the houses more valuable. He estimated that they would be worth an extra £5,000 with a more 'upmarket' Lucan postal address, netting a total of £2.5 million. Lawlor even supplied a fake invoice for the first payment he received. But An Post later maintained, following an investigation, that the postal address of the area had always been 'Lucan, Co. Dublin'.

In one of the biggest property deals of 2004, Menolly paid €95 million for a 50 per cent stake in 450 acres of land between Baldoyle and Portmarnock. The land, once owned by veteran developer John Byrne, had been acquired in 1996 by Seán Mulryan, of Ballymore Properties, for some £30 million after previous rezoning efforts had failed. It has since become the focus of frenetic development, with some 4,000 homes planned in a joint venture between Ballymore and Menolly. A further 7,000 homes and a new town centre are to be built further west on land largely assembled over the years by Gerry Gannon, one of the biggest property owners in north Dublin. Given the volume of its housing production on the city's north fringe and elsewhere, it made sense for Menolly to set up Alcrete Ltd, a company producing precast concrete components, including walls, to speed up construction. This involved a €25 million investment in a quarry and a factory near Kill, Co. Kildare, producing precast units for up to 5,000 new homes per year.

Menolly's glossy brochure for Beaupark, the development it built on the site, was more effusive than most. 'Be part of something beautiful,' it said in 2004. 'On the Baldoyle/Balgriffin coastal fringe of Dublin, Beaupark is opening up a whole new era of city/coastal living, [offering] one of the first opportunities to buy in a new town, Capital North.' Less than three years later, Menolly was testing the foundations of houses and apartments on the estate after discovering that the hardcore used in their construction contained high levels of pyrite, a mineral that expands if it comes into contact with air or water, causing cracks in floors and walls. Large cracks had appeared in at least 40 of the 300 houses in the Drynam Hall estate in Kinsealy, built by

Menolly in 2004, and tests were being carried out on 60 houses in that estate. The same infill material had been used in the construction of Beaupark and Myrtle, another Menolly-built estate near Baldoyle. 'The vast majority of houses that have been tested have come back positive for the presence of pyrite and many more householders are expecting the worst,' according to local Labour councillor Seán Kenny. Tommy Broughan TD (Labour, Dublin North East) has raised the issue in the Dáil, on behalf of affected constituents, though he conceded that Séamus Ross 'is quick to put his hands up when there are problems'; he also took legal action against Irish Asphalt and the Lagan Group, which supplied the infill material, claiming €18 million in damages. But whereas Menolly faced up to the task of carrying out repairs, Beaupark residents complained that another builder, Killoe Developments, which had developed more than 160 homes on the estate, didn't even respond to phone calls.

One of Menolly's most ambitious projects is the Hansfield Strategic Development Zone, west of Blanchardstown in west Dublin. Along with Manor Park Homes, the company became impatient over the length of time it was taking An Bord Pleanála to approve the master plan and sought permission in 2004 for the first phase of 920 homes. But both Fingal County Council and the appeals board rejected this proposal on the basis that it pre-empted approval of the master plan. The latter finally came in January 2006, nearly five years after Hansfield had been identified as a potential SDZ – a mechanism that, ironically, was intended to speed up the planning process. The single biggest problem for Fingal was its inability to control aspects of the project – such as getting agreement from the ESB to put 110-kilovolt power lines underground (this was eventually refused) and from Iarnród Éireann to reopen a section of the disused Navan railway line to serve the area (this wouldn't be open until 2010 at the earliest).

A more unusual scheme involved 83 luxury houses and apartments at the K Club in Straffan, Co. Kildare, where residents were promised a grandstand view of the Ryder Cup. When it was revealed in September 2006 that the company had offered all

26 members of South Dublin County Council free tickets to the prestigious golf tournament, the Irish branch of Transparency International – a global organization that fights corruption in public life – issued a statement urging public representatives not to accept such corporate gifts or hospitality. Government ministers were also told not to accept corporate invitations to attend the Ryder Cup, because the value of such hospitality might exceed the level officially permitted. A government spokesman said ministers had been 'reminded of their responsibilities under the code of conduct for public office holders'.

Ross has also become involved in hotels, buying the former Hibernian Hotel off Upper Baggot Street in 2004 and investing €15 million in its refurbishment as a 50-bedroom 'boutique hotel', known as the Dylan. Another Menolly hotel, Mount Hybla, was due to open at Farmleigh Wood, on the former Guinness land at the edge of Phoenix Park. Menolly's latest scheme is at Grange Castle, Clondalkin, where Ross plans to build a 132-bed hotel, leisure centre, crèche, local shop, replacement golf clubhouse and 290 residential units on 37 acres adjoining Kilcarbery House. In these uncertain times, Ross is in the happy position of being able to hand over more of the day-to-day running of Menolly Homes to his 28-year-old son Séamus junior, meandering across Europe and the world, expanding his empire to eastern Europe and New York and picking up ideas for boutique hotels.

5. The Brickies

Micheál McMahon was among the 35,000 young people who emigrated from Ireland in 1993. For the then 20-year-old carpenter from Co. Donegal, who had left school at 16 to learn his trade, there was only despair at home, as he told the *Irish Times* in 2007: 'There was no work. I was on the dole. I remember I was in my apartment in Bundoran one winter night at around 11 o'clock and looking out the window and it must be that a bale of hay fell off a truck but it was like something you'd see in a Western, hay blowing down an empty street and it was like a sign from God . . .' Within weeks, he and his future wife, Cheryl, were on a plane to New York. As they left for the airport his father, Mick, was too distressed to get out of bed to say goodbye.

Broken-hearted Mick McMahon could never have predicted that within a year, a construction boom would be under way in Ireland. A Canadian construction workers' union, hearing intimations of the boom, wrote to the Services, Industrial, Professional and Technical Union (SIPTU) 'asking if we could take a few of the brothers', in the words of Eric Fleming, SIPTU's construction branch secretary.

And did we? Fleming, plain-talker, musician and trade union activist since his teens, raises a sceptical eyebrow. 'I'm not sure they even got a reply . . . I personally thought we could have taken some workers. But we're an insular country. We're an island nation. And I can tell you that at that time, we were very, very protective of whatever jobs were there . . .'

To be fair to the protectionists, while direct employment in the sector grew by about 12,000 a year in 1994 and 1995, history had taught us that Irish booms were fleeting things. So the outward flow of youth and energy continued and the US was not the only destination of choice. With a building slump in Britain, Germany seemed happy to welcome foreign workers aboard its construction boom following reunification. Some 10,000 Irishmen were labouring there in 1996, when a new law was enacted requiring German employers to pay all foreigners the same rate as their German counterparts and to enact new training standards. In short, earnings would double and standards would rise for many Irish workers. Pints all round down the ersatz Irish pub, then? Not exactly. The unions scented problems for our boys. The change was not 'in the best interests of the Irish worker', said the regional secretary of the Union of Construction, Allied Trades and Technicians (UCATT), Noel O'Neill. 'There are certain basic minimum standards that the Germans have that can't be achieved in this century . . . They weren't too particular about qualifications standards before, but now it looks like if you cannot prove your bona fides you could be out of a job.'

From the German viewpoint, the facts were stark. The new law was not about fair play for the foreigners; in fact, they were fed up with them flying in and selling their labour on the cheap while four million Germans were on the dole. Foreign construction workers were regarded as 'poachers' by their German colleagues, said Heike John, then of the Irish Trade Board in Düsseldorf. They worked for bargain-rate wages in subcontracting deals and this 'wage dumping' had led to profiteering by middlemen. The executive director of the German-Irish Chamber of Industry and Commerce in Dublin, Dr Dieter Tscherning, explained soothingly that there were always problems created in bringing people from one working environment to another. 'What it will mean is that EU workers in the construction trade will be entitled to a minimum wage in Germany irrespective of what they get in their own country.' But from an Irish standpoint, the new requirements for training and certification threatened the status quo. Evidently, solidarity with the brothers anywhere, whether in Germany or Canada, had its limits. Where there was undercutting to be done or jobs to be minded, the Irish were up for it.

What no one could have predicted was how soon the tables would be turned. By 1998, employment in the Irish construction industry stood at 150,000 – nearly double the 1995 level – and there was concern about the supply of construction craftworkers. By July 1999, the Irish were back in Germany, only this time in a bid to woo German job seekers to Ireland. Fás, the Construction Industry Federation (CIF) and Irish contractors joined forces in the hunt for manpower, first stop Cologne, then onwards to Britain, France, the Benelux countries, and the US and Canada, generating intense, intercontinental media interest on the way, centred on little Ireland's extraordinary reversal of fortunes.

Meanwhile, for many Irish construction workers back home, it was bonanza time. Labour shortages combined with frantic building schedules meant unlimited overtime and fat bonuses that virtually doubled the basic wages of carpenters, electricians and other craftsmen.

So that partly explained the booming sales in four-wheel drives and 5-series BMWs, then? 'Yes and no,' says 'Darren', a craftsman cum minor developer in his early 40s, speaking on condition of anonymity but still wary. 'You see very well-off fellas around the place now – painters, plasterers, plumbers, bricklayers – who you'd think made barrowloads of money off the job. But the vast majority would have made it through property. The money you'd earn from the job would give you a bit of a lifestyle all right, but what it really gave you was the contacts, the insight into different avenues that gave you the development opportunities.' Darren's first investment was a house in Drumcondra in 1993, for which he paid £50,000. 'I had the skills to strip it down and do a lot of the work myself. I had the mates to rewire it and all that. In two years, the house was worth £100,000 – double what I paid – and that gave you the collateral to keep going on. We'd have seen a good turn in the business in '95 and '96 and I just kept moving on, taking the collateral from one site to the next, getting mates in to help do it up, renting it out.'

'It's called sweating the asset,' interjects his friend cheerfully, 'and the key is knowing lads with the skills.'

'It was still a big struggle, though,' Darren continues. 'Interest rates were at 14 per cent and it was tougher to get a mortgage.'

But he pushed on, building up a cash flow from rentals, then buying sites and getting into small developments himself.

By 2007, the original Drumcondra rental had been sold for €900,000 – 'top dollar', as he puts it – and Darren was living in a €4 million house in north Dublin with designer-clad wife, Juicy Coutured children and a hairy dog called Prada, running the job out of smart company-owned offices overlooking Dublin port, driving a €160,000 S-class Mercedes, taking three holidays a year and keeping an eye on his investment properties scattered around Dubai, Spain, Portugal and Nevada. The day we meet, he is sporting an unseasonal tan under a magenta Tommy Hilfiger shirt and pinstripe Versace suit.

'We just had two weeks in Dubai,' he explains.

Who takes two weeks at Easter?

'Yeah, well, we work hard and play hard,' he says, grinning for the first time. He grins some more about the 'useless' attempts to compile an accurate Rich List in boom-time Ireland. 'They're not even close. I know fellas – plumbers and that – who are worth millions and you'd never know it. There's one who was an electrician to start with, now he owns a $6 million place in the Bahamas. To look at him you'd say he was basic but he's worth €300 million easy. The way he lives now, he works stints of 10 weeks of 12-to-14-hour days, then he's away to the Bahamas for up to 6 weeks, then he's back working for another 10 weeks ... Among the smaller lads, the common denominator would be their houses. They'd be worth €3 million up and that's what they'd pump their money into. Some would be happy enough with the 5-series BMW but the house is where it's at. Most would have a second property. Spain has lost its buzz so now it's Portugal – Quinta do Lago – with the kids, Cannes, South Africa, the Bahamas.'

Then again, good craftsmen could forgo the risks taken by Darren and still live the good life. They could earn multiples of the average site worker's wage simply by continuing to do their job. Electricians could expect to earn up to €100,000 a year, skilled tilers up to €150,000. For a bricklayer, an average income was €120,000. The bricklayers were the kings of the sites, working on special terms negotiated directly with the main contractors by the Building and Allied Trades' Union (BATU). Under this arrangement they managed to hold on to the rates and productivity premiums from the old days on the lump, but with the security of working within the system. So they could bring tears to developers' eyes – and did – by charging a euro a brick while availing themselves of industry pension schemes and tax regimes. 'Superb negotiating,' whistled a member of another union. 'You'd have to admire them.'

Together, the ready cash, drive and optimism of these men were changing the face of Ireland. Economist and author David McWilliams distilled them into the genus Breakfast Roll Man, 'the new face of suburban Ireland ... its chief architect, head financier, town planner and designer'. He was the guy who pitched up at a Spar counter somewhere in Ireland every morning and ordered 'the full Irish' in a roll, plus 20 John Player Blue, the *Daily Star*, a couple of bottles of Lucozade, a six-pack of Actimel and a Twix. BR Man lived in the future, one 'based on the chimera that tomorrow will always be better than today ... The financial engine fuelling the dream is housing wealth . . . Breakfast Roll Man has no time for the ordinary blokes down the pub who are going nowhere; he respects people who are making a fist of their lives, who are aspiring and who, like him, are moving upwards, always on the make, always dreaming of the bigger car, house, kitchen or plasma screen. He rightly admires the man who is sending his children to a better school than the one he went to.'

If McWilliams's Breakfast Roll Man was a gross homogenization of hundreds of thousands of hard-working men pulling themselves up by their bootstraps in the construction boom, many saw a germ of truth in it. Breakfast Roll Men had a vision beyond the daily grind – maybe a little subcontracting to start with, before aiming higher. In the frantic rush to lash up the buildings, pull in the money and move on, some got a glimpse of the boss's operation, saw the possibilities and became subcontractors themselves.

If the ultimate boss – the big culchie developer, now barely visible from his Bell Ranger helicopter overflying the site – had started out as a plumber, bricklayer, electrician or roofer and shot for the sky, well so could they. The beauty of the property business is that no one is disbarred. There was nothing new about it apart from the scale of it.

Given the nature of the business, the ready supply of money and the sense that everything was possible, the accelerated drive towards subcontracting was inevitable. But so was its vulnerability to abuse. Directly employed workers were entitled to pensions, death-in-service payments and holiday entitlements. As the buccaneering years would reveal, the designation of workers as 'self-employed' or 'subcontractors' would prove a handy way for builders to evade those obligations. Like Canute striving to repel the waves, the bricklayers' union, BATU, stood firm against the subcontracting trend, sensing a threat to its enviable deal with main contractors. It was the odd one out in 1996 when the CIF and eight of the nine construction unions agreed on a framework in which subcontractors could operate. From 1997 onwards, BATU's unofficial strikes were a plague on the industry, as it fought for its members' right to be directly employed. The strategy was to drive all bricklaying subcontractors, even specialist firms, off big sites, using methods that were often intimidatory and sometimes violent.

Amid the headlines about Irish construction companies scouring the Continent in search of building workers, few would have noticed the one in the *Irish Times* in 1999 that read 'Contractors May Leave State' above a short report about the travails of Kilburn Developments, a large brick- and block-laying contractor. Its owner, Martin Young, a bricklayer himself and former BATU executive, was threatening to withdraw from Ireland because of unofficial industrial action by BATU bricklayers. 'Unofficial pickets by members of BATU have disrupted work at four sites in Dublin where Kilburn Developments is carrying out work for McNamara Construction,' read the story. 'On one site at Beaumont Hospital, gardaí had to be called on Wednesday to escort workers past the pickets. The dispute has arisen because McNamara Construction is not prepared to employ bricklayers directly.'

BATU repeatedly targeted Young's company, even though his workers were also BATU members, insisting that his men be replaced by staff directly employed by the main contractor, McNamara. 'The intimidation began on May 4, 1999, as men arrived for work,' Young told the *Sunday Times*. 'They tried to turn one man's van over with him in it – a young apprentice also inside quit on the spot.' One of Young's employees claimed that his mother had been told to get good insurance on her house because she was going to be burnt out. Young himself was forced to change his number after he received threatening late-night telephone calls. 'This was about money,' he said, alleging that he was offered peace on his sites in return for a cash payment, which he declined. He left Ireland in 1999, after his business was 'destroyed' by BATU. 'No builder in the country would take me on. If you wanted a bricklaying contractor, you were not going to ring me because I was going to bring these fellows [BATU mass pickets] to your gate. That was the impression and I could understand that.'

It would not be the last the country would hear of BATU, whose membership comprised all the bricklayers and half of the carpenters in the industry: it had the wherewithal to shut down every building site in Ireland. In a high-level report commissioned by the National Implementation Body, the monopoly issue was repeatedly raised by employers and disaffected or former members of BATU. Many referred to the 'list' system operated by the union, which made it impossible for a contractor to offer employment to a bricklayer, even an in-benefit member of BATU, prior to offering the employment to members who had previously worked with that employer or to nominees of the union. 'Bricklayers not having this "preferred status" are . . . unable to secure employment from the vast majority of main contractors . . . Many documented cases were presented involving withdrawal/denial of membership cards, expulsion for refusal to support list system etc,' reported Phil Flynn and Tom Mallon in their 2006 report on the brick- and block-laying sector. In effect, BATU had arrogated to itself the extraordinary power to decide whether a man could make a living or not, and where. BATU denied 'the context and circumstances of any such decisions, but not the impact', the report noted. 'There is no doubt that, at least in relation to the main contractors, BATU can decide who works ... This power brings with it grave responsibilities and needs to be balanced.' In its submission, BATU claimed that the CIF had 'made no effort to address their concerns, did not mind what kind of subcontractor operated on their member sites and by extension enabled widespread abuse of the pension scheme. They argued that the only way to achieve and protect employment conditions would be to work directly for the main contractor on a PAYE basis.'

Acknowledging that there was 'much in the history of the industry to justify these concerns', the authors noted that 'in recent years, significant improvement has taken place in a number of areas ... This, however, did not lead to an improvement in the climate of relations; unofficial industrial action became more frequent, often involving activities which seemed to be unlawful or at least having no place in normal industrial relations.' They addressed the bricklayers' concerns, however, recommending that a formal registration system of subcontractors be set up to ensure compliance with their various obligations and that contractors be obliged to ensure that their subcontractors were bonded sufficiently to meet notice payments, redundancy payments, pension contributions and employer liability insurance. They also confronted BATU's 'list' system, recommending that the ICTU and relevant unions implement an appeal/dispute resolution scheme, 'with real power', to deal with any individual complaints from workers alleging interference by union with the freedom to work within the industry. Both sides could claim a degree of vindication.

However, something had to give, during the long years of strife and uncertainty – and that was the developers' patience. They had begun to design brickwork out of their plans. Architects and engineers worked to freeze the bricklayers out through the design of new projects. It was estimated that the replacement of brick with precast concrete cladding on a Trinity College hall of residence and an office block on Kevin Street cost bricklayers €4.6 million in lost wages. The Ulster Bank development on George's Quay and blocks of the Irish Financial Services Centre were built without bricks. 'It is quite staggering,' said Martin Young, 'that in the middle of the biggest construction boom this country has ever seen, the employment of bricklayers fell drastically and they were virtually unemployable because of the antics of their trade union.' Just like the Dublin taxi drivers – who took an uncompromising stance on the maintenance of their cartel, only to end up with a regime in which the number of taxi licences was unlimited – BATU had shot itself in the foot. One former craftworker turned major developer, still bristling about having been 'threatened on every site' by BATU members, says: 'We take no chances now. We try to ensure that we have no union members on our sites and to do that, we generally pay 10–15 per cent over the union rate . . . There are still a lot of good, sound tradesmen around. It's true that builders have tried to come up with faster construction methods that can add quality to a scheme, but they're expensive and I think that precast panelling has not been too successful in mass house-building. Bathroom pods [prefabricated bathrooms] and Techcrete wall panelling could add 10 per cent to your building costs. So in slower times for the industry, you'll probably see builders going back to the traditional methods. It's certainly not a dying trade.' Anyway, he adds, common sense seems to have returned in the last three or four years.

Kilburn Developments' High Court action against BATU took nine years to wend its way to a settlement. In March 2008 the union agreed to pay punitive damages of €400,000 to the company. It also accepted responsibility for Kilburn's legal costs and those of two former union figures, estimated at more than €1 million in total. A comprehensive victory for the Construction Industry Federation, then? Hardly. It soon emerged that in 2000,

Michael McNamara and Co., the company for which Kilburn worked as a subcontractor, had secretly agreed to indemnify BATU against any costs arising from its dispute with Kilburn. Some builders were incensed to hear of such an agreement being reached at a time when the federation had determined on a tough, united front against BATU's tactics. Indeed, McNamara and Co. itself had sought legal injunctions against BATU in the High Court in September 1999, armed with copies of cheques and photographic and surveillance evidence to prove involvement by trade union members 'in the active support and organisation of unlawful industrial actions which were seriously damaging the company'. In that context, the deal with BATU seemed bizarre. Nine years on, however, a philosophical Martin Young said he understood Bernard McNamara's predicament. 'They were caught in a desperate situation. It was not something they wanted, but they had building deadlines to meet.'

That frenetic rush to meet deadlines, to finish buildings and to move on to the next site had consequences for more than workers' and builders' pockets. It meant there was little time to rest workers, short cuts were taken, and shoddy practices were tolerated. As SIPTU's Eric Fleming noted, there was no one to monitor even such obvious transgressions as a worker who returned drunk to the site after lunch. In the quiet, uneventful days of the week after Christmas 1995, Fleming recalls standing in his kitchen with the radio on, listening to the Health and Safety Authority chief 'waxing lyrical about how pleased they were about the figures for that year. I was so frustrated I let out a scream – "I'm fuckin' sick of it." I rang the *Irish Times* and lashed out at the HSA in a statement. Then I asked the *Times* woman who took down the statement to fax a typewritten copy to our local sweet shop and spent the afternoon copying it and passing it out to the media. It got great coverage because it was such a quiet time . . .'

The issue had come out into the open, but as the boom gathered pace the situation continued to deteriorate. Within a two-week period there were three scaffold collapses; a worker in

Lower Mount Street, Dublin, sustained a broken back. 'You didn't require any qualifications to put up a scaffold – your da or a mate could help you,' says Fleming. 'It was a risky oul' job done by lads who couldn't read or write. And by the time scaffolders got to the age of 52 or 53, their backs were gone.' When Frank Burns, a 71-year-old bricklayer, fell to his death while working as a subcontractor on a Zoe Developments site in Dublin's north inner city, in March 1996, the court heard that plasterers had probably removed vital supports from the scaffolding earlier and forgotten to replace them.

Judge Frank O'Donnell said it was 'inconceivable' that a company of Zoe's size and experience had failed to provide the correct scaffolding for its workers. 'Some accidents are inevitable – this was not,' he said, when it came to court in June 2000. Zoe had no qualified witness to give evidence about safety issues, and although it had been suggested that the company had only 4 previous convictions, the judge calculated that it was more like 11. He fined the company £15,000.

Less than a year after the death of Frank Burns, 24-year-old James Masterson was killed on another Zoe site at Charlotte Quay in the Grand Canal Docks. One of seven children of a small farmer in Geesala, Co. Mayo, he had been the mainstay of his father, Donal. His devastated sister said her father was considering selling the farm because James would no longer be around to help him. 'I went up to the site where James Masterson was killed, after the cops had gone,' recalled Eric Fleming. 'It was a complete mess. I couldn't believe it. There was an electrician on a ladder in the basement in the middle of a mound of rubble, and no helmet.' James Masterson's death was the third on a Zoe-managed site in six years. Back in January 1990, a worker at Grove Road, Rathmines, had been crushed to death when a crane collapsed on him. For that, the company had been fined £1,400.

With James Masterson's death in 1997, Zoe Developments and the 16-storey apartment block on Charlotte Quay where he died were fast becoming symbols for the unacceptable face of the building boom. An inspector from the Health and Safety

Authority described the company's record over seven years as one of 'shocking heedlessness'. Within weeks, Mr Justice Peter Kelly in the High Court laid down a marker, describing the firm as a 'recidivist criminal'. The learned judge told Carroll in the High Court: 'You are not entitled to make profit on the blood and lives of your workers. You are a disgrace to the construction industry and ought to be ashamed of yourself.'

Under prompting from the judge, Carroll offered to make a £100,000 donation to charity; the judge directed that the donation would be paid to the St Vincent de Paul night shelter at Back Lane, Dublin, and to Temple Street Children's Hospital. After a two-hour meeting with the HSA, Carroll was asked if he had anything to say about the company's safety record. 'We are committed to improving our sites,' he said; and by all accounts, his construction business has since become a model for health and safety practices.

The case seemed to mark a turning point. 'For the first time, a judge has actually said society cares about what is happening in the industry,' said the HSA development officer, Sylvia Wood. 'This is a landmark case for us. At last we have a judge who says, "If you have a case, bring it." Previously, court awards were derisory.' Fleming points out that when he subsequently visited all the Zoe sites with the company's design director, David Torpey, he was struck by the loyalty of many workers to Liam Carroll. 'I could see why, to be honest. The pay wasn't bad at all and the pension scheme was up to scratch. I'd say he certainly wasn't the worst . . . And it would be true to say that Liam Carroll and Zoe, by and large, turned over a new leaf and turned into a [health and safety] model for others.'

Meanwhile, protest marches by building workers became a familiar sight. At one stage, SIPTU members occupied the office of the Minister of State for Labour Affairs, Tom Kitt – 'good sturdy married men', says Fleming, 'fighting for their lives'. Builders were deeply unhappy with the unions' very public activities, according to Fleming. 'The CIF treated me with a fair amount of contempt. Their attitude was: "Why don't you shut your fuckin' mouth, you're making a show of this industry." That's the kind of language they used. Their story was that the majority of them were good, decent builders. I kept saying they were not.' In any event, progress was made, inch by inch. In 2001 and 2002, some €140 million was channelled into the implementation of new training and safety measures and around 1,000 specialist safety personnel were put to work on site. The 'Safe Pass' scheme, under which no worker could step on a site without a certificate confirming that he had done a one-day safety course, was introduced. But legislation remained weak. Although Tom Kitt had promised tough new legislation and on-the-spot fines, nothing happened. The Health and Safety Authority still had only 17 inspectors, with responsibility for thousands of construction sites in an expanding industry.

As the boom intensified, so did reports of unscrupulous employers and subcontractors sacking workers who complained about dangerous conditions, and relocating injured men to prevent an accident being registered. With millions at stake, the closure of a site for an accident investigation was to be avoided at all costs. 'I certainly know of cases where limbs were broken, the men were moved outside and then a van would appear,' says Eric Fleming. 'Companies will do anything to show there are no serious accidents on the job. If an injured worker takes three days off work, it must be registered as "serious" and the Health and Safety Authority has to be involved. I heard of one serious accident where, on the third day, they wheeled the man on to the site to clock in, so the accident wouldn't be registered.'

There were signs that the courts were adopting a more punitive line. In November 2001, a Co. Kildare construction firm, Roseberry Construction, and one of its directors were fined a record £240,000, following the 1998 deaths of two men after the trench in which they were working collapsed. The HSA hailed the fine as 'a milestone'. In 2002, the figures began to creep up again. There were three separate construction site deaths in a single week in December, a week in which a HSA study revealed that three-quarters of the industry's fatal accidents were down to site management failures and company headquarters' actions; just a quarter were attributable to errors on the part of the victim. A month later, Judge Peter Kelly put down another marker: he actually sent a builder to prison. Jason Madden, a director of Kilkishen Homes, was jailed for a weekend for contempt and fined €10,000 after the court had ordered the closure of a Tipperary building site for the second time in two months. In February, 3,000 building workers marched through Dublin to draw attention to safety conditions. In just over four years since 1998, 111 people had died in construction-related accidents while 1,121 had been injured.

In July 2003, Judge Harvey Kenny laid down another milestone at Castlebar Circuit Criminal Court. He imposed a record fine of €500,000 on a Galway construction company, Oran Pre-Cast Ltd, for breaches of health and safety legislation, after the death of 25-year-old Thomas Farragher, who fell from a height of nine metres while replacing a damaged roof gutter. The company had had a number of previous warnings and prohibition notices.

The statistics were moving in the right direction. Despite the massive increases in numbers on building sites, the figures for fatal accidents remained at under 20 a year between 2002 and 2007, with the exception of 2005, when 23 workers died. 'The situation now is by no means grand,' says Fleming, 'but I do believe that without all that protesting and activity, the death rate would have doubled. I'm very happy that we have the Safe Pass system – we're still the only country in Europe to have it. I'm happy that scaffolders, crane drivers, machine drivers have to have training in law and that if there are over 20 workers on a site, they must select a safety representative and he has to be trained.'

There were plenty of other battles to be fought, not least the continuing struggle to force compliance with pension payments to the industry's statutory pension fund. In 2006, Pensions Ombudsman Paul Kenny singled out the construction sector when criticizing the 'theft' by employers of pension contributions deducted from employees. In October 2007, more than 145 builders were facing prosecution for failing to contribute a total of €1.5 million to pension funds. In 2008, one north Co. Dublin company, Limestone Construction, was found to have deducted pension contributions of over €100,000 in little over a year from 200 workers' salaries but had failed to pay the money into the pension fund. It was ordered by the High Court to pay total arrears of over €180,000. The Irish Pensions Board had concerns, however, as the company 'no longer owned its assets, was not paying its creditors and owed a substantial amount of money'.

The trend towards distancing the site worker even further from the main contractor gathered pace with the increasingly widespread use of employment agencies to hire construction workers. In 2007 a survey would show that Ireland had the highest proportion of workers employed on temporary contracts across the EU, while trade unions estimated that well in excess of 500 labour agencies were operating out of Ireland. In 2001, however, there were only glimpses of the phenomenon. 'The first time I noticed the big influx of foreign workers was in 2001,' recalls Eric Fleming. 'A complaint came in that there was a load of lads from Portugal on a site out in Leopardstown. Every day you'd hear back from fellas saying, "I met another Portuguese lad out there." They had no English at all and I remember thinking, "Jaze, what's bringing them here?"' When SIPTU investigated, it emerged that a couple of the 30 labourers working for a sub contractor on the Crampton site were indeed Portuguese. Another few were from other EU countries such as France and Italy and others were from Morocco, Egypt and Algeria. Most of them, however, were Romanian and illegal. None spoke any English and – in a taster of things to come – when a translater was found, it emerged that their gangmaster, a Moroccan, had extracted between £120 and £150 from them to obtain a job and was charging a further £30 a week per man for 'expenses'.

When SIPTU assistant branch secretary Mick Finnegan looked more closely, he found their conditions to be 'absolutely unbelievable, like something out of the Middle Ages', and he estimated that they were owed between £80,000 and £100,000 in unpaid overtime and travel-time payments. The Irish sub-contractor on the site would only say that he 'didn't short-change anybody'. Crampton, one of the country's most reputable builders, knew nothing of the scam; when alerted, they agreed not only to pay lump sums of £600 each to the 16 illegals to get them by, but to take on all those with work permits as direct employees. Unsure what to do about the 16 illegal men, SIPTU officials, Crampton and the CIF turned to Tom Kitt, and thence to what Fleming describes as a 'diligent' civil servant, to sort it out. 'Nobody had a clue how to deal with this,' he says. 'Nothing like this had ever come up before. We were all in it together, in a kind of partnership.' A civilized agreement was reached whereby the government would allow the Romanians to return to Bucharest, where there would be a letter awaiting them, giving them permission to return. 'They were back in Ireland within days,' says Fleming. 'I can say they were very, very good workers and became ardent union members. But what I remember best about that time,' he says, almost nostalgically, 'was the great element of empathy and sense of "live and let live" that was there from everyone.'

Three months later, on 4 July 2002, came an intimation of a practice that was probably rampant around the country by then. When a 31-year-old Polish man, Marek Sliwinski, then living in Co. Meath, appeared before District Court Judge John Brophy on a drink-driving charge, the court heard that Sliwinski was earning just £4 an hour with a local construction company. The judge dispatched his solicitor to check on the national minimum wage, and discovered it was £4.70. 'It's a form of cheap, semi-slave labour . . . a disgraceful trend,' protested the judge. In fact, it was worse than the judge imagined. For construction workers, the legal minimum wage was at least double what Sliwinski had been receiving. Other stories of underpayment began to break the surface. In January 2003, nine Romanian carpenters and steel-fixers, in Ireland under an intracompany transfer scheme which waived the need for work permits, were discovered to be working 60-hour weeks for a Maynooth subcontractor, for €6 an hour –

half the agreed hourly industry rate. In 2005, four Polish workers, who said they were sacked when they queried their wages of between €100 and €125 a week, were awarded compensation of €3,000 to €4,000 each in the Labour Court. They had earlier been receiving between €200 and €250 for an 84-hour week, SIPTU told the court. It was only when even this derisory payment was halved that they asked why; they were told that 'taxes had increased'.

Later that year, SIPTU found a Slovakian and six Polish workers, all legally in this country, being paid €2 an hour by a Dublin plastering company. After eight days' work, Artur Junkiert, one of the seven, had been given a cheque for €796.25, and told to divide it between them. He was also told that five of them were no longer needed. Although he should have been on PAYE, Junkiert's payslip stated that he was working on a self-employed basis. Later, there would be heart-sinking cases such as one involving a Dublin-based company, which was charging Romanian workers €200 a week for housing them in caravans. When one of them moved out, the company continued to deduct €100 a week from his wages.

The difficulty of policing the industry was captured in an *Irish Times* piece by Carl O'Brien in May 2007, describing a building site somewhere in Co. Waterford:

The senior trade union official scratched his head. He had just arrived at a building site ... as part of a blitz to monitor pay and conditions for construction workers. What he happened upon was more complicated than he bargained for. The foreman was German. But the workers were Polish and employed by a separate labour agency. The management were employed by someone else. The supermarket they were building was owned by another consortium. It's difficult to know who you're dealing with. The workers, it turned out, were being paid around half of the industry standard rates. Soon they will have moved on to the next construction site. Within weeks, the workers will be back in Poland, leaving a cloud of dust behind them. 'They're moving so fast that it's hard to keep up with them. It's hard to even find out who is responsible for workers, and by that time, they've gone,' said the official.

Ireland, which had turned a blind eye when its own workers had sold their labour on the cheap in other countries, was getting a dose of its own medicine. O'Brien wrote of a 'labyrinthine world of labour agencies and outsourcing, where employment is never quite as it seems. It's an environment where workers are contracted through complex supply chains of agencies which can bypass industry-agreed pay rates by using a ready supply of cheap and temporary labour from poorer countries.' BATU's nightmare had materialized. According to the Comptroller and Auditor General's report in 2005, there were 33,800 principal contractors in the state, over 40,329 registered subcontractors and nearly 56,580 unregistered subcontractors. And these were only the ones that the C&AG knew about.

In 2005, Trevor Sargent, the then leader of the Green Party, told the Dáil about a 'scam' by big construction companies to avoid paying subcontractors what they were owed. Over the previous month, he had met representatives of 10 small and medium-size indigenous construction companies who described what was going on. 'A construction company, in this case Glenman Corporation, in Galway, won a government contract to build council housing in Fortunestown and Ballymun, Dublin. It hired subcontractors to do most of its work. When the work was completed and the subcontractors presented invoices, in one case for €374,000, and €254,000 in another, some fault was found in the documentation or the work. They were told they would not be paid. When the subcontractors threatened legal proceedings, they were told it would take three years to get to court and by then they would be bankrupt. Instead they were made an offer of approximately half of what they were owed to take or leave.' He mentioned a plant hire company that was owed €180,000, a site security company that was owed €10,000 and a haulage company that was owed €206,000. 'I spoke to one [subcontractor] who owes €400,000 to the people he hired to carry out this work. His apartment has been ransacked – we suspect by the creditors – his wife and children have been obliged to move out of the family home and he has not slept there for four weeks because he fears for his life.'

Sargent was seeking reform in the prompt-payment legislation. Meanwhile, others were pondering definitions. In the chaotic mix of a Klondike-like industry, what exactly was a 'subcontractor' any more? What precisely did 'self-employed' mean?

A key ingredient in this chaotic mix were the tens of thousands of non-Irish workers who were entering the system with no knowledge of their rights and less English. Tagged as 'self-employed', the subcontractors took no responsibility for them. 'We've seen fellas carrying shovels and working in canteens who we've been told are self-employed,' said Eric Fleming. 'People with good jobs are being made redundant.' An examination of sites across Dublin by 30 SIPTU officials revealed 'not one that wasn't deregulated. We've met employers who employ nobody,' said Fleming. There was evidence that foreign subcontractors were employing foreigners only, men who knew nothing of their entitlements. In one grim two-week period in March 2006, three cases of exploitation by foreign subcontractors of foreign workers came to light, all involved, embarrassingly, in some of the country's highest-profile construction projects. A Polish company engaged in the refurbishment of the ESB power station at Moneypoint, Co. Clare, which employed only Polish workers, was found to be paying them just €5.20 an hour, less than a third of the legally binding construction industry rate. Hungarian workers employed by a Hungarian subcontractor on the Spencer Dock development in Dublin were alleged to be working 69 hours a week for a third of the legal minimum wage. And it was discovered that 100 Serbian linesmen and electricians working on the ESB's €3 billion renewal of the electricity network were being paid less than €5 an hour, and were said to be owed thousands of euro each – in some cases up to €40,000 – by a Serbian subcontractor. It was noted in each of these cases that the abuses were exposed by Irish trade unionists and not by the scandalously understaffed Labour Inspectorate. The work of the trade union movement was all the more commendable given the language obstacle and the natural reticence of foreign workers, terrified that their work permits would be withdrawn and that they would never work again in their native countries. A glimpse into the extent of company compliance with employment rights was given by the National Employment Rights Authority, which revealed that 56 per cent of more than 400 inspections of the construction sector in 2007 detected breaches of legislation, and had led to the recovery of €1.33 million in arrears.

But all of these stories were dwarfed by what Socialist Party Councillor Mick Murphy discovered in October 2004, when he travelled out to Lucan, Co. Dublin, to give support to three BATU workers. The main contractor on the site was a Turkish multinational called Gama. The three workers had already garnered media attention while occupying a crane to protest about non-payment of three weeks' wages, claiming that Gama, and not the subcontractor, was their employer. In the event, both the High Court and the Labour Court upheld Gama's contention that it was not the men's employer, but this turned out to be a pyrrhic victory for the company. The visit stirred Murphy's curiosity about Gama: 'I talked to the [BATU] lads about their own situation and also about the 130 non-nationals living on the site, who the lads felt weren't being given the agreed rate of pay.' As was often the case in these situations, language was a problem. Using a stick, the foreign workers had written '600' in the dirt on the ground, 'which I took to be €600 per month' said Murphy, in a video on the Gama affair produced by the Socialist Party and Framework Films. When he tried to talk to them, however, the men were 'very, very nervous . . . they literally ran away from us'. He contacted the council and Gama. Both assured him that everything was above board and the agreed rates – a minimum of €12.96 an hour – were being paid. He contacted trade union officials who had had dealings with Gama, but they were unable to confirm what the rates were. So Murphy tried the direct route. He wrote a leaflet in English and had it translated into Turkish 'mainly to say that we had no problem with them being here, and saying what Gama had said'. He also added a calculation table which showed that their pay should have been around €6,000 a month, rather than €600. Then he threw the flyers over the hoarding into the site where the Turkish workers were both working and living.

After many hours of subsequent discussion between Gama workers, Murphy and Socialist Party officials, the truth emerged: they were receiving €2.20 an hour, one-fifth of the rate that Gama said they were being paid. 'We knew immediately we had a major scandal,' said Murphy.

On 8 February 2005, Socialist TD Joe Higgins rose in Dáil Éireann to tell a shocked nation about Gama Construction Ireland Ltd, a Turkish company with some 10,000 employees in total, some 2,000 of them in Ireland, a company that had been the recipient of 'massive' state and local authority construction contracts, now a company revealed to be engaged in a 'major scandal of immigrant worker exploitation, of massive proportions'. Yes, Gama had built the Ennis and Ballincollig bypasses and had come in six months ahead of schedule, but Higgins argued:

That's easy when you have a bonded labour force working eleven or twelve hours a day with two Sundays off in a month. And then can underbid because of these rates of pay. This company imports workers who do not speak English from their home base, controls their passports and work permits, accommodates them often in company barracks, demands grotesque working hours and, incredibly, pays unskilled construction workers between €2 and €3 an hour, and skilled [workers] something over €3 an hour . . .

Within days, the country would be treated to the sight of 'payslips' – actually, scraps of paper with no names, just a few handwritten figures showing the amount owed – that were handed out to Gama workers. Gama's Irish solicitor would appear on television, denouncing the allegations as 'absolutely untrue' and denying that these were payslips handed out by the company: 'I can absolutely assure you we would never ever produce payslips like that.'

Joe Higgins pounded away, producing examples of workers like Jamal, who worked a 'monstrous' 80 hours a week and who should have been earning €4,200 a month. 'He got less than €1,000 a month,' said Higgins. 'Where did the €3,200 go?' Gama eventually responded that Jamal's and others' money had been lodged in bank accounts in Finansbank in Amsterdam. But it was not clear whether workers were aware of this arrangement, and Higgins alleged that Gama had had to 'coach' workers, 'under duress', to say that they had known that their money was in those accounts. 'They had to be coached because no workers knew they had accounts in Finansbank,' he thundered. When Higgins visited the Dutch bank with Turkish workers, he reported: 'Within 20 minutes, they supplied us with a full account of the money that had gone into each account and what happened to it – which of course they hadn't furnished to a single worker in the three years it was there.' He reckoned there were 'probably €30 million in workers funds' there.

Sevinc, a worker interviewed on the party's video, said that Gama had made the workers sign a lot of papers when they were employed: 'The papers were in English and they told us it was nothing important.' It emerged that one of the forms they signed had authorized the establishment of their account in Finansbank, while a second authorized transfer of all monies out of the account. The day after the money was put into the accounts system, it was transferred to a company called Ryder Investments. Both Gama and the bank refused to say who the beneficiaries were. Higgins then made the point that even if all this money were repaid to Gama workers, it only brought the funds up to what workers were owed for a 48-hour week, whereas the reality was that they had worked 80-hour weeks – 'which explained why the projects managed to be ahead of schedule'. The Turkish workers and their supporters hit the streets, marching to the Dáil, with their Turkish-language banners and hi-viz jackets, chanting

Turkish slogans, clapping, whistling and breaking into their national dance. As the protests and strikes stretched into weeks, charged with emotion and allegations of intimidation of workers by Gama, amid headlines about a threatened hunger strike by Gama workers, the company's auditors PricewaterhouseCoopers resigned, citing Gama's refusal to furnish 'information and explanations . . . in relation to alleged breaches of employment rights'.

The political system gasped and wished it all away. But it could hardly say it had not been warned. In February 2001, Gama's first successful tender in Ireland for a contract to build a power station at Huntstown, Co. Dublin, had come in at a startling 36 per cent below that of its nearest rival, P J Walls. Armed with the knowledge that 40 per cent of construction costs were determined by wage rates, a child could have calculated that the Turkish bid was based on hourly rates that were 10 per cent of those applying in the Republic. Some months later, Gama was celebrating another successful bid, this time for a National Roads Authority contract to build the Ballincollig bypass in Cork. Its bid of £56 million was a whopping £12 million below the next-lowest Irish bid. In response to sceptical inquiries, an NRA spokesman said that Gama was aware it would have to comply with Irish labour law and construction industry wage rates. With some prescience, Mick Finnegan, SIPTU's construction branch officer, cautioned that if the Turkish workers were housed in special camps, it would be impossible to ensure they were properly paid. The NRA responded that it was setting up a monitoring system to ensure compliance with Irish statutory requirements.

By January 2002, as Gama was about to celebrate another major contract for a local authority housing development at Balgaddy, in west Dublin, Irish building unions were threatening industrial action at the Huntstown site. They wanted clarification on whether the company was paying agreed industry rates. At the same time, a rival construction company was also expressing concern to Mary Harney, Minister for Enterprise, Trade and Employment, informing her that Turkish workers at Huntstown were being paid 'the equivalent of five dollars an hour'. 'We have no doubt that, if challenged, this figure will be elaborately camouflaged by Gama,' wrote the company. 'It is clear that [we are] not in a position to investigate this abuse. This is a matter for your department . . .' The department's reply to the Irish company, couched in curtly dismissive terms, said that Gama had been 'fully cooperative in meeting our requests for documents and data and that, following our consideration of the information supplied, there are now no further issues which we wish to pursue with the company in this context. In short, we are satisfied with the outcome of these discussions.'

By now, as well as the projects at Huntstown, Ballincollig and Balgaddy, Gama had landed contracts at the power stations in Lanesboro and Shannonbridge. The one thing that no one could criticize was the quality of Gama's work. Or its PR strategy. It gave donations to local communities and won awards from the likes of the National Standards Authority. Its managing director had become a leading member of the Dublin Chamber of Commerce. When trade union officials visited the Huntstown site, SIPTU's Eric Fleming recalls being 'astonished' at the gleaming modern workers' kitchens. As for the work: 'A union colleague said it was the best work he'd ever seen,' says Fleming. 'All the workers were dressed in modern overalls, protective gear, good sturdy boots – better than you'd see on Irish workers . . . When our officials visited there, they came back to say facilities were fantastic and that the Irish workers were invited to dine with the Turkish workers for nothing. Even with an interpreter, the Turkish lads would say everything was great.' A flavour of how business was done, Gama-style, can be gleaned from Fleming's description of a meeting in Liberty Hall, not long after Gama's arrival in Ireland. The company was represented by three lawyers, three accountants 'and a man from Ankara with excellent English . . . I have no doubt that this was the officer corps of the Turkish army, impeccably dressed and manicured to the nines. The man from Ankara took out a massive box of Turkish Delight and handed them around to officials. One official, a guy with false teeth, couldn't talk again for most of the meeting.' At a later stage, when yet another enormous box of Turkish Delight was being presented, the man from Ankara explained the significance: 'There is a saying in our country, "Eat sweet, talk sweet."' It appeared to work. Gama had turned out to be a magic wand for a government determined to shake up a heavily unionized and regulated construction sector, in the interests of delivering major National Development Plan projects on budget and on time. Irish companies watched impotently as a besotted government enabled Gama to benefit from massive income tax, social insurance and work permit concessions – de facto grants worth millions.

Gama was the major beneficiary of a scheme exempting employers from paying social insurance for employees from abroad, hoovering up over 70 per cent of such exemptions between the beginning of 2003 and May 2005. Out of a total of 1,867 workers covered by the scheme, a startling 1,324 were Gama employees. 'We have no explanation as to why Gama workers made up such a high proportion,' said the Department of Social and Family Affairs.

Turkish employees of Gama also benefited from reduced income tax, as most of their wages were paid directly into accounts in Turkey and the Netherlands. The Department of Enterprise also ensured that a certain type of work permit, banned since 2003, continued to be available to Gama for its workers. Other companies would have been required to seek to fill positions through FÁS, but a super-satisfied Department of Enterprise official noted in a 2003 report that the department had continued to issue these permits to Gama 'liberally and quickly to ensure that contracts for these projects are delivered on time. To date the company has met our requirements and we have had no problems with compliance.'

In fact, this official had no problem with Gama in any respect, attributing all the allegations in relation to Gama to 'one source', BATU, and surmising that they all related to an inter-union dispute (with UCATT). In any event, the official was happy to confirm that the plasterers', carpenters' and painters' unions had had no significant problems with the company. Thus was BATU dispatched. Next, the official got to work on the 'disappointed Irish rival contractor', which had had the temerity to complain about pay levels at Huntstown. This of course was precisely the sort of thing about which the department had been warned when Gama first arrived, as well as the fact that dodgy payments would be elaborately camouflaged. But the official ploughed on regardless: 'This, too, led to a concerted letter-writing campaign to public representatives and, on investigation by this department, the allegations were found to be without substance.' He/she added. 'We have invited interested parties to provide evidence in support of allegations, if such evidence exists.'

A question that was asked then, and that has never been answered, is what kind of investigation was carried out by the department that allowed it to dismiss legitimate concerns with such thoroughgoing complacency? Whatever they did, they obviously found nothing. Yet three years on, when sent in again by Minister for Enterprise Micheál Martin, inspectors found enough to warrant referral of their report to the Department of Social and Family Affairs, the Revenue Commissioners, the Director of Public Prosecutions, the Competition Authority, the Office of the Director of Corporate Enforcement and the Garda Commissioner. In fairness to the complacent department official, it could be said that no one, with the exception of Higgins's Socialist Party, had acquitted themselves with credit in this affair. A flavour of the feeling around the Dáil might be gleaned from Conor Lenihan's shouted suggestion across the chamber to Joe Higgins to 'stick with the kebabs', during a debate about Aer Lingus. No flags had been raised in SIPTU either, even though all Gama's general operatives were SIPTU members. Why did the workers not complain? Because they believed the bosses' men were planted among them. 'The bosses ran it like a military operation,' says Eric Fleming. 'They would set it up when they knew visitors were coming. For instance, where they'd have had four men in a two-bed room, they'd reduce it back to two men in the room, that kind of thing ...' Even BATU, whose members had made most noise about Gama over the years, readily conceded that it had encountered no difficulty with the company regarding its own members. 'We have been doing good business with Gama,' said the union's general secretary, Paddy O'Shaughnessy, a few days after Joe Higgins's first Dáil statement. 'They pay the appropriate rates and stick to agreements.'

It had been a wildly different scenario for Gama's Turkish employees, of course. In August 2005, despite earlier widespread scepticism about Higgins's allegations, the company agreed to pay its workers €8,000 per year of service and one month's extra salary in respect of overtime worked up to March 2005. It was nothing like the amount they were owed, of course, but as SIPTU's Noel Dowling pointed out, 'The system would not allow for justice for workers who can't afford to hang around and wait for 18 months to two years.' In May 2006, Minister for Enterprise Micheál Martin was still pursuing Gama for documentary evidence that its workers had received all the money held in their names in Finansbank. Large sums of money from the Dutch bank accounts did eventually find their way to their true owners.

As for Gama itself, although copies of the inspectors' report into allegations against it were forwarded to several bodies, no prosecutions ensued. There is, therefore, no way of knowing how or why Gama felt it could operate in Ireland with such impunity. Despite the many questions swirling around it, Gama continued to prosper from public contracts in Ireland, winning a €50 million contract for the new N2 Dublin/Derry bypass at Castleblayney in 2005 and a joint €400 million contract with GE to build a Bord Gáis power plant in Co. Cork in 2007. In evidence to the Labour Court in 2008, regarding SIPTU workers' claim for a 'finishing bonus' of between one and two weeks' additional pay – which, the union said, was becoming the norm on large projects – the company claimed that it had lost up to €45 million on the 21 km Ennis bypass. By then, the numbers in the industry had reached a peak at just over 280,000 – a far cry from the 80,000 when it was all kicking off 12 years before. Figures from the

Central Statistics Office showed that 38,000 non-Irish nationals were employed in the industry at that stage, with around 30,000 of those hailing from the EU accession countries, such as Poland, Latvia and Lithuania.

As the boom fades into memory, there is the question of what the future holds, not only for Irish construction workers but for the men who flocked here from eastern Europe to become the modern counterpart of the Irish navvy who built the roads of Britain. Many returned to their own countries with the anticipation of entering their own fledgling boom. Meanwhile, Breakfast Roll Man conjures with the realization that 'for the first time in a generation the future is not so bright', in the words of David McWilliams. Those who climbed on the buy-to-let train in the past few years 'are probably having a few sleepless nights' says Darren, the craftsman turned developer. In December 2007, Micheál McMahon, the Donegal emigrant in New York, faced a dilemma. Still illegal after 15 years and under pressure to return to Ireland with Cheryl and their two small children, he was standing his ground. From his vantage point in the Bronx, the cracks in the Celtic Tiger had been evident for a while. Emigrants who had gone back to Ireland were returning to New York, disillusioned and heartsick at the changes they had seen. Worse, at that stage no one in the Irish political establishment wanted to hear that jobs were not as plentiful on the ground as the returned emigrants had been led to expect; and McMahon was witnessing the arrival of new young emigrants in New York every day.

Meanwhile, Eric Fleming notes wryly that companies in Canada's north Alberta are 'begging for workers'. Is it really only 14 years since a Canadian union asked us to take 'a few of the brothers'?

The controversy, and the negative public attention it involved, must have been traumatic for a man more accustomed to seeing the words 'financial wizard' after his name and whose bright blue and yellow signs festoon big construction sites all over the place: 'Better Built by McNamara'. The name McNamara is also likely to be emblazoned on the jibs of tower cranes lifting long steel beams or huge buckets of concrete for Michael McNamara and Company Ltd, one of Ireland's top building contractors. The blue and yellow livery is no accident: the late Michael McNamara came from Lisdoonvarna, and blue and yellow are the Clare GAA colours. Bernard, his son, then took over the company, becoming not only one of the most successful building contractors in the state, but also a prolific property developer and investor.

Bernard McNamara was involved in a splurge of acquisitions during the latter years of the boom, including the Burlington Hotel (bought for €288 million), Carrisbrook House in Ballsbridge (€46 million) and his biggest joint venture, the Irish Glass Bottle site in Ringsend (€412 million). He also led the consortium that bought the Shelbourne Hotel on St Stephen's Green for €140 million and then spent nearly €90 million on a lavish refurbishment of the property, adding 75 bedrooms to give it a total of 265. In February 2007 he spearheaded the group that bought the Montrose Hotel on Stillorgan Road for more than €40 million. This group, Select Retail Holdings, includes his Shelbourne partners Jerry O'Reilly and David Courtney as well as Simon Burke, who formerly headed Hamley's toy store chain in Britain. It had already bought Superquinn's chain of 21 supermarkets in January 2005 for almost €450 million, and sold six of the properties for €142 million in May 2007. Five months earlier, McNamara purchased a 45 per cent stake in the Conrad Hotel, on Earlsfort Terrace, for around €45 million, having snapped up the Great Southern Hotel in Parknasilla, Co. Kerry, the previous summer for almost €40 million. He also controls the Mercer Hotel in Dublin and the Radisson in Galway. Meanwhile, his construction firm continues to win lucrative contracts, heading the Leargas consortium named in April 2007 as the preferred bidder to build a new prison at Thornton Hall, in north Co. Dublin, to replace Mountjoy; his partners in this public-private partnership deal are Barclays Private Equity and GSL, which runs prisons in Britain. A month later, he was dubbed 'Bernard the Unstoppable' in the *Irish Times* property supplement.

Files in the Companies Registration Office show that the McNamara group is owned by an unlimited holding company called Adenway, in which Bernard McNamara has a 90 per cent stake, with the remainder split half-and-half between fellow director Christopher Hirst and Michael O'Brien of Bohola, Co. Mayo – a place that has produced a sizeable crop of property developers. Another unlimited holding company, Belltrap, is the ultimate parent of a number of vehicles used by McNamara and Jerry O'Reilly for joint ventures. The accounts for the year to November 2006 show the company paid out €9.3 million to its two shareholders, plus a dividend of €4 million on the previous year's retained profits. Radora Developments, the company they set up with David Courtney to do their biggest scheme yet at Elm Park, on Merrion Road, had bank loans totalling €303 million at the end of November 2006, mainly from Anglo Irish Bank, though the guarantees given by the three-man syndicate behind it were limited to €62 million.

Although McNamara's roots lie deep in Co. Clare, he is a long way from the mould of his generation of west-of-Ireland builder-developers. In his interview for Ivor Kenny's book *Leaders: Conversations with Irish Chief Executives*, he mentioned his father's purchase of a house on Dublin 4's Raglan Road for £34,000 in the mid-1970s, not as a home, but as a place for his children to live while attending college – an introduction to Dublin life and lodgings that most country students could only dream about. His siblings include Shelley McNamara of the highly regarded Grafton Architects, who was the first architect to be admitted to Aosdána; Grafton designed his corporate headquarters, built above the remains of a Scots Presbyterian church on Ormond Quay in the late 1980s.

The Raglan Road house was significant in the context of his

eventual colonization of Dublin. That privileged Dublin base, plus 12 years of unwitting networking with future movers and shakers on holidays at Renvyle House Hotel in Connemara, followed later by sociable Friday evenings at the Shelbourne Bar with his petite and stylish wife, Moira, chatting with architects while nosing around for business, all made him realize that he 'knew an awful lot of people' in Dublin. And awfully useful people at that.

Back then, he was working to take his father's small, Clare-based construction company to the next level. Michael, an astute gentleman, had encouraged him to study business rather than engineering, on the basis that: 'A lot of builders . . . get into trouble because they think that cash flow means they own the money.' Another lesson he learned – from a sign in Joe McHugh's pub in Liscannor, Co. Clare – was that: 'Experience is what you get when you didn't get what you wanted.' That's how he learned most of what he knows, he told Ivor Kenny. A key part of that experience was a spell in party politics. In his mid-twenties, single, in the quiet Clare winters, he got involved in local voluntary organizations, through which he was invited to take a co-opted seat on the county council in 1974. A natural and unflappable politician, with the gift of remembering names, he was twice elected as a Fianna Fáil councillor. But at the end of his second term, he told Kenny, he and Moira had 'two or three kids, and it was time to give up and devote myself to them a little more'. What he failed to mention was the scalding experience of contesting his first and only general election in the cauldron of 1981, in which he polled just 2,700 first-preference votes. That was surely fuel for the 'fear of failure' that he mentioned to Kenny. In 1984 he moved back to Dublin to win contracts for the family business.

McNamara perfected the role of contractor-developer, making tight margins in the highly competitive world of tendering for big projects – and much fatter margins as a developer who built up a big property portfolio. The rewards were irresistible at a time when the market was booming, when every developer wanted a piece of the action. But he had an inside track as someone who knew the nuts and bolts of construction, and had a vast network of political friends to call upon, which he is known to cultivate with great charm and energy.

His monthly dinner parties featured an impressive assembly of figures from business, politics and the arts, while his lavish lunches in Antibes during the annual MIPIM real estate jamboree are legendary. His Galway racing festival dinner at the Radisson SAS Hotel, held on the evening of the Galway Plate – a vastly more discreet venue than the infamous Fianna Fáil tent – was another opportunity to gather highly influential guests from politics, property and investment banking.

'His Fianna Fáil connections are no burden,' as one industry source puts it. McNamara has been, at one time or another, on several state boards, including those of Great Southern Hotels, the National Roads Authority and the National Gallery. He is a close friend of Clare TD and junior minister Tony Killeen, an affable presence in the Fianna Fáil tent at the Galway races when it was in full swing, and a regular at the visitors' bar in Leinster House, notably in the company of Jim Nugent, a former director of the Central Bank and one of Bertie's 'dig-out' men, who acted as an industrial relations adviser to McNamara during troubles on site, such as when he had to confront a wildcat strike by insatiable bricklayers.

Significantly, his successful venture into property in the early 1990s, he told Kenny, 'largely came about from the capacity to use tax breaks', employed to build the Central Statistics Office in Cork as well as a host of Section 50 student accommodation projects. Losing that election was the best thing that ever happened to him, he has told friends, unsurprisingly.

A measure of the damage inflicted by the PPP imbroglio can be gauged from comments about him before the cloud descended. He could do no wrong. While his notorious flashes of temper had been known to leave those on the receiving end quaking and angry, on the whole he was that rare animal, a man who had risen to the top of a cut-throat industry while remaining widely liked and admired. A random selection of descriptions included: 'a badge of quality', 'a fantastically clever operator', 'smart, never petty', 'remarkably unpretentious', 'great fun'. 'Put his name to something and it will fly,' said an industry source. A fellow developer described him as 'dead sound' and 'a very straight operator'. Ciarán Cuffe, the Green TD, named him as 'one of the good guys'.

McNamara's choice of a landing pad for his helicopter beside Booterstown Marsh – a bird sanctuary – was a rare gaffe and attracted Cuffe's ire in print. When they subsequently met at McNamara's request (after he had stopped the landings), the developer offered to speak at a Green Party-organized housing meeting. 'There were about 150 there, and he was fairly nervous,' said Cuffe. 'He got a lot of heckling. Essentially, he said. "Here's land that I control and I will build affordable houses [on it] if I get planning permission." With him, what you see is what you get. I warmed to him, not in a palsy-walsy way, but because he's straight up about what he's doing, which is to make money. And that's what these guys do.'

While friends describe him as unpretentious, he is hardly low-key. His home on Ailesbury Road in Ballsbridge, Dublin, on a site formerly occupied by the Japanese embassy (which he demolished), is a mini-palace furnished with a cinema, ballroom, and 'more plasma televisions than the entire street', according to one boggle-eyed visitor. His summer residence in Lahinch overlooks two golf courses. His philanthropy reaches into every stratum of society, from charity golf teams, to giving space in his hotels for charity events, to supporting the 75-strong Lismorahaun Singers from Co. Clare, who performed a sell-out concert of Mozart's Requiem at the RDS.

But the undoubted tough streak was ever present. Back in 1999, he had no hesitation in hiking the rent in Corrib Village, a student housing complex catering for NUI Galway, by nearly 28 per cent despite protests by the put-upon occupants. 'When I see the price being charged, I have to keep reminding myself this is Galway and not an apartment in Manhattan,' said Students'

Union president Paddy Jordan. But McNamara held his ground. The rooms, he said at the time, 'still represent value in terms of what you would get in Galway. If the market is too high, it's something I can't control.' In May 2000, Irish Intercontinental Bank agreed outline terms to purchase a new headquarters building to be developed by McNamara and Jerry O'Reilly on a site at Barrow Street, in the Grand Canal Docks, for £60 million. Just five months later, negotiations with the bank were terminated by McNamara, who said they had 'fallen foul of the current property boom, with values in this prime location increasing daily'; the pair eventually decided to retain the building as an investment, having let it very profitably to McConnell's Advertising, Coyle Hamilton Willis insurance brokers and other tenants.

In 2006, early investors in the Elm Park development on Merrion Road in Ballsbridge were miffed when McNamara and O'Reilly, his partner in the venture, took steps to ensure that they wouldn't be able to resell the apartments for a quick profit. A clause in the contract specified that the developers would get a share of the profits, on a sliding scale, if a purchaser sold up within 10 years – just as those buying affordable housing are subject to penalty 'clawbacks' if they sell on within the same period. If the property was sold within 12 months, a whopping 90 per cent of the profit would go to the developers, and so on down the scale, tailing off to 10 per cent in year nine. McNamara then clinched a deal with insurance company Friends First for one of the Elm Park office blocks, raking in €45 million in up-front funding for the development. The eight-storey block, which overlooks the golf club, comes with access for all employees to amenities on the site, including a gym, heated swimming pool, restaurant, bar and coffee shops.

Again in partnership with O'Reilly, McNamara developed Bishops Court on Upper Kevin Street and pre-let it to the state, as overflow offices for the Department of Foreign Affairs and two other government departments; it was producing an annual rent of €3.2 million in 2006. He also got on with the Exchange, an office scheme in Tallaght, which enjoyed the benefits of urban renewal tax write-offs. In March 2001, after O'Reilly paid a then record price of €46 million for a 14.5-acre site on Merrion Road, beside Elm Park Golf Club, McNamara joined him as a partner in Radora Developments Ltd to plan a new future for this choice property in Dublin 4. The initial idea was a private hospital, to cash in on new tax incentives that the government had introduced for such facilities. It became much more ambitious, however. Several firms of architects were invited to prepare sketch designs showing how much mixed-use development could be accommodated on the site in a form that Dublin City Council's planners might find acceptable. Bucholz McEvoy Architects, fresh from their triumph with Fingal County Hall, managed to fit 100,000 square metres – more than one million square feet, in old money – and they won the commission to design the entire scheme. The fact that these (relatively) youthful architects have such a cutting-edge image made it easier for the planners to indulge them – to the delight of their clients. Apart from a private hospital, the scheme included 330 apartments, 100 terraced houses, more than 30,000 square metres of offices and an eight-storey hotel in an open landscaped setting.

Radora subsequently bought in the adjoining Tara Towers Hotel for €14 million and had plans to add a further 60 bedrooms to bring the number up to 160. But this scheme, also by Bucholz McEvoy, ran into strong opposition because it would have involved replacing the tired old hotel with a 25-storey building. Not only did Dublin City Council refuse permission for the proposed development, but this was confirmed by An Bord Pleanála in May 2007. In its ruling, the appeals board said the new tower on a restricted site would be 'visually intrusive' alongside Dublin Bay and would 'set an undersirable precedent for similar development at such locations'. More than 30 Booterstown residents had objected to the scheme; a woman from Dornden Park claimed the high-rise tower would be 'an alien erection against an otherwise beautiful landscape'. Cllr. Eugene O'Regan, then cathaoirleach of Dún Laoghaire-Rathdown County Council, described it rather more diplomatically as 'unacceptable'. Nonetheless, McNamara and his partners can take pride in the scale of what's built at Elm Park. The office blocks – raised on stilts to give unobstructed views across the beautifully landscaped site, naturally ventilated and with rippling double-skin façades – are radically different from anything else in Dublin. 'The resulting buildings raise, push and twist the bar beyond the designs of many other commercial developments,' wrote Emma Cullinan, in a rave review in the *Irish Times* in February 2008. 'These concrete-framed structures dance in so many ways, from the timber shuttering systems, the sky conservatories, cantilevered rooms, red windows, atria with high, nerve-tickling walkways and views from offices right down the glass façade, all eliciting an emotional response, from the high that comes from mild vertigo to the pleasure that is derived from appraising various forms that can be gradually pieced together and understood.' The result, she wrote, was both 'gorgeous' and 'awe-inspiring'.

In October 2004, McNamara paid more than €23 million for a seven-acre site with town centre zoning in Navan, Co. Meath – the highest price ever for land in this fast-growing commuter town. Ten months earlier, he bought a 1.25-acre site at Fair Green, near Galway's Ceannt Station, for €6 million. He also led one of the three groups bidding for the National Conference Centre, with Leopardstown Race Course as the proposed site, but pulled out of the contest in March 2005. He was among the underbidders for the Bank of Ireland headquarters in Baggot Street, bought for €200 million by rivals Landmark and Quinlan Private. But when the bank offloaded 36 of its branches in a sale-and-leaseback deal, he managed to buy three of them – at Arran Quay, Merrion Row and Upper Leeson Street – for his personal pension fund. He also led a consortium that bought the Champion Sports retail chain for €60 million from Paddy McKillen and Paul McGlade, who built it up.

McNamara's biggest coup was to put together the consortium that bought the 24-acre Irish Glass Bottle site, at Ringsend, in October 2006, with the Dublin Docklands Development Authority as one of his partners. Not only was the deal arranged to minimize stamp duty, but having the authority on board meant that the redevelopment of the site would be easier from a planning perspective because of the DDDA's powers under Section 25 of the act that established it. McNamara raised the bulk of his €57.5 million stake through loan stock placed with Davy Stockbrokers, whose memorandum to clients noted that the DDDA had 'fast-track planning powers, which guarantees the authority's ability to make things happen for its development partners'. The deal was also backed by a €288 million Anglo Irish Bank loan. Given that the DDDA's then chairman, Lar Bradshaw, was a director of Anglo Irish and that the bank's chairman, Seán Fitzpatrick, was on its board, the authority issued a statement saying it operates within a strict code of conduct on conflicts of interest and, in this case, it had a long-standing interest in seeing the Poolbeg peninsula redeveloped.

The Davy memorandum also provided a glimpse of the type of calculations that developers make. It estimated that site clearance, construction and finance costs would come to €1 billion, or around €3,300 per square metre, while the office space being developed there would fetch at least €7,700 per square metre in five years' time and apartments even more – over €8,000 per square metre. The former Irish Glass Bottle site is so large that it could accommodate a whole new city quarter, including new homes for up to 10,000 people and all of the local facilities they would need. But it's unlikely to be the 'mini-Manhattan' that the Progressive Democrats had in mind for Dublin Port, and the low-lying area will need to be protected against the prospect of rising sea levels. Meanwhile, at the height of the controversy over the PPP schemes, the *Sunday Business Post* reported that McNamara was due to begin paying back the €52 million borrowed from Davy private clients – the remaining €5 million-plus had come from his own funds – from the beginning of 2009. While noting that he had until 2013 to pay back the sum, interest of 17 per cent per annum would kick in from 2009. 'If he wants to clear the debt in one go . . . it will cost him €73 million.'

In 2005 and 2006, McNamara won the €900 million tender for

five PPP housing schemes in Dublin, all of them long-overdue regeneration projects. For long-suffering residents, it would be the third attempt over many years to achieve a decent quality of life in areas plagued by desperately run-down dwellings, crime and antisocial behaviour. The schemes included 820 new homes at O'Devaney Gardens off the North Circular Road, 700 at St Michael's Estate in Inchicore, 360 in Dominick Street, another 179 on Sean MacDermott Street and 162 on Infirmary Road. By May 2008, McNamara – with Joe O'Reilly's Castlethorn Construction on board – had signed contracts on two of the schemes and was the preferred bidder on the remaining three. Although the five PPP deals were not identical, they followed a common model whereby the council gives the entire site to the developer. In return, the developer rebuilds the social housing on the site, and also provides a number of units for the council's affordable housing scheme. Meanwhile, the developer is free to build private housing to be sold profitably on the open market. In the McNamara-Castlethorn scheme, the private-sector players were to fund their end of it by selling some 800 of the approximately 1,800 homes that were due to be built.

By any standard, PPPs are big business. Some €43.5 billion is scheduled to be spent on such projects in Ireland in the five years up to 2011, and about a quarter of the PPPs in the pipeline are housing schemes. Politicians love PPPs because they keep the cost of the project off the balance sheet and – in theory – proceed efficiently and speedily. Developers love them because they look like a one-way bet. McNamara's deal, struck at the giddy height of the property boom, was one such – or so it seemed. The snag, blindingly obvious in hindsight, is where boom turns to bust or, in this case, where some 25,000 new homes are lying vacant and the private component of the PPP looks like a beaten docket.

After-the-fact analysis raised questions about the nature of this particular PPP model. 'If the debacle over St Michael's illustrates anything, it is that public-private partnerships should be kept simple,' Michael Flynn, the director of the Deloitte PPP division, told the *Irish Independent*. In this case, there were important variables – such as the number of units which could be fitted on the site (which kept changing), as well as the price for which they could ultimately be sold (which kept falling). 'You really have to look at this as a property deal with elements of the public sector involved. I would not even call them a PPP; essentially it's a land swap,' said Flynn. McNamara himself had cause to question the model, describing PPPs to Marian Finucane as 'a very sophisticated, difficult process that is usually only used for major infrastructure projects. . . . I often wonder what is suitable at all for the procurement of public housing.'

'This was a property deal,' said another figure familiar with the arrangement. 'And when the property market goes wallop, property deals run into trouble.'

And so it unfolded. McNamara pulled out of all five schemes. 'The decision needed to be taken in the interests of the group,' said his spokesman when the news broke. The man who in the good times had been christened 'St Bernard' and 'the acceptable face of capitalism', was suddenly plunged – as the *Irish Times* property supplement put it – 'from hero to zero . . . When the Clare builder pulled out of the housing plans for a run-down estate in Inchicore, he could hardly have foreseen the extent of the reaction. By the weekend, he was being trounced in the Sunday papers as some kind of social pariah, catering for the rich (The Shelbourne) while abandoning the poor (Inchicore).'

While the tone of the piece was sympathetic, describing McNamara as 'undoubtedly a hard-working, decent man who built up an amazing construction empire during the heyday of the property boom', the writer added: 'He is clearly out of touch with popular sentiment, which has the ability to bite back. Like another titan of business, Jim Flavin of DCC, he is not immune to the knock-on effects of one decision made at the time for what appeared sensible reasons. How that one decision to pull out of Inchicore may have effects way beyond its location is another example that the test of any chain is its weakest link.'

In fact, the fall-out should have been no surprise to anyone. After all, here was one of Ireland's business elite, a man with reported personal wealth of €230 million and a trophy home on Ailesbury Road with glass-ceilinged swimming pool, a tycoon who could afford to buy three banks for his personal pension fund and ran a company boasting a €611 million turnover in 2007, abandoning projects designed to benefit the poorest of the poor.

McNamara told Marian Finucane that it was Dublin City Council which initiated the break-up, claiming that the assistant city manager, Ciarán McNamara (no relation), had called the company in and said they 'wanted to go a different route ... We never pulled out.' The letter to the council blamed a number of factors, including changes in the rules governing the minimum size of apartments, under regulations that were introduced after he won the tenders. McNamara also cited delays in achieving planning permission and the fact that, where he was granted planning, it was either for a reduced number of units or it was appealed to An Bord Pleanála, causing further delay. The other main factor, he said, was the slowdown in the market. 'The adversely changed circumstances of the current private housing market to that of 2005/2006, when the bids were submitted, along with the significant additional costs of increased apartment sizes and new energy regulations, have rendered the whole concept of using the sale of private housing units to fund social and affordable housing and community services, along with a balancing site purchase figure, unsustainable in the current market, despite the best efforts of everybody involved.'

He repeated some of those points on radio, saying that: 'If the planning had been applied at the beginning of the process and then you knew what numbers you were involved in, we would never have been caught in the new size guidelines for the project.' New guidelines had added 25 per cent to the building space, he said. But, as Richard Curran pointed out in the *Sunday Business Post*, he had signed only two contracts, and these were for the two schemes where planning permission had been granted; and where planning permission had been granted, the new apartment size regulations did not apply.

In any event, Curran argued, McNamara was one of the most

experienced property developers in the country and 'it is hard to imagine that, when he won these tenders by submitting far and away the lowest tender price, he didn't realize the normal planning process would still apply. Just because Dublin City Council agrees a tender with a developer to provide new units, [this] does not mean that the normal rules of planning, where members of the public can object, are scrapped. McNamara would have known this.' (McNamara had argued on radio that the PPP process needed to be fast-tracked and suggested that the council could, under planning regulations, give itself planning permission 'without appeal in a period of 10 weeks'.)

McNamara and his spokespeople murmured about rivals whose housing PPPs had also stalled, implying that the problem was more widespread than was being acknowledged and therefore deserved greater understanding. Meanwhile, industry figures suggested reassuringly that this setback need not hinder other major PPP construction projects – for state offices, public facilities and infrastructure – which were not reliant on selling residential property.

David McWilliams, writing in the *Sunday Business Post*, raised another question: was it wise for Dublin City Council to embark upon five major urban renewal projects with a single developer? 'The impression that a small number of builders have benefited from state business during the boom is overwhelming. This has to change. There is little point in abandoning the tent at the Galway Races if the philosophy that underpins it remains alive and well.' McWilliams referred to another multimillion-euro state contract for which McNamara was the preferred bidder. This was for Thornton Hall, the new prison in north Co. Dublin – 'a much less risky deal than a PPP to build social housing, which is dependent on the housing market cycle. In a prison deal, you simply build the prison for the state, get a stream of income and take no risk. This is a no-brainer for a developer. There is a strong argument that McNamara's action [in] cherry-picking the PPPs he wants, should come into the equation when the government is deciding how to dole out this contract. If you mess with the government – taking projects when they suit you and abandoning them when they don't – you should pay a penalty.'

For the McNamara group, undoubtedly the most damaging aspect of the whole affair was the spotlight consequently thrown on its financial situation. Journalists noted that it was cashing in large assets – such as the Ormond Hotel and two retail properties on Grafton Street. McNamara also sold his 14.5 per cent stake in Superquinn. On the Marian Finucane programme, he hotly denied a *Sunday Independent* headline that the group was €1.5 billion in debt, and revealed that it anticipated an income stream of €340 million over 20 years from 300,000 square feet of offices applied for on the stupendously costly Burlington site. The company was also confident, he said, of making a 'bankable return' on his joint venture in the Irish Glass Bottle site. 'The bankers certainly haven't been jumping all over me, which seems to be the impression that has been given. We have sufficient assets to cover what's given ... Unless the world collapses, we don't believe we're exposed in the kind of situation that people are talking about ...' All the more reason, surely, not to walk away from O'Devaney Gardens, Inchicore, Sean MacDermott Street, Dominick Street and Infirmary Road?

Meanwhile, one of his more pressing priorities was to devise a scheme that would be acceptable to Dublin City Council's planners to redevelop the Burlington Hotel, occupying a site of almost four acres with frontages on Upper Leeson Street, Sussex Road and Burlington Road, plus the adjoining 1.3-acre Allianz site, which he had also acquired for €100 million. The slab-like hotel, developed by P.V. Doyle, opened in 1972 and quickly became a Dublin institution; it was the first hotel in the city with an indoor swimming pool. Famous guests in the Burlo's early years included Muhammad Ali, Maureen O'Hara, Cliff Richard and John Wayne. Without any show of sentiment, but with €288 million added to its already bulging coffers, the Jurys Doyle hotel group closed it down on 2 January 2008, laying off 447 full-time and part-time employees. McNamara, who got the keys to the hotel shortly after noon that day, was negotiating to purchase its fixtures and fitting with a view to reopening it on a temporary basis as he progressed plans for the site. A month later, planning permission was sought – and granted in May 2008 – for a mixed-use scheme in three blocks up to eight storeys high comprising 33,340 square metres of office space, 185 apartments, a leisure centre, gymnasium, three restaurants, café, wine bar, six shops and a crèche, all laid out around a public landscaped plaza and new pedestrian routes linking Burlington Road and Sussex Road. Contrary to expectations, there was no provision for a hotel to replace the Burlington.

Over the years, 'The Burlo' had been part of Dublin's social fabric, hosting countless banquets, conferences, charity balls, post-match parties and other big events in its vast ballroom. Among the biggest bashes throughout the boom years were the annual dinners of the Construction Industry Federation and Society of Chartered Surveyors, not to mention the Fianna Fáil's President's Dinner, at which party members paid their respects to their leader. Now much of this valuable business will move to the Citywest hotel, leisure and conference complex in Saggart, out on the fringes of the city, where the ebullient Jim Mansfield plays host to the annual ardfheiseanna of both Fianna Fáil and Fine Gael.

Mansfield reputedly bought the land in 1990 for only £1 million, using a small fraction of his profits from the purchase and resale of scrap after the Falklands War; by 2007, the complex was said to be worth at least €400 million. The Citywest Hotel had become the largest in Ireland, with over 1,400 bedrooms, and plans to add even more. It also had a conference centre with a capacity of 4,000, but Mansfield didn't think it was big enough for his growing business, so he started site development work in 2003 for a new facility to fit 6,000. South Dublin County Council had no problem granting approval and construction soon got under way, even though an appeal by An Taisce had been accepted by An Bord Pleanála. Mansfield's planning consultant, former South Dublin county manager Frank Kavanagh, said his client was 'quite well aware of the element of risk' in jumping the gun. He was always a man in a hurry to get things done, whether at Citywest or his other properties, Palmerstown Stud in Co. Kildare and Weston Aerodrome, near Lucan, which he was developing as an executive airport; he even hoped to line up Bill Clinton to open it in May 2005, just weeks after the High Court ruled that he had carried out unauthorized works there.

Now in his late sixties and with a life behind him that reads like a guide to derring-do, Jim Mansfield gives the impression of a man not indifferent to his legacy. 'I'll probably be remembered for what I am, a fucking idiot,' he joked in a 2005 interview with the *Sunday Times*. 'I've never given that sort of thing any thought.' The first part is clearly untrue, the second even less so. For reasons best known to himself, Mansfield has taken to issuing 'updates' on his wealth in recent years, an unheard-of approach for an Irish property mogul. But, clearly, money matters to him. Thanks to an 'update' from the man himself in January 2008, we know that his property portfolio has been valued at a 'conservative' €1.7 billion, although his chief executive, former Football Association of Ireland boss Bernard O'Byrne, let it be known that he reckoned the true value was over €2 billion. We are told that he owns more than 2,250 acres of land in Dublin and Kildare, including Citywest in Saggart, the nearby barracks-style West Park Hotel on the N7, Weston Aerodrome and the PGA golf course at Palmerstown Stud. And, frankly, he is pleased with himself. 'This success is all down to good planning, foresight and hard work,' he modestly told the *Irish Times* in 2008. It might also be said that he has been a victim of a degree of snobbery. 'Mansfield has often been unfairly portrayed by the media as some sort of millionaire Del Boy,' said the *Irish Independent*, 'and there is a lot of snobbiness about the whole blingy, darts-tournament hosting, chopper-infested Ireland that is on display out at "CountryEast". It works, though . . .'

Mansfield is an old-fashioned buccaneer who left school at 14 and, after odd jobs working on a farm and a gravel pit, bought a truck and launched himself into the haulage business aged 17. He had bought another six before he realized that he was making 'less with seven than with one', whereupon he moved into buying and selling trucks and heavy machinery – following a path that was also trod by his friend Robert 'Pino' Harris. While Mansfield's vision might have seemed a tad counter-intuitive in the recession-ravaged Ireland of late 1970s and early 1980s, with the construction industry in virtual collapse and tons of plant machinery lying idle, he looked towards the US, where the Reagan-era economy was soaring and the exchange rate mightily attractive. He assembled over 100 diggers, Caterpillars and the like, chartered a ship, and sent the lot for auction in Florida. It paid off handsomely. Next he cast an eye on the Falkland Islands in the South Atlantic, where 1,100 earth-movers brought in by the British government to rebuild the islands after the improbable 1982 war with Argentina were now surplus to requirements. When they went to auction, anyone who wanted to bid 'had to be flown down in an RAF plane ... The catch was that you weren't allowed on the jet unless you were able to prove that you were worth £6 million sterling,' one machinery man recalled. Jim Mansfield obviously was and, afterwards, he transported the earth-movers thousands of miles north to Atlanta, Georgia. In an auction said to be the biggest of its kind seen in the US, he netted around £19 million; the rest he sold in Liverpool Freeport, netting another £7 million. A subsequent row with the British authorities – who tried to charge VAT to both Mansfield's company and the shipper, despite Liverpool's Freeport status – was finally won by the shipper at the European Court of Justice, but by then Mansfield had lost interest. He was, as he told an interviewer a few years ago, 'doing other things'. The 'other things' were property, of course, specifically the Citywest campus in Saggart, Co. Dublin, with which he has become synonymous.

At one point, Mansfield lost three senior executives within a short period, including the hotel general manager, John Glynn, as well as Séamus Kearney, formerly Willie Walsh's sidekick at Aer Lingus, after one of the shortest chief executive officer stints in Irish corporate history. Mansfield robustly defended himself against charges of being 'difficult' and Glynn made it clear that he did not find him so, adding that he had 'great admiration' for him. Those who work for Mansfield say that it's a 24-hour job and that his attention to detail makes him a tough taskmaster, but, like many of his ilk, he walks the walk, living to work, and working 12-hour days, despite a thyroid condition which 'makes my eyes bulge' and has left him ill at times. 'The amount of satisfaction I get out of working here night and day is unbelievable,' he has said. He takes no holidays, hasn't been to the cinema since he got married and never reads books. But he is 'big into metal', says one acquaintance, meaning cars and planes. The blingy Citywest image is boosted by the spectacle of two Rolls-Royce Phantoms, one black, one silver, parked outside. His passions are the GAA, Formula 1 motor racing and flying. Over the years, he has owned a Beech 18 aircraft once used to transport Dwight D. Eisenhower, the US president, a relatively modest Bell 206 LongRanger and a Cessna Citation V1.5, which he was reputed to use 'as a taxi'. Meanwhile, his sons are rarely seen flying with a commercial airline, having acquired pilots' licences of their own.

Home for Jim Mansfield and his self-effacing wife Anne is the restored old Tassagart House at the heart of his empire, containing busts from Humewood House in Co. Wicklow, an obelisk from Santry Demesne and a lake built by his sons. The three sons, Tony, P J and Jimmy, all work in the business and he clearly takes pride in his relationship with them, saying in a 2006 *Sunday Tribune* interview, 'It's very unusual for an oul' lad like me to get on so well with them.' For a long time, he and the sons seemed happy to operate well below the media radar. This all changed when a succession of events thrust them centre stage in recent years. The most embarrassing of these was in 2006, when an Englishman who chartered a plane owned by Jim Mansfield and destined for Weston Aerodrome was found by Belgian police to be in possession of €10 million worth of heroin. Mansfield immediately issued a statement that he was unaware that the plane was in Belgium at the time. In 2007, his youngest son, the Ferrari-driving, helicopter-flying P J, married a former Miss

Ireland, Andrea Roche, in a highly publicized wedding. Some months later, in the wake of the equally highly publicized death of model Katy French, following a reported cocaine overdose, Jimmy junior confirmed that he had been her secret lover.

Meanwhile, their father's single largest project at Citywest has been the highly contentious new conference centre he's been trying to build for several years. Its vast shed-like steel structure was already completed by the time An Taisce lodged an appeal against it and Mansfield agreed to halt work on the project and await An Bord Pleanála's ruling on whether it should be allowed to proceed. In April 2004, by a majority of seven to one, the board refused permission – primarily because its location, relatively remote from the centre of Dublin and from good public transport, would make the centre heavily reliant on private cars. Experience elsewhere had also shown that a city-centre location is much more attractive to anyone attending a conference than somewhere out on the edge. Six months later, HSS was fined €1,750 and ordered to pay almost €30,000 in costs after being convicted in Tallaght District Court of carrying out an un-authorized development. Mansfield was not deterred by the modest judgment. He aimed to bid for the National Conference Centre, putting forward Citywest as the venue, taking on Treasury Holdings, Bernard McNamara and a consortium involving Bennett Construction and the Gallagher Group. He managed to persuade the county council to rezone his site for conference centre use, and the steel structure, which should have been demolished after An Bord Pleanála's decision, was reprieved. The council again approved Mansfield's plan and again its decision was appealed by An Taisce, this time joined by Harry Crosbie, owner of the Point Theatre on North Wall Quay and member of the Treasury-led consortium planning to build the National Conference Centre at Spencer Dock. In May 2006, An Bord Pleanála again refused permission, on the same grounds as it had two years earlier.

And just as Mansfield had initiated judicial review proceedings to have that decision overturned, he took another High

Court action against the latest ruling. One of his claims was that the board had not taken into account a planned spur from the Tallaght Luas line to serve Citywest, for which he himself was shelling out €13 million as a contribution towards its capital cost. He also claimed that the board was 'ignoring the democratic process', since his site had been rezoned by South Dublin councillors for a conference centre. One of the main advantages of the legal actions was that the council couldn't take steps to get rid of the unauthorized steel structure, which had to be screened from view during the Ryder Cup gala dinner at Citywest in September 2006. But Mansfield wasn't going to leave it there as a skeletal white elephant, so he made a third planning application in April 2007 to turn it into a conference centre, with a reduced capacity of 4,000. Former FAI chief Bernard O'Byrne, who had taken over as Mansfield's head of group operations, expressed confidence that this new, improved offer would find favour with the planners. South Dublin County Council – for which the Citywest complex is a huge commercial rates honeypot – yet again gave its approval. And yet again, predictably, An Taisce lodged an appeal. But in July 2008, An Bord Pleanála, rather surprisingly, decided to grant permission for the project. By then, the steel hulk of the conference centre had been standing forlorn for four years. Meanwhile, Mansfield was packing them into his existing Citywest conference centre, which has taken the place of the Burlington. The big difference, of course, is that nearly everyone has to get there by car.

By contrast with Mansfield, Michael Cotter has always played it by the rules.

From Galway and a mechanical engineer by training, he was a project manager with Roadstone when he had the good fortune to fall in love with Angela McInerney, the daughter of Frank, who had founded Park Developments in the 1960s. With substantial McInerney assets at his back, he bought vast tracts of land for £3,000 an acre in the 1970s. The word around the industry is that he was more lucky than good: planning delays worked in his favour, as they did for many other developers who built up land banks in the 1970s and 80s. In a rapidly rising market, you could end up getting twice as much money for houses and apartments if your scheme was ensnared by appeals to An Bord Pleanála from the likes of An Taisce and local residents who didn't like the density.

Park made headlines in 1999 for Dublin's first scheme of £1 million-plus homes at Carrickmines Wood, off Brennanstown Road – and it was a runaway success. The five-bedroom detached houses, with floor areas of 300 square metres, were described by Jack Fagan in the *Irish Times* as 'easily the most lavish to have come on the market in recent years', all hidden behind high walls on a 28-acre site that Cotter had banked since the mid-1980s. The scheme also included 45 smaller and somewhat cheaper detached houses and 72 two- and three-bedroom apartments, none of them in the 'shoebox' category. Over 5,000 sightseers turned up on the launch day, and all 16 of the most expensive houses were snapped up within the first four hours, mainly by upwardly mobile professional couples in their thirties.

The Carrickmines Wood frenzy showed just how much the market had heated up. At Cotter's earlier Carrickmines development, simply called 'The Park', it took eight years to sell 650 houses, starting in the mid-1980s; even this slow-burn brought a huge profit of around €110 million, from a site that had cost the equivalent of €10 million to buy. Not far away, at 'The Gallops', Cotter also took a measured approach to the development of 150 acres, with a keen eye on the changing market. First launched in 1990, when its three-bed semis sold for less than £60,000, the scheme's most recent phase wasn't completed until 2006, when the latest batch of houses fetched €925,000 apiece; one of the factors in this price inflation was the proximity of the Sandyford Luas line and the M50. Four blocks of apartments are to follow, in line with the general trend in recent years. 'We've made a jump to the contemporary mode,' Cotter told the *Irish Times*. 'There were no Belfast sinks or Neff appliances in the old semi-d's. People are much more sophisticated, and like apartment and duplex living.'

Mount St Anne's in Milltown was Park's flagship scheme for the new era of development in Dublin. Cotter had bought the 18-acre site from the Sisters of Charity in 1995 for £9 million, including their old convent, chapel and school buildings. But his plans for a relatively high-density housing development, designed with some flair by OMP, were resisted all the way by residents of low-rise houses in Merton Road and Richmond Avenue South – a preview of similar planning battles in other suburban areas where people felt threatened by high-rise apartment blocks. Its centrepiece, a large crescent-shaped six-storey block, was dubbed 'Áras Ceaucescu' by one of the objectors. Others argued that the green spaces of Mount St Anne's provided a habitat for birds, foxes, squirrels and badgers. Local politicians were equally critical of Dublin Corporation's decision to grant permission, with Ruairí Quinn – a qualified architect, town planner and then Minister for Finance – arguing that such a large concentration of housing in an inner suburban area posed a 'serious threat' to proper planning. The scheme was also opposed by two adjoining schools, Alexandra College and Gonzaga College, both of which feared it would increase traffic problems in the area and leave their playing fields overlooked by residents of the apartment blocks. Much to the surprise of both Park Developments and its opponents, An Bord Pleanála overturned the corporation's decision in April 1997, saying that the layout and density of the scheme and particularly the height of a number of blocks would be 'visually obtrusive'. It took the 1999 Residential Density Guidelines, which encouraged higher-density housing schemes within walking distance of good public transport links, to move the goalposts for Mount St Anne's. Taking its cue from government policy, An Bord Pleanála eventually granted permission for a revised scheme of 480 apartments and town houses, in blocks up to five storeys high, in a landscaped parkland setting. By the time its first phase came on the market in late 2000, property values had soared and Park made a substantial profit on its initial investment.

There was a downside for Cotter, however: when he went back to the Sisters of Charity to negotiate the purchase of a further 3.5 acres adjoining Mount St Anne's, he had to shell out £8 million for the land – almost as much as he had paid for the original 18 acres just five years earlier. A higher-density scheme would be needed to pay back this investment, and that's what Park proposed: six blocks ranging in height from four to eight storeys, containing a total of 217 apartments (a density of 62 units per acre) as well as a crèche, gym, two shops, a replacement parish hall and a new pedestrian route through Mount St Anne's to the Luas stop at Milltown. And while the old buildings on the larger site were retained and converted for residential use, Marian Hall was to be demolished. After Dublin City Council decided to grant permission for a scaled-down version of the scheme in February 2004, there were five appeals to An Bord Pleanála, which reduced the overall height of the scheme by cutting the number of apartments to 175. The board's decision was then challenged in the High Court by two residents of Mount St Anne's, who objected to conditions requiring their management company to maintain a public walkway through the grounds to the nearby Luas stop and also to facilitate public use of the grounds, by providing seating, lighting and other measures. The concern of the litigants was that their privacy would be 'ripped away' by potential boisterousness and vandalism, and this could affect their quality of life as well as property values. Under a settlement reached in June 2006, An Bord Pleanála agreed to replace the disputed condition with a new one requiring that the communal open space of Mount St Anne's and its swipe-card access to the Luas stop would be available to residents of the Marian Hall site on the same terms.

Cotter's Milltown ambitions did not end there. When word got out, in 2004, that Park Developments was in negotiation with Alexandra College, a fee-paying girls' school with an affluent student body, over the sale of athletics grounds adjoining Mount St Anne's, there was uproar. The students marched off and occupied the hockey pitch, chanting: 'Save our Pitch!' All this was observed by a bemused media, with resulting spots on the Pat Kenny and Gerry Ryan shows. Parents, armed with a petition signed by 400 parents and students, picketed Archbishop John Neill's mansion on Rathgar's Temple Road. Meanwhile, the Archbishop – said to be 'on leave' – was advising parents and guardians by letter to 'disregard the rumours and allow the [school] Council the opportunity to finalise the proposals adequately'. Clearly the man had no idea who he was dealing with. It is said that when 30 parents met in the Dropping Well pub down the road to consider their strategy, they included six senior counsel, two junior counsel and four solicitors. 'Enough to take on the House of Lords,' guffawed one, 'and all absolutely outraged at being patronised by the archbishop. And all *free*! No *fees*!'

Michael Cotter, it emerged, had offered €30 million for 3.5 acres of hockey pitch. The size of the bid itself was an extraordinary commentary on the market: it meant that values in Milltown had climbed from around €580,000 an acre in the mid-1990s to €8.6 million some 10 years on. In the end, it was all academic. The lawyers did their research into the precise ownership of Alex, aided by the dramatic intervention of retired Alex principal, Gladys Ruddock, with documents confirming that the state had funded half the cost of the site following the move from Earlsfort Terrace. That made it joint owner and a decisive voice in matters such as land sales. The fact that Alex girls still swing their sticks there today is certainly a testament to parent power, if of a very particular kind.

He may have lost that battle, but Milltown has still been very good to Cotter. At this distance, Mount St Anne's looks like his greatest coup – it is believed that he made €200 million on it. His initial outlay of £9 million for the site was, according to one acquaintance of the time, 'an enormous sum back then'. This aquaintance believes that Cotter's success is largely down to having had a huge amount of cash to work with at exactly the right time. 'You could never say he showed great brightness or vision but he had such wealth behind him and really it was hard to go wrong back then. If Joe O'Reilly had had that kind of money behind him, he'd have taken over Europe. Michael was lucky. He had the money to spend and in that period from 1995 to 2005, you could have been the worst builder-developer on the planet, with no sense of design or landscaping, and the punters would still have been queuing up, literally, to buy your houses. It was just a golden 10 years and it will never happen again.' For Cotter, the delays in the planning process dragged out the Mount St Anne's development by a crucial five years, by which time, bingo, the boom had arrived.

Meanwhile, in 1998, Cotter completed one of his most sensitive deals – the purchase for £26 million of Glencairn in Sandyford, official residence of the British Ambassador for many years, and its 35 acres of wooded grounds. The British government had decided to cash in on the Irish property boom and therefore traded down to a less opulent Victorian house, Marlay Grange in Rathfarnham, worth £7 million. But Marlay Grange needed extensive renovations and was never used as a residence; instead, successive ambassadors continued living at Glencairn, with the British government renting it back from Park Developments. The House of Commons Foreign Affairs Committee found that this U-turn had resulted in the loss of the potential profit and that 'serious mistakes' had been made in the sale of Glencairn and various attempts to buy it back.

Cotter, on the other hand, did very well from the deal. In 2000, he sold 5.7 acres of the Glencairn site, located near the M50's Sandyford interchange, to Galway-based TBD Properties for around €14 million. TBD subsequently got planning approval for an office development of some 35,000 square metres, but didn't go ahead with it because of a downturn in the market for out-of-town offices. In 2004, the company offloaded the site for close to €25 million to Cork developer John Fleming, who was working on the assumption that he would get planning approval for a high-density residential development. He got the green light from Dún Laoghaire-Rathdown County Council in

April 2005 for more than 400 apartments, including a 17-storey tower, designed by HKR Architects. But this decision was appealed by An Taisce and local residents, who took to blocking roads in protest, and then reversed by An Bord Pleanála because of the 'generally excessive height, scale, bulk and mass' of the scheme and the proximity of its apartment blocks to heavy traffic on the M50.

The board's ruling was the fourth refusal in as many months for high-rise/high-density housing schemes, and this provoked an outcry. Leading estate agent Ken MacDonald claimed in January 2006 that the appeals board's 'hardline' approach had resulted in 9,000 new homes approved by the local authorities over the previous two years falling at the last fence. Its refusals, he told the *Irish Times*, were 'leading to a serious curtailment in supply in key locations, particularly in Dublin, and that's already driving prices up'. But the board's chairman, John O'Connor, a former assistant secretary at the Department of the Environment, complained about the poor quality of many large-scale housing schemes, saying these showed 'scant regard' for their location or for the amenities of residents.

Described as a 'low-key kind of guy', Michael Cotter never resorted to such megaphone diplomacy, preferring to operate quietly behind the scenes. He has been particularly adept at acquiring land from religious orders, not just the Sisters of Charity in Milltown but also the Holy Faith nuns in Glasnevin, from whom he bought 18 acres on the Old Finglas Road. This became the setting for Addison Park, a scheme of 140 apartments in long blocks, with southerly views out over the River Tolka towards the wooded grounds of the Botanic Gardens and Glasnevin Cemetery. When it was launched in 2003, prices ranged from €260,000 for spacious one-bedroom apartments to €715,000 for large five-bedroom homes, all finished to high specifications.

Prices were much higher for the apartments and town houses built by Park Developments on the site of St Anne's Hospital, on Northbrook Road, near Ranelagh. Though sold at the same time as Addison Park, they ranged from €430,000 for one-bedroom apartments to €1.25 million for three-bedroom mews houses, tucked away at the rear on Northbrook Lane. Standard features included Junckers wood and limestone flooring, smart bathrooms and lavishly fitted kitchens. The substantial Victorian houses that had provided care for cancer patients for many years were gutted, even though they were protected structures. OMP's James Pike, who acquired one of the mews houses as a family home, said they had been 'knocked about a lot' while in hospital use and had to be demolished behind their façades. Embarrassingly for Park, however, protests by local residents prompted Dublin City Council to obtain a High Court injunction in 2001 restraining further demolition work.

Cotter did another deal with a religious order in 2004 when he bought the seven-acre playing fields of Notre Dame School in Churchtown from the nuns who ran it, paying a cool €30 million. The sisters of Notre Dame des Missions had originally planned to close the school altogether but agreed under protest that it would remain open, to be run by a trust company controlled by parents. When Park proposed to build nearly 300 apartments on the site, in nine blocks ranging from three to six storeys, the Churchtown Residents Association complained that the area was 'fast becoming a concrete jungle', while others expressed serious concern that the influx of new residents would aggravate traffic congestion on the already car-choked Upper Churchtown Road. But Dún Laoghaire-Rathdown County Council gave its approval for the €130 million scheme and, despite appeals, this decision was upheld by An Bord Pleanála in April 2007 – subject to the number of apartments being reduced to just over 250. Always on the prowl for new development sites, in late 2005 Cotter paid more than €20 million for a four-acre site in Sutton, in an attractive coastal setting, that formed part of the grounds of the Dominican Sisters' school at Greenfield Road. As in so many other cases of land sold by religious orders, the argument would be made that they needed the money to look after elderly nuns, brothers and priests at a time when few young people in Ireland had vocations to follow them.

Apart from building major residential schemes, Park Developments has a large commercial portfolio that includes south Co. Dublin's first large-scale retail warehousing park on a 50-acre site strategically located next to the M50's Carrickmines interchange, which was purchased for £36.5 million in 2000. The overall plan unveiled four years later included six office blocks, two hotels, restaurants and shops, as well as at least 10 'big box' retail warehouses and surface parking for no less than 3,500 cars. Woodie's agreed to take the anchor unit, paying a hefty rent for its 6,000 square metres of floorspace, and Australian white goods retailer Harvey Norman later took a similar-sized unit to anchor the second phase of the scheme. By early 2006, Park had an annual rent roll of €5 million from 15,000 square metres of retail warehousing on the site, and Cotter decided to sell the lot for more than €100 million to a small group of investors represented by Warren Private Clients; this was an unusual move, as Park normally retains ownership of its high-value commercial investments. Perhaps the money was ploughed into the second phase of The Park, which was to include a further 11,000 square metres of retail space as well as an office block, hotel and motor mall. Cotter was also responsible for developing the M50 Business Park in the wilds of Ballymount; its most innovative element was Fashion City, a new base for Dublin's wholesale 'rag trade', which had traditionally congregated in and around South William Street in the city centre.

Over on the northside, Park Developments has been building up an industrial portfolio since the mid-1990s, usually involving strategic sites. In 1995, for example, Cotter paid £2 million for 28 acres of industrial land on the North Road, not far from the Finglas interchange of the M50, then still under construction. A year later, he outbid Aer Rianta to acquire another industrial development site of 18 acres near Dublin Airport. But it's on the south side that most of Park's activity is concentrated. One of its associated companies, Viscount Securities, a relic from the Ambrose McInerney era, obtained the go-ahead in 2004 to build yet another money-spinner – a district centre on a 10-acre site at

Ballyogan Road, next door to Leopardstown Racecourse. The €100 million scheme had been euphemistically billed as a 'mixed-use development' of just over 20,000 square metres, including a public library, health centre and three office blocks. But the real meat was its supermarket and 10 retail units, all aimed at catering for the exploding, overwhelmingly middle-class population in an area that Cotter saw as 'under-shopped'. Dunnes Stores agreed with his assessment and was happy to pay €10 million for the anchor store of over 5,000 square metres, anything to keep Tesco out. Park itself had been involved in building much of the new housing in the area, and now it was providing a convenient place for the residents to do their shopping – a win-win outcome for the builders and their principal customers.

Like Bernard McNamara, Michael Cotter is a tycoon who has managed to stay on top of a tough game while remaining widely liked. 'Of course he had luck to begin with, but if I was stuck with a site, he's the first man I'd sit down with for advice,' said a fellow developer. 'He'd have the knowledge and the muscle and he's very well respected within the business, a nice guy with a proven, steady pair of hands.' Cotter is also one of the rare ones whom subcontractors remember with affection. 'Park had a great pay system,' recalled one. 'I would single him out for that alone . . .'

Now in his mid-sixties, Cotter lives a relatively modest existence for a big player on Planet Developer. 'He'd argue over a euro. He's very, very tight with his money,' says an old friend. Stories abound about his determination to travel hundreds of miles out of his way to save a few hundred euro on air tickets. He will generally opt for the house wine rather than a lofty château and has no interest in fancy restaurants, designer suits or private planes. His house in Westminster Road, Foxrock, is modest in every way but its location. 'He's very modest, like Liam Carroll, but more personable. He's a nice man and doesn't stress out. If you needed to be rescued in the middle of the night, you could rely on Michael to come and get you.'

His money is manifest in his life-long passion for cars and boats.

Already the proud owner of a second-hand Porsche when he was 30, Cotter's vast collection of classic cars includes Jaguars, Bentleys and Lotuses. His current yacht is a 120-footer bought for €4.5 million and moored in Palma de Mallorca, where he kicks back for several months a year.

7. The Bold Boys

No two men on Planet Developer polarize opinion quite like the duo who make up Treasury Holdings. 'Of all the developers that have come to the fore in the past 20 years, Johnny Ronan and Richard Barrett are, more than any others, the terrible twins of the Celtic Tiger,' says one who knows them. 'When they are good, they are very, very good, but when they are bad, they are horrid.'

After becoming business partners in 1989, there were 'just the two of us, then us and two secretaries, then an accountant, because you can control large amounts of investment property with very few people', Barrett recalls. 'But when you get into development and you have to do something with property, it takes large numbers.' They decided to set up Treasury Holdings, a vehicle for large-scale development, over dinner at the 1992 Olympics in Barcelona, and it now forms the umbrella for a complex web of some 500 companies, employing around 90 people in Dublin, with plans for that number again in its Shanghai office. Their foresight and willingness to play a long game are exemplified in the Shanghai adventure, instigated when Barrett visited China in 2002. Friends tell wry and hilarious tales of early efforts to adapt to Chinese business culture, involving relentless karaoke, 70-proof *baijiu*, and jellyfish, chicken's feet or yak's penis for dinner. The then Taoiseach's visit in January 2005, to help seal the deal, was a resounding success, as Bertie held hands and gazed mesmerizingly into eyes unaccustomed to that sort of thing.

While the Barrett–Ronan vision, courage and drive for quality are acclaimed and backed by a serious professional infrastructure (Treasury's board includes Kevin Kelly, who previously headed the construction firm Sisk, and Paddy Teahon, former Secretary-General of the Taoiseach's Department), relations with outsiders have been rather less elegant, riddled with tales of ruthlessness, litigation and even 'obnoxious' behaviour. As several campaigners, competitors and public officials know by now, you take on Treasury at your peril. Many individuals and institutions rue the day they crossed swords with the formidable combination of Barrett's cool, calculating legal brain, and Ronan's ferocious drive and hotheadedness. To one industry professional, Ronan, with his glossy black hair and beard, is nothing short of 'a pirate king . . . fantastic, larger than life. He fucks and blinds people out of it. I admire the way he gets the bit between his teeth and pushes things on. We need people like that – with that absolute energy, drive and ambition. And he's a bit of craic, very likeable socially. He's one of the people you'd sit down and have a meal with.' To others, he is 'explosive', 'light on manners and the social niceties'. The more 'polished' half, as Richard Barrett is invariably described, regards tomes such as *Irish Land Law* as holiday reading and is renowned for an ability to pounce on the small print of a Finance Bill or a contract. The pair's litigiousness has become the stuff of legend, and it is reckoned that they have racked up as many as 40 legal actions over the years, many against other developers. 'You were nobody in town unless Treasury was suing you,' one of their targets commented.

On a personal level, Ronan is said to have a 'good heart'. Now separated and with three grown-up children, he is known to be supportive of the Irish Georgian Society and various children's charities, and has participated in cycling challenges in aid of the visually impaired. To help generate much-needed jobs back in his native Co. Tipperary, he is driving an ambitious scheme for a biotechnology park in Carrick-on-Suir, located on a 325-acre site near the existing Merck Sharp and Dohme plant. Champion cyclist Seán Kelly is an old friend from home, and the pair of them have done gruelling days out on racing bikes in the Wicklow mountains and even (in the past) some of the more challenging stages of the Tour de France.

Meanwhile, Ronan clearly enjoys the spoils of his buccaneering life, which include a mini-palazzo (dubbed 'Saddam's Palace' by hostile observers) on Burlington Road in Ballsbridge, a helicopter to ferry him to his country estate in Co. Wicklow, with its stunning glass-and-steel summer house/party pad cantilevered out over the River Dargle, a €640,000 Maybach car, plus a Hummer and a retinue of prominent socialites such as nightclub owner Robbie Fox, radio star Gerry Ryan and, most recently, glamorous young model Glenda Gilson. He is well known for his extravagant gestures, such as the occasion in June 1998 when Treasury invited 50 friends and associates to what the *Irish Times* property supplement described as a 'glittering gig in Modena', where Luciano Pavarotti sang for them in the garden of his villa. Despite all this, sighs a professional acquaintance, he simply couldn't understand why the papers were so interested in him at a time when his Hummer was ostentatiously parked outside the Elephant & Castle restaurant in Temple Bar, where Treasury is the landlord.

Much of Richard Barrett's working life is now in Shanghai, but his elegant lifestyle includes a tasteful house on Upper Leeson Street, a villa in Ibiza, and a house off London's Berkeley Square. In Dublin, he eschews the clubs for the more sedate surroundings of Town Bar & Grill. It was Barrett who persuaded Gordon Ramsay to set up a restaurant in the new Ritz-Carlton at Powerscourt, after having what he called 'the best meal of my life' in Ramsay's restaurant in Tokyo. He is also a self-professed wine connoisseur, having 'travelled extensively in every continent and [developed] an ongoing friendship with restaurant wine lists, especially favouring obscure grape varieties, regional specialities and outright spectacular great wines', as he recalls in the recently published *That'll Never Work: Success Stories from Private Irish Business*, by Mike Gaffney and Colin O'Brien. 'This acquaintance [is] also shared by my partner, Johnny Ronan, who has acute tastebuds when it comes to willingly mortgaging the company's asset base for a rare vintage at lunchtime – he has a pay-by-instalment facility at Patrick Guilbaud's.'

On a serious note, Barrett told the *Irish Mail on Sunday* in June 2008 that he cried along with thousands of Chinese at an open-air concert in Shanghai to raise funds for victims of the devastating earthquake in Sichuan province the previous month. 'There was a picture of a child dying . . . As I looked around me in the venue, I saw thousands of faces and they were all crying. And then I started crying too.' He immediately agreed to launch an appeal to help find foster homes in Shanghai for kids orphaned by the earthquake, and also pledged that Treasury and its offshoot, China Real Estate Opportunities, would donate a percentage of the value of its property deals to fund a children's charity. Barrett also writes poetry at quieter times, while waiting in airports, travelling on planes, or sitting by the swimming pool, where he does 50 laps a day to keep fit. Mostly, he keeps it private, and friends were astonished when he presented long-time buddy John Meagher with a book of 17 poems dedicated to him – three of them written in Spanish – at a lavish party in Ibiza to mark the award-winning architect's 60th birthday.

Though both were born beyond the Pale, Barrett and Ronan were reared a long way from damp little cottages. Ronan's entrepreneurial gene goes back at least three generations. In the 1930s and 40s, his grandfather, John, was already dabbling in property while running a farm near Carrick-on-Suir, as well as a meat factory and leather business in Clonmel, Co. Tipperary. In the 1960s, his father, also John, was still farming while buying up attractive slices of Dublin around Waterloo Road and Pembroke Street. In the 1970s, Johnny himself was already striking property deals, with and without his father, while still a trainee accountant at Price Waterhouse.

Richard Barrett also came from a comfortable background, the scion of a grain-importing family in Ballina, Co. Mayo, who went on to study law at Trinity College, Dublin, and train as a barrister. He speaks fluent French and Spanish and is described by one industry professional as 'the smartest man I ever met'. Having met as boarder-classmates at Castleknock College, Barrett and Ronan made an early attempt to work together in 1981, but were thwarted by the tenor of the times: land could be bought but couldn't be developed because the banks had shut the tills. Barrett went abroad, setting up an import-export venture in Taiwan, which proved to be a useful early introduction to Asia. A few years later, when they met again as rivals for a property, he teamed with Ronan, who had bought the Boland's bakery on Lower Grand Canal Street in 1986. This was revamped to become the Treasury Building, so named even before it won a prestigious tenant in the form of the National Treasury Management Agency, and later familiar to many as the nerve centre of Fianna Fáil's election efforts. In the early years, they specialized in buying prime sites and buildings in Blackrock and promptly reselling them at a tidy profit.

What put Treasury on the road to riches was its acquisition in 1994 of an Irish Life property portfolio, which included the Stokes Place office complex on St Stephen's Green, for the knockdown price of £46 million. Irish Life's unit trust funds were not doing well at the time, and it needed to get cash quickly. Three years later, in partnership with a British company, Treasury bought a UK portfolio, mostly office blocks, from equally hard-pressed General Accident for £62.5 million; three of these blocks – in Banbury, Kingston-upon-Thames and Peterborough – were sold very profitably in June 2006, for £112 million.

Barrett and Ronan also found themselves negotiating with Charlie Haughey in mid-2000 to buy 10 acres on the Malahide Road frontage of his Kinsealy estate for £6 million, which the former Taoiseach needed to pay tax and legal bills. They thought this would be a useful entrée to acquiring the entire 250-acre Abbeville estate, but the Haugheys got a better offer from Manor Park Homebuilders and sold the lot in 2003 for €45 million. Other Treasury projects in north Dublin include the M1 business park on a 188-acre site near Balbriggan, a joint venture with Drogheda Port and Hong Kong conglomerate Hutchison Whampoa to develop a new deepwater port at Bremore, near Gormanston, with an eye towards replacing Dublin Port, and the redevelopment of Ballymun Town Centre, including restaurants, bars, a multiplex cinema and 500 apartments, for which approval was granted in 2004.

Spencer Dock dwarfs them all, however. Formerly occupied by Iarnród Éireann's rail freight marshalling yards, the huge site on North Wall Quay had become redundant after Dublin Port had moved downriver, and its pivotal location in the heart of Docklands turned it into a prime piece of real estate. Treasury got its hands on it in 1998 by doing a deal with CIÉ, under which it would receive 17.5 per cent of the rental income after the site was developed. When these terms became public in 2002, leading to criticism in the Dáil that the state-owned transport company had been short-changed, Barrett said CIÉ stood to gain a lot more from the deal over time than it would have raised by selling the site: 'It is a wasteland and they would have got a wasteland price, and they would have got screwed.' Instead, CIÉ got into bed with Treasury and Docklands entrepreneur Harry Crosbie, who owns a small part of the 52-acre site, to form the Spencer Dock Development Company and tendered for the National Conference Centre. One of the bid's main selling points was that the building had been designed by Kevin Roche, Ireland's most renowned emigré architect; it was Johnny Ronan who flew to the US and persuaded him to accept the commission.

Although the procurement of a National Conference Centre had been a government objective since 1989, it was made clear from the outset that not a single penny in public money would be provided to fund its construction. So the Treasury-led consortium proposed a massively overblown high-rise development of offices, hotels, apartments and ancillary facilities, with Roche as lead architect, for the Spencer Dock site.

Roche, who might have thought he'd be welcomed with open arms like the prodigal son, was astonished to find himself in the midst of a huge planning battle. Lined up on the opposite side were community groups opposed to high-rise development in Docklands, billionaire financier Dermot Desmond, the Dublin Docklands Development Authority and even the then Taoiseach Bertie Ahern, one of the local TDs, who described the scheme as 'a monstrosity'. The NCC was enveloped in a poisonous atmosphere that seriously threatened its delivery. A crisis meeting between Treasury and the DDDA turned into a 'table-thumping session', with Barrett and Ronan seeking an unequivocal assurance that the authority would not take the matter to An Bord Pleanála. Under duress, the DDDA agreed not to appeal Dublin Corporation's decision to approve six million square feet of development on the Spencer Dock site, but its submission at the week-long oral hearing in March 2000 proved crucial in persuading the board to reject Roche's master plan; the DDDA's then planning director, Terry Durney, warned that it would 'irrevocably and irredeemably prejudice the ability of the authority to achieve its policies and objectives in relation to the Docklands area as a whole'. Eight years later, following yet another competition for the NCC project, the 86-year-old architect will finally get the chance to leave a legacy to his native city in the form of a major public building.

Other elements of the Spencer Dock development, including the PriceWaterhouseCoopers headquarters, an office block let to Belgian bank Fortis and the serried ranks of apartment blocks to the rear, were designed by Scott Tallon Walker, and Shay Cleary got the coveted commission to design a 35-storey hotel that would rise up directly behind the NCC; a planning application for this towering scheme, which wouldn't have been permissable under the DDDA's master plan for the north docks, was submitted to Dublin City Council in December 2007. Meanwhile, Treasury remained assiduous in defending its interests in the area by initiating High Court judicial proceedings in June 2008 over the DDDA's decision to grant approval to North Quay Investments Ltd, a company controlled by Liam Carroll, for three large office blocks in the area, arguing that this breaches the master plan because Carroll's scheme is entirely devoid of residential content.

Another big row involving Spencer Dock was sparked off over an ingenious plan by Treasury to build its own combined heat and power (CHP) plant to provide heating and electricity for the entire development, and ultimately for the whole Docklands area. Devised by Richard Barrett in collaboration with Tim Cooper, of Conservation Engineering, who was then Director of Buildings at

Trinity College, it would have been an enormous coup, and Treasury nearly pulled it off. Barrett and Ronan had managed to persuade Minister for Public Enterprise Mary O'Rourke to amend the 1999 Electricity Regulation Bill so that privately run CHP plants would be classified under the 'alternative or renewable' energy heading, with full access to the electricity market in competition with the ESB. But the monopolists in Fitzwilliam Street could see immediately that the amendment was inimical to their objective of emasculating the EU-directed liberalization of the electricity market by limiting access to as few competitors as possible.

A furious round of lobbying ensued, during the course of which ESB company secretary Larry Donald described Treasury's claim that the ESB was unable, or unwilling, to supply power for the NCC as 'palpably false, misleading and . . . clearly designed to promote another agenda'. Barrett responded by characterizing the ESB as 'a clubby band of corporate thugs' in a private letter to then Labour Party leader Ruairí Quinn, which was subsequently read into the Dáil record by Emmet Stagg, the party's spokesman on public enterprise. Senior ESB officials so enjoyed this taunt that they had 'Corporate Thug' T-shirts printed, but O'Rourke took such grave exception to it that she withdrew the amendment, much to the ESB's delight and Barrett and Ronan's chagrin.

One of the best-documented cases of Treasury's litigiousness revolved around their efforts to use two small sites in the Moore Street area of central Dublin as bargaining chips to gain slices of the action in major developments being planned in the area, notably a shopping mall and cinema complex on the former Carlton cinema site in O'Connell Street. Their strategy was to put the other owners under pressure to sell out to Treasury or, at least, to agree to joint-venture deals. Minutes of a lunch meeting with Paul Clinton, project manager of the Carlton Group, at the Hibernian United Services Club in September 1997 noted that Treasury's site in Moore Lane had a 'strategic nuisance value' and said the company was 'torturing' Garrett Kelleher, who had bought a derelict site at the corner of Moore Street and Parnell Street with the aim of building a hotel on it. Treasury's game plan was to ease Kelleher out and consolidate control over a four-acre site, in partnership with the Carlton Group, in the expectation that the entire site would be designated for urban-renewal tax incentives and that its redevelopment would yield a profit 'well in excess of £50 million'. In the meantime, acquisition of further properties in the area was to continue with the utmost discretion and there were to be 'no consultants or business-looking people with suits, shirts, ties and mobile phones floating around Moore Street'. Kelleher, who had invested at least £5 million in acquiring more than 30 property interests on the Parnell Street site, certainly felt 'tortured' when Keelgrove, a Treasury vehicle, engaged planning consultant Frank Benson to object to and appeal against his scheme, and then to seek a judicial review of An Bord Pleanála's decision to approve it. Keelgrove also initiated enforcement proceedings against Kelleher's company, Shelbourne Developments Ltd, challenging the legality of a surface car park it was operating on the Parnell Street site.

Later, after the prospect of a joint venture with the Carlton Group evaporated, Keelgrove took a similar route in pursuing its opposition to Carlton's proposal for a Milan-style galleria linking O'Connell Street with the ILAC centre, topped by a 15-screen multiplex, threatening to 'tie them up in such legal knots that they would never be able to do anything with the site'. Again, Benson was engaged to object to and appeal against the Carlton scheme. The plan was certainly ambitious, extending from Dr Quirkey's Good Time Emporium, owned by Carlton Group chairman Richard Quirke, to the Fingal County Council office block, owned by hotelier Jim McGettigan. He had managed to purchase this crucial piece of real estate in 1996 for £4.55 million after the Irish Airline Pilots Pension Fund had offered it for sale by tender. Treasury had also intended to bid for it, and Johnny Ronan was expecting 'a steer ... either directly or by means of hints' from the agents, Jones Lang Wooton, on the amount of money it would need to offer. When this 'steer' did not materialize and Ronan's late bid of £4.58 million was not accepted, Treasury lodged a *lis pendens* on the property and sued both the pension fund and JLW for breach of contract; it lost this High Court action and McGettigan kept the office block.

After Benson's pleadings failed to deter either Dublin Corporation or An Bord Pleanála from granting permission for the Carlton project in August 1999, Keelgrove took its case to the High Court for judicial review. This action, perhaps unwittingly, opened the floodgates. In a lenthy affidavit, backed up by numerous appendices, Carlton Group project manager Paul Clinton detailed the history of its dealings with Treasury – including a note from Richard Barrett pointing out, with cold understatement, that 'certain opponents of ours have underestimated our ability to cause legal chaos to their detriment'. When this was disclosed, Treasury threatened libel proceedings seeking £20 million in damages, with the *Sunday Business Post* quoting Barrett as saying of Clinton: 'I will sue the pants off him.' By then, the corporation wanted the whole lot of them out of O'Connell Street, and it made a compulsory purchase order in late 2001 for the entire site, having concluded that the Carlton Group had neither the development expertise nor the financial capability to make the Millennium Mall a reality. Even after his erstwhile partner Richard Quirke had settled with the corporation, Clinton engaged in a series of fruitless legal actions against the corporation that had the effect of further delaying the development of this crucial site, as well as putting an end to the prospect that it would accommodate the new Abbey Theatre. Kelleher pursued a separate action against Keelgrove, claiming 'adverse possession' of its site on Moore Street (adjoining the Jurys Inn he developed), but the High Court found in favour of Treasury's subsidiary. The tables were turned in 2007 when both Dublin City Council and An Bord Pleanála rejected plans by Keelgrove for the small but crucial site it owns on Parnell Street, beside Jurys, describing the proposed eight-storey apartment block as 'unacceptably congested' and of 'poor architectural value', though a revised version was later approved.

The battle over Treasury's plans for the Westin Hotel in Westmoreland Street was equally bitter. With the exception of a Victorian banking hall on College Street, only façades were retained under the scheme permitted by An Bord Pleanála, and this led to protracted legal proceedings by Lancefort Ltd, a vehicle set up in 1996 by former An Taisce chairman Michael Smith to fight planning battles through the courts – a startling move that sent shivers through the property development community. Lancefort's action against the appeals board dragged on through 1997, running up an estimated £1 million in legal costs, and was ultimately lost. An attempt by Smith's legal advisers to settle it in return for a substantial contribution to Lancefort's 'fighting fund' was rejected by Treasury because of the conditions attached, which included the retention of threatened buildings and an overall reduction in height. After Judge Catherine McGuinness delivered her judgment in March 1998, Richard Barrett made it clear that Treasury would be pursuing Smith personally for its costs. In 2002, Lancefort suffered the indignity of being wound up at Treasury's behest because it couldn't pay £233,000 in legal costs – a mere fraction of the bill racked up on the site due to delays.

The least popular of Treasury's legal actions was the case involving Bewley's on Grafton Street, housed in a building owned by one of its subsidiaries, Ickendel. The Campbell Bewley Group (CBG) had agreed to allow Jay Bourke to reopen the legendary café as Café Bar Deli and Mackerel, with its familiar interior intact, but Ickendel, wishing to let the premises more profitably to a fashion retailer, sought forfeiture of CBG's lease after the catering group declined an offer of €6 million to relinquish it. Ickendel was refused an injunction in 2005 to halt renovation works, and the action was settled in February 2007. At the height of the controversy, after 20,000 people had signed a petition to save Bewley's, Green Party TD Ciarán Cuffe phoned Johnny Ronan to plead with him. 'My memory of the conversation was that he said: "Business is business." I was saddened that there didn't seem to be any interest in retaining a Dublin institution.' Café Bar Deli remains open, though for how long is questionable; after a three-day arbitration hearing in January 2008, Ickendel succeeded in getting the rent hiked by 93 per cent to €1,475,000 per annum – backdated to the previous January.

Prompted by the availability of tax incentives as much as by any conviction about going green, Treasury was the first major Irish property company to diversify into renewable energy, securing a sizeable share of wind power franchises under successive Alternative Energy Requirement (AER) schemes. Barrett pledged in 1999 that Treasury would 'devote a lot of capital' to this area, with the aim of becoming a major player in the electricity market, based on projections that demand would soon outstrip supply. The early efforts of its subsidiary Eco Wind Power (EWP) were relatively small installations at Drumlough Hill, Co. Donegal, and Arigna, Co. Roscommon, but plans for a much bigger 13-turbine farm near Macroom, Co. Cork, were turned down by An Bord Pleanála in 2002. After losing out to ESB subsidiary Hibernian Wind Power in the following year's AER scheme, Treasury argued that awarding contracts on the basis of the lowest tendered price per unit for electricity was unworkable. 'What's happening is that people are underbidding each other and then finding that they cannot build the wind farms,' a spokesman said. Another major constraint was that the ESB spin-off, Eirgrid, had been dragging its feet in adapting the national grid to provide connections for new wind farms, and planning for electricity lines was taking five years on average and up to seven years in counties Cork, Tipperary, Meath and Donegal. By the end of 2007, EWP had five wind farms up and running, with a total installed capacity of 23 megawatts, two more ready to go and seven others in the pipeline; these would bring it up to a much more impressive 180 megawatts. Treasury's total investment in this area amounted to €250 million, but, with turbine and grid connection costs soaring as wind energy catches on, much more would be needed – especially as EWP, which is chaired by one-time mandarin Paddy Teahon, won an exclusive mandate to develop wind farms with a total capacity of up 250 megawatts on lands owned by Coillte, the state forestry company.

Even more enticing prospects lay offshore – but only if the prices paid to wind power companies were raised to reflect the real value of renewable energy, particularly in meeting Ireland's targets under the Kyoto Protocol on Climate Change. Treasury-EWP saw this coming and did a joint-venture deal in 2002 with a division of Norwegian shipping firm Fred Olsen, which owns the Harland and Wolff shipyard in Belfast, to develop a massive wind farm on the Irish Sea's Codling Bank, off Bray Head. Much larger than the Arklow Bank wind farm further south, being developed by Airtricity and GE Energy, the first phase would have 90 huge wind turbines generating 330 megawatts of electricity at peak production – as much as many conventional power stations. It was steered through the planning process by Teahon and EWP's then chief executive David Tyndall, with former government press secretary P.J. Mara and environmentalist Duncan Stewart acting as consultants.

After some of the main players, including Eco Wind Power, got together to form NOW Ireland, with the promise that its members would invest €4 billion in the sector, Minister for Energy Eamon Ryan announced in February 2008 that the government would guarantee a price of €140 per megawatt hour for offshore wind farms (rising to €220 for tidal or wave energy installations): this made huge projects like the Codling Bank suddenly look like real runners. There is even the intriguing prospect of developing an electricity grid in the Irish Sea, with wind farms on either side of it providing power to both Ireland and Britain. No wonder the Belfast-based Viridian energy group, which is aiming to become a leading player in the market, was prepared to pay an undisclosed sum – believed to be €50 million – to acquire EWP from Treasury in April 2008.

Treasury's sense of the possibilities of green enterprise also led it into the area of waste management. In 2003 the company bought Herhof, a German firm with a proprietary system of mechanical and biological treatment that creates refuse-derived fuel (RDF) from municipal waste. But the venture turned sour because it needed more capital than Treasury was prepared to put up. There were also difficulties in finding outlets for growing volumes of RDF; if it could have been used instead of fossil fuels in power stations or cement kilns, Herhof would have been all the rage with banks and investors. Plans to build plants at Courtlough, near Balbriggan, and Belview, in Waterford Port, were turned down and the company ran into liquidity problems due to overambitious expansion plans, notably the construction of three new waste treatment plants in Germany. Treasury had a financial plan to transfer specified sums to Herhof every year but began to have serious concerns about cash flow, profitability and contracts with local authorities. Quinlan Private was lined up as a major investor, but the promise of more money evaporated in the end. When no payment was made at the end of 2004, the company was put into administration, leaving Treasury to trawl the European waste sector for potential investors in what many still saw as a viable business based on a technology that was probably ahead of its time. But Bernd Ache, the court-appointed administrator, remarked: 'Treasury was prepared to do everything [to save Herhof] except invest money.'

After the attempt to bring in fresh capital from Quinlan Private fell through, Treasury sold Herhof to Helector, the waste management subsidiary of Greek conglomerate Elliniki Technodomiki, which then completed construction of the half-finished plants. They went into operation in 2006 and Herhof is profitable once again, with post-tax profits of €500,000 in 2006 and €640,000 in 2007. 'They're beating down the door for our technology everywhere from Cyprus to England,' a spokesman for the company said. However, after what was described in the German media as a 'bitter battle' with the Greeks, Treasury managed to retain the Irish and UK patent rights for Herhof's technology, which will surely yield dividends in the longer term.

According to its website, Treasury Holdings currently controls a property portfolio valued 'in excess of €4.8 billion'. How much of this is owned by Richard Barrett and Johnny Ronan is not revealed and their company, Treasury Group Holdings, which has unlimited liability status, has not had to file accounts to the Companies Registration Office since 2001. However, as the *Irish Times*'s Colm Keena discovered, Ronan's 50 per cent stake in Treasury is held by way of a company he owns called Ardquade Ltd, and notes to its accounts for 2005 state that the group's total reserves at that time amounted to €457 million, up from €288 million the year before. A calculation based on the net asset or capital and reserve figures of companies owned or controlled by Ardquade, and given in the notes, comes to €362.5 million. The biggest assets are Ronan's half share in Treasury Holdings, and his one-third share in the Spencer Dock Development Company Ltd, which had capital and reserves of €107 million at the end of 2005. Barrett has equal shareholdings to Ronan in both these ventures. Filed company accounts show that Ronan personally owns a number of very valuable properties around south Dublin city, including 3 Burlington Road, valued at €16.8 million, and an office building on Herbert Street, with a value of €42 million (both at the end of 2005). A company called Jayfield Investments, owned equally by Ronan and Paddy McKillen, owns the Treasury building on Lower Grand Canal Street, which was valued at €59 million.

Barrett and Ronan's 2001 bid to buy the ill-fated Millennium Dome, in partnership with British developer Robert Bourne, collapsed amid a welter of lurid stories, including a front-page article in the *Financial Times* suggesting that Treasury might be a vehicle for IRA money. This wholly unfounded allegation led Barrett to believe that a break-in at his London hotel room was the work of MI5 agents; the British security services may have read too much into the fact that Cillian Ó Brádaigh, son of former Sinn Féin president Ruairí Ó Brádaigh, was senior vice-president of Lehman Brothers, the US bank which provided funding for some of Treasury's projects. The *Guardian* described Barrett and Ronan as 'two highly ambitious Irish tycoons, whose Treasury Holdings has thrived more than most in the murky waters of the Dublin property market'; some of these negative media reports were planted by their enemies at home, with the avowed aim of scuppering the Legacy Consortium's bid for the Dome and 63 acres of development land on the Greenwich Peninsula. Bourne, a substantial donor to New Labour (having abandoned the Tories), had a 15 per cent stake in Legacy, with Treasury holding 80 per cent and the Bank of Scotland, which had agreed to lend £50 million to the consortium, taking the remaining 5 per cent. But there were serious doubts about the viability of the scheme to turn the Dome into a 'high-technology campus', housed in a series of 'space-age' office blocks within the tented structure; the real agenda was to develop the Dome as a casino if a licence could be obtained.

Bourne was well connected with New Labour and was famous in London for his perspicacity in selling shares just days before the Black Monday crash of 1987; he also owns the legendary Ronnie Scott's jazz club in Soho, the Old Vic and Criterion theatres, and the Chinatown and Queensway markets. Ronan and Barrett had previous dealings with him, buying a portfolio of properties for £80 million three years prior to the Dome bid and selling them off over time. The proposed sale was also targeted by the Tories as an example of New Labour's 'cronyism' and it was clear that it could become an election issue in 2002. In the end, the British government peremptorily stopped the sale and held a new competition for the prize of taking over the country's best-known white elephant. It was finally sold to Meridian Delta, a joint venture between property companies Lend Lease and Quintain, with realizable plans to turn the Dome into a sports and entertainment arena and develop nearly 10,000 new homes in a mixed-tenure residential quarter on the adjoining land. Renamed as 'The 02', in a £6 million-a-year deal with the mobile phone company, it was successfully relaunched in the summer of 2007 with a rock concert featuring Bon Jovi.

In November 2006, Treasury again hit the headlines in London after buying the long-disused but iconic Battersea power station for £400 million (€573 million), on behalf of the publicly quoted Real Estate Opportunities (REO), which it controls. The site was purchased from Hong Kong developers George and Victor Hwang, whose plans for a leisure complex never materialized; apart from the usual range of entertainment, it was to include a seriously exclusive single-table restaurant in one of the power station's four huge chimneys. To complete the deal, REO assumed £250 million in debts and issued £150 million of loan notes to the Hwangs, who had bought it in 1993 from John Broome, the man who developed the Alton Towers theme park and had plans to do something similar in Battersea.

Treasury had been trying to get its hands on the 38-acre site for four years, because it's one of the best in London. 'If there was a bridge going diagonally across the river, it would be within walking distance of Sloane Square tube station,' says Richard Barrett, who negotiated the deal at a series of lavish dinners with the Hwangs in Hong Kong, Shanghai, London and Dublin. George Hwang and Barrett had something in common: a love of fine wine. 'He discovered, in a chance remark I made about a dusty Sassicaia, that I knew a thing or two about wine, garnered from all those Malbecs and Syrahs and Grenaches and Cabernets and Tempranillos and Merlots that I had spent years around the globe slurping, never thinking it would come in useful,' Barret recalls in the 2008 KPMG publication *That'll Never Work . . . Success Stories from Private Irish Businesses*. 'It's difficult to describe George's great joy when he found someone that enjoyed the pleaures of the grape as much as himself. And when he did, the wine flowed and the vintages kept coming one after another after another.' The elder Hwang also had a taste for cigars, and one of the dinners at his home was finished off with 1891 Havanas 'from a sunken galleon'.

The price paid by REO for Battersea power station began to look like a bargain compared to the record £900 million shelled out by a consortium headed by London developer Christian Candy in April 2007 for the 13-acre site of Chelsea Barracks, on the north bank of the Thames. And, like everywhere else in the northern hemisphere, 'views from south of river to the north bank are much better than the other way round' because of the direction of sunlight, as Barrett noted. With a 380-metre river frontage, just 2 km from the Palace of Westminister, the site was clearly ideal for a substantial scheme with a good mix of uses, particularly high-value residential.

But there were constraints. As the largest brick building in Europe, designed by Giles Gilbert Scott, the former coal-fired generating plant, which ceased operation in 1983, was already a Grade II listed building. Ten months after REO purchased the site, it was upgraded to Grade II* by English Heritage in response to representations from the ever-watchful Battersea Power Station Community Group. The much-loved London landmark, which was featured on the sleeve of a Pink Floyd album showing a huge inflatable pig suspended between the chimneys, was on English Heritage's Buildings at Risk register and also on the World Monuments Fund's Watch List of the world's 100 most endangered sites. But Treasury assured English Heritage in March 2007 of its commitment to 'repair, refurbish and bring the site back into beneficial use'. By then, it had scrapped Hwang's master plan and hired Montevideo-born starchitect Rafael Viñoly, who is chiefly known for the 'Walkie-Talkie' tower he designed for Fenchurch Street in the City, to draw up an alternative scheme. Three additional properties in the vicinity were purchased in November 2007 for a total of £58 million, including the site of two still-functioning gasholders, which are to be demolished; had they continued to operate, a swathe of the power station site would have been sterilized for development by a safety zone imposed under the EU 'Seveso' directive.

Even jaundiced observers were quite astounded by the ambitious master plan unveiled by REO in June 2008. Not only was the old power station to be retained, in line with solemn assurances given to English Heritage, but part of it was to be brought back into use as a CHP generating station, with biomass as its fuel; the rest of the structure, which will cost an estimated £150 million to repair, would be renovated for a hotel, apartments and shops. Alongside, Viñoly envisaged a series of serpentine apartment blocks and one of the tallest buildings in London – a

300-metre glass cylinder called 'The Chimney', rising out of an 'eco-dome' modelled on the Eden Project in Cornwall. 'This will be a power station for the 21st century – a truly sustainable, zero carbon development,' Rob Tincknell declared. It would have 'the largest solar-driven natural ventilation system ever conceived' to reduce overall energy demand by more than two-thirds. He also revealed that Treasury Holdings UK, which he now heads, was talking to Transport for London and other landowners in the area about building an extension of the Tube to bring it to Battersea, with a new underground station beneath the 'eco-dome'. Referring to the old power station, he said: 'Londoners have a strong emotional attachment to this building but most of all they want to see something positive happening on this site. We will meet and exceed their expectations.' But with the planning process yet to be negotiated, he didn't expect construction to start until 2012, to finish in 2020 – so there was some prospect that the market might recover in the meantime.

The Battersea deal put a spotlight on the relationship between Treasury Holdings and REO, which was set up specifically to raise money from a wide range of investors – managed funds, financial institutions and high-net-worth individuals – while Treasury maintained a firm grip on its operations. It also provided a highly valuable new income stream for Treasury. 'Irish duo set to make a mint in London,' trumpeted the *Sunday Times* in an April 2007 story on the terms under which REO operates. 'Even before the [Battersea] purchase, Treasury was entitled to fees under "management agreements" for overseeing REO's properties in Ireland. But with the Battersea deal, Treasury also became responsible for "the provision of advisory and property management services for the company's global property assets" outside Ireland,' Ben Laurance reported. This entitled Treasury to receive a basic annual fee equivalent to 0.5 per cent of the value of REO's assets, a 'development management fee' of 1.5 per cent of the cost of any construction that it oversees for REO, and a further 1.5 per cent of construction costs for day-to-day project management. 'On top of that, Treasury will be entitled to huge bonuses – a "performance fee" – if REO increases net assets per share. If the net assets rise by 7.5 per cent, then Treasury receives 3 per cent of the increase. If net assets rise by more than 15 per cent, then Treasury receives 7.5 per cent of the gain.' By the end of 2005, Treasury had earned accrued performance fees of more than £6 million from REO, plus other fees totalling €5 million and a further €3 million from a firm jointly owned by Treasury and REO, which Laurance described as being 'domiciled in Jersey, quoted in London and controlled from Dublin'.

Treasury has significant overheads, employing nearly 90 staff at its headquarters in Connaught House, a swish office block on Burlington Road, plus almost as many in Shanghai and others in London and elsewhere, depending on what's happening. Those on the payroll include such high-flyers as former AIB Investment Managers chief John Bruder, who is now managing director of Treasury Ireland; Rob Tincknell, who returned from Shanghai in 2007 to take charge of the group's UK and international divisions (apart from China); and Richard David, who came in from Macquarie Bank to become head of its operations in China. Then there are all the consultants, none of whom come cheap, including accountants, architects, engineers, chartered surveyors, estate agents, lawyers, project managers and planning consultants. 'Treasury is quite misunderstood. People assume we're a fairly successful Irish property company,' Devon-born Tincknell told blogger Neil Michael in 2005. 'The reality is that we're a pretty sizeable international real estate machine, with valuable interests all around the world. We have significant growth plans and a very clear agenda.' As for its lack of interest in bidding for the Jurys/Berkeley Court sites, he quipped: 'We prefer Shanghai to a few acres in Ballsbridge.'

But Johnny Ronan and Richard Barrett had to fight hard to secure Treasury's highly favourable position in REO, against challenges from solicitor-developer Noel Smyth and London-based investors Dawnay Day. Smyth had entered the fray in 2003 not long after losing his epic battle with Liam Carroll for Dunloe Ewart, and built up a 10 per cent stake in REO at a time when the Treasury boys controlled only 37 per cent of the company. He joined forces with Dawnay Day, which had just under 30 per cent, in publicly querying the payment of €11 million in fees to Treasury for managing REO's Irish properties and projects. Smyth went for broke, hiring a private plane to fly himself, other shareholders and even some journalists to Jersey for a show-down at the company's annual general meeting in St Helier's Grand Hotel. During tetchy exchanges, as Colm Keena (who travelled under his own steam) reported in the *Irish Times*, he suggested that Barrett had 'something to hide' in relation to a mystery Isle of Man company called Calyx, which had an 8 per cent shareholding and always voted with Treasury, and went on to query notes on the accounts. Barrett, who was chairing the meeting, asked him: 'Are you accusing the board of producing misleading accounts?' Smyth replied: 'I am.' Somewhat exasper-ated after explaining the point three times, Barrett said: 'Am I speaking slowly enough for it to get into your head?' This withering remark was followed by a long pause in the room, which then erupted in laughter, prompting a rather embarrassed Smyth to sit down with his wad of speaking notes. 'And not a further peep was heard from him,' Barrett recalled later. His put-down line made it to No. 3 in the *Sunday Business Post* 'Quotes of the Week', pipped only by Jacques Chirac and George W. Bush. He also received more than 20 emails and letters from accountants, bankers and lawyers 'congratulating me on putting Noel Smyth in his box'.

The row over REO was eventually resolved in April 2005, with the dissident shareholders being bought out for £46 million. Since then, Barrett and Ronan have controlled at least 60 per cent of the company and 54 per cent of its offshoot, China Real Estate Opportunities (CREO), through Treasury and other vehicles. This complex arrangement has worked well for Treasury, but it also produced healthy returns for other investors after a rather shaky start. The good news for them came in 2005 when REO recorded a four-fold increase in pre-tax profits, due mainly to the then healthy state of its Irish property portfolio, which was stated to be worth €1 billion. By the end of 2007, the value of REO's fixed assets had grown to £1.85 billion (from £1.2 billion in the previous year), including the acquisition for £120 million of Treasury's interest in Havenview Investments, a 50–50 joint venture by these two very closely related companies.

Meanwhile, in December 2006, it was announced that Treasury had clinched a conditional deal to acquire Xidan Centrepoint, an office, hotel and shopping complex then under construction in Beijing, for €362 million. Its scale was massive, with the retail element alone some four times the size of St Stephen's Green shopping centre, and Treasury intended that Xidan would be the crown jewel in CREO's initial property portfolio. But the deal fell through after state-owned China Metallurgical Construction, parent body of the company developing the complex, decided to sell its subsidiary to Chinese buyers only, in the expectation of getting a better price.

This setback highlighted some of the difficulties of doing business in China and caused the flotation of CREO as a public company to be postponed for several months. But a gruelling 'roadshow' in summer 2007, which saw Richard Barrett criss-crossing the world to make presentations to potential investors, raised more than €380 million to fund property deals involving CREO. Since then, CREO has teamed up with Treasury's part-ner, Shanghai Industrial Investment Corporation (SIIC), to buy two water-front sites in Qingdao for almost €19 million. Located halfway between Shanghai and Beijing, this flourishing port city with a German imperial past hosted the 2008 Olympics' sail-ing contests, and has a population of more than seven million. Treasury and SIIC already had a joint venture to develop a marina-based resort on Tangdao Bay, so CREO's two sites are being added to create an integrated residential, retail and hotel scheme extending over 15 acres that could end up being worth €500 million. By the end of 2007, according to analysis by char-tered surveyors CB Richard Ellis, the aggregate value of CREO's property portfolio had risen to €870 million and it was expected to continue growing by 30 per cent per annum.

The first and by far the biggest joint venture involving Treasury and SIIC is Dongtan, China's first 'eco-city', a four-million-square-metre development to be built on Chongming Island, north of Shanghai. More than 80,000 people are to live there, in what the *New Scientist* described as a 'zero-pollution, largely car-free ... green-fringed utopia'.

It came about in a curious way. Some Chinese interests were looking into bringing horse racing, which is enormously popular in Hong Kong, to the mainland, and an approach was made to David Tyndall, a Dubliner who had worked as finance director for racing entities controlled by Sheikh Mohammed bin Rashid al Maktoum, the noted horseman and ruler of Dubai. As it happened, a friend of Tyndall, Cavan-born businessman Des O'Connor, was in Shanghai scouting for business opportunities when he came across SIIC and the prospect of the eco-city at Dongtan. O'Connor put the idea to Tyndall, who was immediately intrigued by it and flew out to Shanghai early in 2002 to have a look for himself. The pair set up a partnership to pursue it and agreed to do a joint venture with SIIC.

By then, Tyndall had got a new job as chief operating officer of Treasury Holdings and felt in all fairness that he should put the Dongtan prospect to Richard Barrett. Barrett was as intrigued as Tyndall, so the two of them flew there a couple of weeks later to meet SIIC. Barrett was amazed by what he saw in Shanghai. The 88-storey Jin Mao Tower, then China's tallest building, was already finished and there were dozens of other skyscrapers built or under construction. He thought, 'How could all of this be happening and we don't know about it?' As a sharp businessman, he could see that Treasury would have to throw itself into this new market and take over as SIIC's partners from Tyndall and O'Connor's fledgling company.

Barrett went back again and again to Shanghai, operating from the Westin Hotel before purchasing an apartment in Xintiandi, a trendy part of town, then a three-storey house in the leafy French Concession and a swanky office block on Huashan Road, which was renamed the Treasury Building. Over 60 staff are employed, half of them Chinese, and the number is expected to rise to 100 as more architects, engineers, planners, surveyors and marketing people are taken on, with Barrett predicting that CREO-Treasury Holdings was poised to become 'the largest western real estate company in China' by the end of 2008. 'Shanghai was the most valuable land on the planet in 1929, so it's only reclaiming the status it previously had, and we're on the ship that rises with that tide.'

For Barrett, as he told the *Sunday Times* in February 2008, Treasury's success in China has been 'all about relationships . . . You know someone who knows someone else. You go to the right places.' That means making contact with senior government figures, including Prime Minister Wen Jiabao. 'A framed picture of a smiling Wen, Barrett and Mary Harney, the former Tánaiste, sits on a shelf in the corner of his office. The eldest daughter of Deng Xiaoping, the country's former leader, is a close friend,' Mark Paul reported. 'Barrett has an impressive knowledge of Chinese business culture. The maintenance of good connections, he says, also extends to the bosses of other companies with whom you might want to do a deal. "The Chinese believe that if they do you a favour during a deal, maybe by bringing the price down, some day you might reciprocate . . . maybe getting someone's daughter into Trinity or helping to get a visa. If you were able to help when it comes to making a representation with the visa office, that would be highly appreciated. It's worth much more than money," he said.'

Despite Barrett's diplomacy, progress on the €1.2 billion Dongtan project, which was announced with great fanfare in January 2005, has been painfully slow. No development could be started on Chongming Island before the completion of a 10-kilometre suspension bridge and 9-kilometre tunnel connecting the island to the city and its new container port. The project was also stalled by investigations into corruption following the sensational dismissal in September 2006 of Chen Liangyu, Shanghai's once powerful Communist Party chief and protégé of former president Jiang Zemin, over allegations that more than

$400 million had been looted from the municipal pension fund to finance major property and construction deals. Chen was detained a year later to await trial on charges that could result in his receiving the death penalty; 10 other senior officials involved in the scandal have already been sentenced to jail terms ranging from three years to life imprisonment. As part of the wide-ranging police investigation, all contracts between municipal undertakings and foreign investors were scrutinized to ensure that they were untainted by corruption, and this led to numerous projects being delayed, including a Shanghai satellite of the Pompidou Centre in Paris, a Saks Fifth Avenue department store on the famous Bund and the Dongtan eco-city. Mayor Han Zheng has called for systematic supervision of construction, land and property transactions, and pledged in January 2008 to build a 'clean government committed to fighting corruption'; the last thing he or new Communist Party chief Xi Jinping want is for Shanghai to regain its old title, 'Whore of the Orient'.

Richard Barrett insists that the Dongtan deal was as clean as a whistle and, though frustrated by the delays, he remains confident that this hugely ambitious project will go ahead. The enormous bridge–tunnel project linking Shanghai and Chongming, comparable in scale to the Öresund crossing between Copenhagen and Malmö, is ahead of schedule and will be finished before the end of 2009. The Dongtan site has been rezoned for development, but Treasury still needed some 30 administrative pieces of paper certifying that its scheme complies with a Chinese quota system designed to regulate development in the interest of protecting agricultural land. There may also need to be more investors. 'The Dongtan project cannot be completed by just one company,' Ma Chenliang, SIIC's managing director, has said. 'Definitely we need to invite a lot of partners who have expertise in this sort of project.'

It was through Treasury's well-connected Shanghai partners that Richard Barrett negotiated the purchase in 2005 of 900 acres of parkland surrounding the Catherine Palace, outside St Petersburg, two years after the city founded by Peter the Great celebrated its 300th anniversary. Plans include a five-star hotel, 500 villas, a health spa and two golf courses; Russia has very few golf courses, but a fast-growing army of golfers. In Sweden, Treasury is planning a golf resort in Gothenburg, with two 18-hole courses, a 200-bedroom hotel and 800 villas on a 390-acre site called Landvetter Park, not far from the city's airport. Another golf resort is planned for Milverton, in north Co. Dublin, a historic parkland demense of some 425 acres, with views over Skerries Bay. Two Arnold Palmer-designed golf courses are planned, plus a five-star hotel and 'exclusive residential accommodation'. And yet another is planned for the 377-acre Roundwood Park estate in Co. Wicklow, once the home of President Seán T. O'Kelly and later Galen Weston; it would be turned into a clubhouse for a 27-hole championship golf course laid out in the grounds. The scheme also includes a 300-bedroom hotel, with bar, restaurants, conference centre, gym, spa and swimming pool. Sixty 'tourist lodges', some as large as 370 square metres with six bedrooms, are also planned as well as an equestrian centre, outdoor riding area and surface parking for over 600 cars. But Roundwood Park is likely to face stiff competition from a strikingly similar €250 million scheme planned by Galway-born developer John Lally for the 450-acre Humewood Castle estate near Kiltegan, Co. Wicklow, which he bought from socialite Renata Coleman for €25 million in 2006.

Meanwhile, some long-running sagas remain to be resolved. In Sligo, Treasury was selected in mid-2000 to develop a £70 million shopping centre on a large surface car parking site at Wine Street, in the heart of the town. The site, owned by Sligo Borough Council and a number of private interests, had been identified by the National Building Agency as the right location for a development that was seen as vital to the future of Sligo, which had failed to develop retail facilities comparable to those of other towns of similar size. The NBA got agreement in principle on a plan and was represented on an advisory panel that chose Treasury on the basis of its track record, financial capacity and commitment to implement the scheme. 'It's really the way planning should be done,' NBA managing director Matt O'Connor said at the time.

But Treasury fell foul of Sligo Chamber of Commerce, which claimed that some of its members were 'completely unaware' that their properties had been included in its development proposals, and an ad hoc group of traders who branded the scheme as a 'travesty'. (Treasury's John Bruder admitted to the *Sligo Weekender* years later that the initial plan put on public display was 'quite misleading'.) Sligo Borough Council could have used its compulsory purchase powers to expedite the development, but instead Treasury was left to engage in tortuous negotiations with adjoining property owners, one of whom stubbornly held out. He also happened to be one of the legendary 'Seven Sisters', a small group of businessmen who meet for coffee every morning in the Adelaide, off Wine Street and are said to 'run' Sligo. It was not until 2006, three years after it was all supposed to be built, that Treasury unveiled new plans for the long-delayed shopping centre, which was to have 18,000 square metres of retail space and nearly 100 apartments in blocks ranging from 6 to 15 storeys high. By then, Sligo Borough Council was losing its patience and, in January 2008, it sought to rescind the sale because Treasury had failed to secure planning permission for the project more than five years on. But, for all the objections it had to face, the company maintained that it was 'ready to go ahead'. Three years earlier, however, Treasury had shelled out €16 million for a 12-acre 'prime landmark development site' adjoining the Summerhill roundabout on Sligo's 'inner relief road', a continuation of the N4, which had been driven through the centre of the town like someone hacking their way through the jungle with a machete. A retail-based scheme is also being planned here, in what looks like an each-way bet on Sligo's shopping future.

Treasury's plan to redevelop the Stillorgan shopping centre – an open-malled complex dating from 1966, which Barrett and Ronan bought 30 years later from the Bank of Ireland Pension Fund for £38 million – has also turned into a protracted drama. A scheme by Polish-born architect Andrzej Wejchert that would have doubled the amount of retail space on the site was approved by Dún Laoghaire-Rathdown County Council, but rejected on appeal by An Bord Pleanála. Wejchert resigned the commission almost immediately and his clients adopted a more site-sensitive scheme by Gilroy McMahon, who had been runners-up in an architectural competition for the £50 million project. But their plans were also turned down – twice – after local residents appealed, leading Barrett to brand An Bord Pleanála as 'maverick and unpredictable ... Normally a board decision is a road map by which we make the necessary amendments to a development but in this case they keep making up new grounds each time.' It was not until August 2006 that the board finally gave its approval for a revised scheme by Duffy Mitchell O'Donoghue. A few months earlier, Treasury acquired the five-acre Stillorgan Leisureplex for €65 million from Ciarán and Colum Butler, whose plans to redevelop the site for more than 300 apartments, including a 15-storey tower, had also been been rejected by the appeals board. It is located directly opposite the Treasury-owned Blake's site, where a scheme for 215 apartments – including a 12-storey block – was approved in 2005. The Leisureplex acquisition brought Barrett and Ronan's portfolio in Stillorgan to 13.5 acres on three pivotal sites, giving them major leverage in shaping the local area plan in consultation with Dún Laoghaire-Rathdown County Council and local residents.

And then there was Central Park. In what seemed at the time to be an each-way bet on the Dublin office market, Treasury was involved in pursuing two major office development plans in 1999, one at Spencer Dock and the other way out in Leopardstown. The Clyde Road Partnership, a joint venture between Treasury and British property company Jermyn Investments, with David Arnold as its partner, had acquired a 20-acre site on Leopardstown Road from the Legionaries of Christ a year earlier for more than £25 million. Given its close proximity to the route of the M50, and with rents soaring as the economy really took off, it was an obvious candidate for an out-of-town office scheme, which someone had the bright, rather Orwellian idea of calling 'Central

Park'. Dún Laoghaire-Rathdown County Council, with its eye on capturing a share of the office market for commercial rates revenue, had no problem granting permission to the Clyde Road Partnership in August 1999 for 150,000 square metres of office space in 12 blocks, as well as a 160-bedroom hotel, conference and fitness centre, crèche and neighbourhood shops. The only major constraint was that half of the overall development, which was billed as having an 'end value' of £500 million, could not be built until the final phase of the M50 was opened and the Sandyford Luas line extended southwards to serve the scheme. And even though the developers were required to pay a whopping levy of £7 million for infrastructural improvements, including upgrading Leopardstown Road to a dual carriageway, they were 'extremely satisfied' with what they got from the council.

The Clyde Road Partnership – which by then included Quinlan Private – made rapid progress on the first phase of Central Park, pre-letting the largest office block to Eircell (now Vodafone) in April 2000 at an annual rent of £5.25 million for 24,400 square metres of space. The largest office letting on record in Ireland, it was negotiated by colourful estate agent John Finnegan, who was empowered to offer an attractive package of incentives, including a three-year rent-free period. Such inducements were needed to snatch Eircell from the jaws of Green Property, which had been talking to the mobile phone company for several months about taking one of the two blocks in Green's Atrium office development on Sandyford Industrial Estate, which subsequently became Microsoft's European headquarters. But it took a long time to land other major tenants, including First Active, Merrill Lynch and ABN Amro, mainly because so much office space was being built in Dublin that the shortage driving all of this development was turning into oversupply.

The availability of lucrative tax incentives for hotel schemes led to Bewley's taking the hotel in Central Park, but it was clear that some housing needed to be thrown into the mix. Planning permission was secured for 450 apartments in three blocks, and the six-acre site was put up for sale in April 2005; the temptation was hard to resist, given that 300 apartments in the nearby Beacon South Quarter had been sold off the plans by Sherry FitzGerald over a single weekend. John Lally's vehicle, Lalco, snapped up this 'ready-to-go' site for €60 million, judging that the proximity of Luas would add to its appeal. It was not Lally's first deal with a Treasury-led consortium; two years earlier, he had purchased the former Rowntree Mackintosh chocolate factory opposite Kilmainham Gaol after Treasury had fought off strong opposition from local residents and conservationists to win planning permission for 173 apartments and a Hilton hotel, designed by Anthony Reddy and Associates. Another consortium involving Treasury, David Arnold and Derek Quinlan scored a spectacular coup on the Allegro site in Sandyford. In November 2005, just a week after securing approval for 880 apartments as well as major retail and leisure facilities, the 7.5-acre site was sold to Fleming Construction for €165 million – 10 times what was paid for it in 1997. It was a profit opportunity that no property developer would have passed up.

Treasury will also benefit from the designation in 2006 of 400 acres of land at Balgaddy-Clonburris as a Strategic Development Zone, even though its plans to develop the 15-acre site it owns there were fought tooth-and-nail by South Dublin County Council and Barkhill, the O'Callaghan-Grosvenor consortium that owns Liffey Valley. But Barrett and Ronan have another plan up their sleeves for a rival shopping centre, with up to 50,000 square metres of retail space, at Collinstown, near Leixlip, Co. Kildare. They paid €43 million for its 39-acre stake in the designated town centre, which would also serve Celbridge and Maynooth, as well as sucking some business from Liffey Valley. In February 2007, Treasury suffered a setback when its plans for 119 apartments and 54 houses on an eight-acre site at Brennanstown Road, in Cabinteely, Dublin, were rejected by An Bord Pleanála as premature, pending the adoption of a local area plan. It also had to withdraw plans for a 32-storey tower at Barrow Street, for the same reason. But it got planning approval for two other high-rise schemes at either end of the Grand Canal Dock's inner basin – Shay Cleary's Altovetro, billed by its agents as 'the most beautiful building in Dublin', and OMP's Montevetro, next to the area's DART station. Treasury also partnered Sisk in bidding to build the U2 Tower at Britain Quay, at the confluence of the Liffey and the Dodder, with Baghdad-born superstar Zaha Hadid as their architect. The 'twisting tower', designed by Blackrock-based architects Burdon Dunne Craig Henry, had emerged from a competition held in 2003 that turned into a debacle when the original winner chosen by the adjudicators proved impossible to identify because the number assigned to this entry could not be matched with a name. The DDDA subsequently decided to double the tower's height to 120 metres, throw in an adjoining site to make it more viable and hold a new competition.

The contest attracted four top-flight competitors: Treasury Holdings/Sisk, Seán Dunne's Mountbrook Homes (with trendy Danish architects 3XN), the Riverside II Partnership (Anthony Reddy and Associates/Rafael Viñoly) and Geranger, a consortium of Ballymore Properties, U2 and Paddy McKillen (Foster + Partners). In response to concerns by other bidders about U2's involvement in the competition to build the tower that would carry its name, the DDDA made it clear that members of the rock band had no role in setting the ground rules, nor would they have 'any role or involvement, directly or indirectly' in assessing the bids. According to its brief, the 'shoulder height' of the tower 'should not exceed 100 metres . . . above existing street level' and the maximum overall building height, including any architectural features, was capped at 120 metres. So there was considerable surprise in October 2007 when the DDDA awarded the project to Geranger for a tilted triangular tower designed by Foster, openly admitting that it would rise to a height of 180 metres, including a battery of vertical wind turbines topped by a huge solar panel, with the band's egg-shaped recording studio suspended above an observation deck. Having invested at least €1 million apiece in preparing their entries, the other bidders were understandably miffed and there was even talk that one or more of them would challenge the result in the courts. In the end, however, they accepted that in the property game, as in every other, you win some and you lose some.

At 53, the terrible twins show no signs of a slowdown, although Ronan is training his 24-year-old son John into the business. 'He wears a hairstyle just like his dad,' says a friend, 'and they go around town like the Men in Black.'

8. The Battle of Ballsbridge

It was the longest letter ever published by the *Irish Times*, 1,937 words from property developer Seán Dunne bristling with anger, indignation and sarcasm over an editorial in the paper. 'The number of grossly inaccurate and misleading articles which have been written over the past two years about my company and the Jurys/Berkeley Court site by now outnumber the number of rugby fans who claim to have been in Thomond Park when Munster beat the All Blacks in 1978,' Dunne wrote on 24 August 2007; but the editorial was 'so vindictive, misleading and inaccurate that it trumps them all'.

The *Irish Times* had blamed him for the closure of two Ballsbridge hotels – Jurys and the Berkeley Court – with the loss of 600 jobs. It argued that:

... these hotels were an important part of the social and economic infrastructure of the city ... From the hardball negotiations between Albert Reynolds and Dick Spring in 1992 that led to the formation of the first Fianna Fáil–Labour coalition to the frivolities of Jurys Irish Cabaret, from press conferences and corporate AGMs, to wedding receptions and debs' dances, they staged important events in public and private life. As well as business people and tourists, rugby and soccer fans going to Lansdowne Road, farmers attending the Spring Show, equestrian enthusiasts going to the Horse Show, fans going to rock concerts and bleary-eyed revellers desperate to keep the night going, all passed through their doors.

All of this, the newspaper charged, had been 'ruthlessly ... swapped for an audacious bet on property development'.

Seán Dunne was outraged, and hit back hard, asserting that the hotels had been closed by the Jurys Doyle group and not by him, and taking issue with the whole thrust of the editorial. 'You talk of changes in Dublin 4. One change I would personally welcome is a change in the current trend among certain members of the media of blaming property developers for the ills of all society,' he wrote. The paper's condemnation of Dunne's supposed 'ruthlessness' was 'hypocritical given that the *Irish Times* itself embarked on a controversial rationalisation programme over the past four years . . . namely: disposing of its head office – a Dublin landmark; moving to rented accommodation; and laying off approximately three hundred staff'.

As for the 'audacious bet' he had taken, Dunne pointed out that other developers had spent a lot more than him on sites in Ballsbridge and 'one does not need a degree in construction economics to know the position all would prefer to be in'. There was even a patriotic angle in his argument: 'The business of property development involves risk-taking, and, in this case, a belief in the sustainable success of the Irish economy,' he wrote. 'While others have chosen to sell up now while the going is good and depart with their profits, I have chosen to put my trust, faith and money in the future of my country and its economy.' As he saw it: 'A unique, once in a lifetime opportunity has now arisen for the development of an eleven-acre triangle of land in Ballsbridge . . . in the ownership of five developers.' And his own vision for the Jurys/Berkeley Court sites, which included a 220-bedroom hotel and more than 500 apartments, would 'enhance, enrich and enshrine this area of Ballsbridge for the next hundred years and beyond'.

Months before the sale was first announced, in June 2005, speculation had been rife among Dublin's property development fraternity that Jurys Doyle Hotels were about to offload Jurys Hotel and Towers in Ballsbridge, and possibly even the nearby Berkeley Court. The group, then a plc, was in the throes of contesting a takeover bid from developer Bryan Cullen's Precinct Investments, which had already acquired the Gresham Hotel group, and other developers were waiting in the wings to see what would happen. Precinct was interested in taking over Jurys

Ballsbridge as a going concern; what the others wanted, however, was to redevelop its prime site of nearly five acres. The hotel was relatively old, having been built as the Intercontinental in 1963 with 315 bedrooms, making it Ireland's largest hotel at the time; Jurys took it over in 1973. Now it was to sell out at a time when the property market was booming, having been advised that the Ballsbridge site could be worth €200 million.

Thirteen tenders were submitted and the biggest bid came from Seán Dunne, who offered a whopping €260 million. Incredibly, four of the bidders were within €2 million of each other, with Bernard McNamara just €300,000 behind Dunne. The other underbidders offering similarly large sums were Alanis (controlled by the McCormack family) in partnership with veteran developer Paddy Kelly and not-so-veteran John Flynn; Derry-based Taggart Homes; and Ray Grehan, of Glenkerrin Homes. It seemed almost beyond belief, at least to ordinary mortals, that developers were prepared to pay such extraordinary money for a development site; Dunne's purchase price worked out at €53.7 million per acre; the previous record was €35 million per acre, paid by Liam Carroll for the Brooks Thomas site on North Wall Quay in Docklands.

Clearly, all of the developers who bid for the site were bullish not only about Dublin's property market but also about the prospects of building out the Jurys site with a high-rise, high-density scheme – as were Dunne's bankers at Ulster Bank, who had agreed to lend him most of the money. Within hours of winning the tender, he was talking about transforming Ballsbridge into 'the new Knightsbridge'. A landmark tower up to 32 storeys high would be the centrepiece of a 'top-class residential development' of between five and six hundred luxury flats that would offer residents the lifestyle of 'top apartments in Manhattan' with a 24-hour concierge service, swimming pool and gym. 'The only better site is St Stephen's Green, and I don't think they will sell that,' he famously declared.

Just a month earlier, An Bord Pleanála had upheld Dublin City Council's approval for a 32-storey tower near Heuston Station, so there was reason to assume that the planners would be similarly indulgent towards equally tall buildings in Ballsbridge. Dunne had two objectives: to nail down Jurys Doyle board approval for his offer, and to put himself in pole position to grab the Berkeley Court Hotel site next door. So he started building up a significant shareholding in the hotel group, with the avowed aim of preventing a takeover by Precinct's Bryan Cullen and his British backers, billionaire brothers Simon and David Reuben. Within three months, he had built up a 28 per cent stake in the company with the aid of more bank loans, advanced by the likes of French private equity house Orion Capital. He had also hired former Investment Bank of Ireland chief Richard Keatinge as a corporate adviser. (Keatinge died in February 2008 at the age of 60.) In October 2005 Dunne sold his shares – at a profit of €20 million – to JDH Acquisitions, the Doyle family-led consortium seeking to take the group private; the group returned the favour by selling him the Berkeley Court Hotel for €119 million. Given that it stands on a site of just over two acres, the purchase price this time equated to €57.5 million per acre. Now, Dunne had what he wanted – control over seven acres of prime property in Ballsbridge with frontages on Pembroke, Lansdowne and Shelbourne roads. The only drawback (which the bullish tycoon managed to overcome) was that Jurys Doyle sought to impose a covenant in the terms of sale that no 'hotel, motel, inn, guesthouse, apart-hotel or hostel' could be built on the site. P. V. Doyle's family, watched over by his eagle-eyed son-in-law John Gallagher, still had its residual hotel interests to protect. Although they had earned more than €700 million from the disposal of assets in Dublin (Jurys Hotel and Towers, the Berkeley Court, the Montrose and the Burlington), their remaining hotels in Ireland, Britain and the United States were estimated to be worth as much again or more.

Seán Dunne's two acquisitions sparked a Klondike-style gold rush in the heart of Dublin 4. Even the state cashed in on the frenzied mood by inviting tenders for the former UCD Veterinary College on Shelbourne Road, right next to Jurys. Ray

Grehan, one of the disappointed underbidders for the hotel property, emerged as the victor on this occasion with his offer to pay €171.5 million for the 2.1-acre site in November 2005, setting a new record price of over €81 million per acre. Describing this acquisition as a 'once in a century' opportunity, he forecast confidently that the Irish housing market would 'not slow down in the near future' because of the projected rise in population, continual inward migration and the emergence of a younger society.

Grehan's splurge was trumped the following May when Jerry O'Reilly and David Courtney paid €36 million for the adjoining state-owned Faculty Building when it was sold by tender, pipping both Dunne and Grehan himself for the tiny (0.378-acre) site; the price equated to just over €95 million per acre, well above what the Office of Public Works or its agents, Lambert Smith Hampton, expected the property to fetch. A month later, David Daly of Albany Homes bought Franklin House, a dark and brooding five-storey office block opposite the US embassy, from land speculator Gerry Gannon for €25 million. The price Daly paid worked out at a staggering €133 million per acre; at the time, this made the huge sums shelled out earlier by other developers look like bargains. It also seemed very extravagant compared to the acquisition in January 2007 of Carrisbrook House by a Bernard McNamara-led consortium for €46 million, which represented a relatively trifling price of €92 million per acre. This cheap and tatty hexagonal office block, pure rubbish even when it was built in 1968, is expected to be replaced by a much larger building that will extend over the adjoining site of a disused petrol station, which was also snapped up by the same consortium. While nobody would regret the loss of Carrisbrook House, where the Israeli embassy is the last remaining tenant, McNamara knew that to win planning approval for a replacement, the best strategy would be to propose a fine piece of architecture for the junction of Pembroke and Northumberland roads.

Meanwhile, Seán Dunne continued to accumulate property in Ballsbridge. In April 2006, just six months after buying the

Berkeley Court, he joined forces with Hibernian Life and Pensions to acquire the AIB Bankcentre for €378 million in cash, leasing it back to the bank at an initial annual rent of €11.6 million. For his portion of the complex, which included its extensive landscaped forecourt on Merrion Road, Dunne paid €200 million, or €55 million per acre – described as 'good value' by a spokesman for Dunne's Mountbrook Homes. The bank had previously raked in €368 million when it sold a large extension to the rear of its headquarters, fronting on to Serpentine Avenue, to a syndicate of 'high-net-worth individuals' who had been rounded up by its private banking unit and Goodbody Stockbrokers, which is now an AIB subsidiary. No wonder bank chairman Dermot Gleeson was able to predict a 'bright' future for AIB at its annual general meeting a day after the deal with Dunne and Hibernian had been announced.

But there were others who thought there was something fishy going on. 'These fellows and their lenders have steely nerves – and optimism that is without bounds,' observed the 'Current Account' commentator in the *Irish Times* business supplement in April 2006. 'Sweet as the latest deal is, questions should be asked when a big property lender such as AIB chooses to cash in on its site in one of the wealthiest parts of Dublin. Why is it moving now? Does it think the top of the market is near? And did it decide to avoid the possibility of a lesser profit by selling out as soon as possible?'

Dunne didn't allow any such suspicions to put a brake on his buying spree. In August 2006, he acquired the eight-storey Hume House beside Jurys by doing a swap with Irish Life, which received an office block on Sir John Rogerson's Quay in exchange. What made this unusual deal more remarkable was the disparity in the age and size of the two buildings. The L-shaped Hume House dates from 1966 and has less than 7,500 square metres of offices, whereas the Riverside IV office block in Docklands was still under construction at the time it was swapped and contains just over 12,000 square metres of high-spec modern working space. What Dunne really wanted, of course, was the

0.65-acre site of Hume House, rather than the building itself; the swap deal was estimated to be worth €130 million, which meant the price on the Ballsbridge site equated to an all-time record of €195 million per acre, one of the highest ever paid for real estate anywhere in the world.

Seán Dunne was well used to playing hardball in the rough-and-tumble world of property development, but his beginnings were typically modest. In an interview on RTÉ radio in March 2008, he spoke of his childhood in Tullow, Co. Carlow; when he and his siblings needed a bath or shower, they went for a swim in the River Slaney. He was the fourth of five children of Tom Dunne, a town clerk and part-time fire-fighter, and his wife, Maureen. 'I worked from the age of 12. We had to. Making hay, thinning beet, picking potatoes, working on building sites.'

Dunne qualified as a quantity surveyor in 1977 at Bolton Street College of Technology in Dublin and then spent two years working on the environmentally devastating extraction of oil from tar sands in the Canadian province of Alberta. After returning to Ireland, he got a useful job overseeing the construction of local authority houses in the misnamed Jobstown area of Tallaght, before going on to set up on his own and build more social housing in Sallynoggin, Mulhuddart and Bray.

His first venture, set up in 1983 with the help of Séamus Ross and Mick Whelan, was DCD Builders. 'Even then,' says one who knew them, 'Dunne was flamboyant and would never get his shoes dirty – not like Ross or Whelan.' DCD is still his holding company; one of its subsidiaries, Padholme, was the vehicle he used to purchase the Jurys and Berkeley Court sites. Times got so tough in the mid-1980s that he left for London to make some money during the boom period of Thatcher's Britain. Back home again in 1989, he was one of the lads in Donnybrook Tennis Club and Lansdowne Rugby Club, where he played prop forward, knocking around with up-and-coming movers and shakers like Kyran McLoughlin and David Shubotham of Davy Stockbrokers. They were putting together a consortium to buy

St Helen's in Booterstown, one of the finest surviving 18th-century houses in south Co. Dublin, and its 70 acres of grounds, from the Christian Brothers; it had been their Irish headquarters for many years. McLoughlin and Shubotham had no experience of building or property development, but they were well aware that Dunne did, and he was invited to become a shareholder in Berland Homes, which agreed to purchase the property for £17.75 million. Other investors lined up by Davy included multi-millionaires Martin Naughton and Lochlann Quinn, of Glen Dimplex, and the British Merchant Navy Officers' Pension Fund.

Despite its prime location, just off the Stillorgan dual carriage-way, and the relatively high quality of the development, jitters caused by the first Gulf War and a surge in interest rates made it difficult to sell apartments, and prices had to be slashed to attract ready buyers. Tensions between the partners flared up in 1993 when the British Merchant Navy Officers' Pension Fund sold its 25 per cent stake to Davy's vehicle, Mulroy, and Mulroy promptly demanded repayment from Dunne of £4.5 million in loans. Dunne responded by initiating a High Court action, claiming he was entitled to half of the pension fund's shares. He also claimed that he was being oppressed by the Davy side, which counter-claimed that he had acted in an oppressive manner and with disregard for their interests.

The case was eventually settled out of court in 1996, with Berland going into voluntary liquidation, leaving £6 million to be distributed among its shareholders. Dunne did well from the deal, getting full title to an undeveloped slice of the St Helen's site at a time when it could only rise in value, and his newly formed company, Mountbrook Homes, cleaned up on it. He was also well capable of doing a quick turn, as he showed with Grattan House in Lower Mount Street; having bought the office block from Irish Life for £5 million in December 1996, he jacked up the rent for its state tenants by 30 per cent and put it on the market for over £6.5 million just nine months later.

With the bitter Berland experience behind him, Dunne knew what he had to do to thrive in this cut-throat business: buy land on his own account, and plenty of it. His first coup was the acquisition of Woodtown Manor, a Georgian house on 150 acres of wooded farmland at Stocking Lane, Rathfarnham. In 1997 he managed to buy it for the bargain-basement price of £1.4 million from an agent acting for Garech Browne, the most colourful member of the Guinness brewing dynasty and founder of Claddagh Records. 'That was a risk – you were buying on the side of the mountain,' Dunne said in 2005 when the Stocking Lane land was valued at more than €250 million.

Having got Stocking Lane for a song, Dunne could afford to hold the land for several years. Planning permission to convert its manor house to hotel use, with a 98-room bedroom block tacked on to it, was secured in 2004. And with 30 acres rezoned for housing, there were plans to build 500 new homes in the grounds, probably as the first phase of a major residential development in an area that is being transformed beyond recognition. Among Dunne's other acquisitions was a parcel of 50 acres between Malahide and Swords, which he has since agreed to swap with Malahide Rugby Club for its 10 acres of zoned residential land. He also bought large sites on the edge of Celbridge, Co. Kildare, to roll out hundreds of suburban houses in schemes marketed under the names Oldtown Mill and St Raphael's Manor. Completed over a four-year period, the terraced and semi-detached houses were aimed mainly at first-time housebuyers and sold like hot cakes, earning substantial profits for Mountbrook.

Seán Dunne wasn't neglecting the top end of the market. In June 1999, he outbid everyone else at a Lisney auction and paid £8.3 million for Hollybrook, a five-bedroom detached Victorian on Brighton Road, Foxrock. Its real value lay in the three-acre site – if the planners would agree to release its development potential. Dún Laoghaire-Rathdown County Council refused permission in September 2000 for the demolition of Hollybrook and its replacement by 42 luxury apartments, saying the density and bulk of the proposed development would 'seriously injure the special amenities of the area' and set an 'undesirable precedent' for similar schemes. But this decision was overturned on appeal by

An Bord Pleanála, much to the distress of local residents, who later complained that Foxrock was 'under siege' from developers seeking to replace its fine homes with blocks of luxury flats. Hollybrook was aimed at the rich, with prices ranging from €745,000 for spacious one-bedroom apartments to €2.5 million for much larger penthouses when the first phase was launched in June 2002. The U-shaped three-storey block, designed by CCH Architects, also has a leisure suite with a sauna, steam room, jacuzzi and gym. 'Hollybrook bears all the hallmarks of an exclusive private club, from the 24-hour concierge to sumptuous common areas with seating and formal Italianate gardens,' enthused the *Irish Times* property supplement in February 2006, when the last of its penthouses was put up for auction with an advised minimum value of €2.7 million. Coincidentally, that was also the price Dunne himself had obtained six years earlier when he sold his Foxrock home, in The Birches, on Torquay Road, to move to what is billed as Dublin's most exclusive residential address – Shrewsbury Road, Ballsbridge.

The move to Ballsbridge involved a deal with Niall O'Farrell, owner of the Black Tie dress hire chain, to split a site of less than half an acre that O'Farrell had bought from the Pharmaceutical Society of Ireland in December 1998 for a then record price of £3.6 million. Just six months later, Dunne agreed to pay £3 million for half of this valuable property, with the benefit of planning permission for a detached house next door to O'Farrell's new home. Not long afterwards, he formed the impression that O'Farrell had encroached on his half of the site, and initiated legal proceedings to force him to comply with the terms of the planning permission for the house he was building next door. This squabble was finally settled in July 2000 after six days in the High Court, with Dunne emerging triumphant and O'Farrell facing a hefty legal bill.

In the meantime, Dunne joined forces with another denizen of Shrewsbury Road, solicitor-developer Stephen MacKenzie, in a sustained campaign against O'Malley Construction's plans for the former Chester Beatty Library site. In 1999, before the library moved to Dublin Castle, O'Malleys had agreed to pay £7 million for the site, and obtained planning permission in 2004 and again in 2005 for a modest residential development, despite strenuous objections from Dunne and MacKenzie. They took their case to the High Court in 2006, arguing that An Bord Pleanála's most recent decision was invalid because O'Malleys had not specified how they would comply with the 2000 Planning Act's requirement for a modicum of social and affordable housing. The court ruled that, although there had been some technical breaches of the regulations, these were not serious enough to warrant quashing the planning permission.

Even Dunne's friends concede that he has a talent for making enemies. 'I'd say he's generous to a fault and there's no doubt that he puts his balls on the table, but, having said that, I'd hate to work for him,' one says. 'He can be abrasive and suspicious. Often there are rows with whoever he's working with. He likes to do things his way.' He flies friends (using Netjet, typically costing €4,000 an hour) to rugby matches, and he has purchased a coveted 24-seater corporate box at the newly developed Lansdowne Road, costing €475,000. He also takes a private suite for Punchestown race week, directly opposite the winning post. Clongowes Wood College, the Co. Kildare Jesuit private school where his two older sons were boarders, has benefited from his largesse in the shape of a €1 million floodlit, all-weather rugby pitch. Meanwhile, he – or rather, his chauffeur – drives an environmentally conscious Lexus Hybrid.

His spending and socializing have become more and more conspicuous in recent years. His heavily publicized wedding to gossip columnist Gayle Killilea, in Thailand, was celebrated with a two-week cruise for 30 guests, including Irish Nationwide boss Michael Fingleton, rugby international Ronan O'Gara and fashion designer Karen Millen, on the *Christina O*, Aristotle Onassis's legendary yacht and the scene of his wedding to Jacqueline Kennedy. For Killilea's 30th birthday celebrations, they booked the five-star Park Hotel in Kenmare, Co. Kerry, where Dunne dressed as an admiral for the *Pirates of the Caribbean*-themed party. Such was the macho posturing among the guests, according to local gossip, that one of them felt obliged to ask if he could park his embarrassingly small helicopter elsewhere.

Dunne, his son Stephen and daughter Elaine found themselves at the receiving end of High Court proceedings in 2005 when the management company of Merrion Grove, an established apartment complex near UCD, got an injunction to stop them turning one of the nine blocks into student housing; they were seeking to avail themselves of lucrative tax incentives for the provision of such accommodation. The court halted the alteration works being carried out by Mountbrook Homes on eight duplex apartments after hearing that residents of the complex had rejected the proposal by 69 votes to 2. The Dunnes later got planning permission from Dún Laoghaire-Rathdown County Council to turn the apartment block into a 'residence hall', despite a strong objection from the Merrion Grove management company arguing that the 'transient nature' of student accommodation would have a negative impact on the residents in terms of noise and nuisance. After an unsuccessful appeal to An Bord Pleanála, a case was taken to the Circuit Court on the basis that the Dunnes were 'thumbing their noses at the management company' by breaching a strict covenant in all of the leases for apartments in the complex specifying that they could not be used other than as single private units and prohibiting any alterations without the company's approval. Counsel for the Dunnes countered that consent in this case was being unreasonably withheld. By then, it was already clear that young Stephen Dunne was following his father into the property development business. His first scheme was a swanky architect-designed mews house on Pembroke Lane, not far from Jurys Hotel, which he developed on the site of a run-down garage and then put on the market in September 2003 for a cool €1 million.

The most high-profile legal battle involving Seán Dunne was his High Court action in 2006 against financier Kevin Warren over the newly opened Whitewater shopping centre in Newbridge, Co. Kildare. Dunne told the Commercial Court that he was 'dumbfounded and astounded' when Warren had claimed that he had a binding contract to purchase Dunne's 50 per cent stake in the centre for just €37.5 million. After almost eight expensive days of intense argument in May 2006, a settlement was reached under which Warren agreed to pay a 'basic price' of €197 million for Dunne's share in Whitewater, to be topped up later with a deferred payment of €23 million if the rents went up as expected.

Dunne needed the Whitewater money. At first, he was going to put it into the Jurys/Berkeley Court acquisitions, but his row with Warren delayed things and he now needed it urgently to finance his share of the AIB Bankcentre deal, on which he had only paid a deposit of €20 million in April. When there was no sign of the remaining €180 million at the end of May, the bank served him with a completion notice and followed this up with a reminder at the end of June. By then, Warren's initial €197 million Whitewater payment had come through, and Dunne was able to meet AIB's demand for the outstanding cash. He was also raking in a lot of money – estimated at between €80 and €100 million – from his joint venture with Seán Mulryan in developing Charlesland, south of Greystones, having sold 1,800 new homes there over the previous two years; one scheme of apartments, The Fairways, gave residents views over the local golf club towards the Irish Sea. Their latest coup was to persuade Wicklow County Council in December 2006 to rezone an 80-acre site in Charlesland for a district shopping centre of some 20,000 square metres, in return for providing sites for a primary school, garda station, and enterprise and community centres.

But Dunne remained firmly focused on Ballsbridge. He engaged the formidable Joan O'Connor, first (and only) woman president of the RIAI, as project manager, and on her advice invited no fewer than 13 top-flight architects from Ireland and abroad to participate in a design competition for the project. Eight of the invitees ended up taking part and, famously, he flew all of them over the hotel sites by helicopter, so that they would get a bird's eye view of the terrain which had cost him €379 million; some of them needed this orientation tour because they had never been in Dublin previously.

Ulrik Raysse, design director of Danish architects Henning Larsen, who won the competition, was one of the first-timers. 'I didn't know much about Ireland then, except that it had blossomed a lot while Denmark was growing more gradually,' he said later. 'But I think Dublin is quite like Copenhagen. Both are historical cities with centres that haven't been destroyed.' This gave him a 'strong understanding of scale', pointing to the need to be 'bold and at the same time humble' in designing for Ballsbridge. It was while walking around Dublin on his first visit that Raysse spotted the Peppercanister church in Mount Street Crescent and realized that it was one of the city's few perfectly aligned landmarks. But what he proposed was far more grandiose – a 'diamond-cut' skyscraper, 12 metres higher than the Spire in O'Connell Street, placed on the axis of Pembroke Road as a 'gateway between 19th- and 21st-century Dublin', and seven other buildings ranging in height from 10 to 18 storeys. The scheme also exploited the 'great potential' of opening up the two hotel sites with pedestrian routes going right through the combined site to link Pembroke, Lansdowne and Shelbourne roads. Altogether, it would include over 600 apartments as well as offices, restaurants and bars, a theatre, arthouse cinema, jazz club and outdoor ice rink in winter. Raysse managed to offend many Irish architects when he said, 'Ireland, and especially Dublin, is very strong on literature, poetry, music and theatre. But where is the excellence in architecture? What we're trying to do is to raise the bar here, by daring to create a place that's unique.' Gate theatre director Michael Colgan had become cultural adviser for the project, and saw it as an opportunity to inject some life into Ballsbridge by giving it an element of 'burlesque', as the great impresario put it himself.

The audacious scheme was first unveiled at a private meeting with local TDs, councillors and senior council officials in November 2006. When Jim Barrett, then City Architect, described the proposed tower as 'a very sculptural tapered piece', it must have been music to Dunne's ears. His acquisition of the Jurys/Berkeley Court sites and the subsequent transactions involving other developers had put pressure on Dublin City Council to produce a local area plan (LAP) for Ballsbridge, to provide a statutory framework for regulating the scale and type of development that would be permitted in the area. Drawn up by planning consultants Urban Initiatives, the draft LAP did exactly what it was intended to do: open up opportunities for higher-density development on certain sites, notably the pieces of real estate that had been bought up at staggeringly high prices. But the plan, unveiled in January 2007, didn't go far enough to meet the vaultingly ambitious visions of the developers. The 'contextual height' it proposed was just four to five storeys, so as not to overwhelm the area's mature Victorian houses; the 'standard height' in the centre of the urban village would be six to eight storeys, while clusters of eight-to-ten-storey buildings might be permitted in the middle of larger sites. The only real comfort for the developers was a vague provision for 'landmark buildings' of unspecified height and location. But local residents branded the LAP as 'a developers' charter which ... will irreparably damage the character and heritage of the area' and called on the city council to scrap it 'unequivocally'. In a joint statement, 14 residents' associations said it was 'simply not acceptable that poor planning decisions in the 1960s and 1970s, which resulted in a number of excessively high buildings [in Ballsbridge], should now be used to justify even more excessively high buildings'.

Senior council officials, including city manager John Tierney and assistant city manager Michael Stubbs, who is in charge of the Planning Department, were on the opposite side of the argument. They sought to persuade the council to rezone a series of sites for 'mixed-use development' of offices, residential and shopping, in a move that was seen as opening the door to much higher densities and buildings of up to 20 storeys on key sites. However, the council could not be persuaded. Local Labour councillor and former Lord Mayor Dermot Lacey said the LAP was 'flawed beyond redemption', while his party colleague Cllr. Mary Freehill criticized Stubbs for even bringing the plan to the members for adoption in June 2007. 'It is hard for us not to believe you are being driven by more powerful forces outside this city council,' she said bluntly. Tierney said that 'it was irrelevant to us who buys the sites and what they paid for them' and rejected any allegation that the plan was 'writing blank cheques' for developers. But there was no stomach among any of the parties on the council to adopt the proposed rezonings, and the plan was rejected without a vote. One source close to Dunne saw this as 'a pre-emptive strike by the Nimbys' – a reference to the 'not in my backyard' view adopted by the coalition of residents' associations, and the political response to it.

At first, the LAP's rejection was interpreted as a setback for the developers, with several sources suggesting that it could be a year or more until the council returned to the issue of what to do about Ballsbridge. In the absence of an LAP, the schemes put forward by Dunne and other developers would have to be adjudicated on in the context of the Dublin City Development Plan, which did not envisage tall buildings in the area. Its Z1 zoning of the hotel sites – 'to protect or improve residential amenity' – didn't seem to offer much leeway but, on closer examination, the range of permissable uses included everything other than offices and heavy industry; even pigeon lofts and halting sites are Z1-compatible. And as for the height issue, developers could point to how the new stadium at Lansdowne Road, in the midst of a residential area, had sailed through the planning process even though it would be nearly 15 metres taller than Croke Park.

Ray Grehan was first into the breach. In August 2007, Glenkerrin sought planning permission from the city council for a development on the former Veterinary College site, with a 15-storey residential tower – perhaps aptly named 'No. 1 Ballsbridge' – as its centrepiece. Designed by HKR Architects, the plan also included three office blocks up to nine storeys high as well as cafés, restaurants, boutiques and an arts centre, laid out around a central square and a dog-legged pedestrian street linking Pembroke and Shelbourne roads; it seemed almost modest compared to Seán Dunne's scheme for the hotel sites next door.

Grehan told the *Irish Times* that he had taken on board the concerns of local people over the impact of high-rise development and that Glenkerrin's scheme would have a 'minimum visual impact on residents and the general area'. In terms of height, he insisted that it was 'comparable with Hume House' – which was true if you subtracted six or seven storeys.

In an expression of solidarity among developers, Dunne's planning consultants, RPS, suggested that Glenkerrin's proposal would complement Dunne's vision of creating a 'new world-class urban quarter' in the heart of Ballsbridge. The city council's planners and senior officials obviously agreed. In what local Fine Gael TD Lucinda Creighton said was a 'worrying signal', they approved the 40,000-square-metre development as proposed in February 2008, just eight months after the councillors had thrown out the Ballsbridge LAP. Labour councillor Dermot Lacey asserted that the city manager's decision 'flies in the face' of what the council itself wanted. It was also seen by local environmental campaigner Damien Cassidy as the 'thin end of the wedge', a harbinger of worse to come in Ballsbridge. But a delighted Ray Grehan said it showed that the planners had accepted the idea that they would have to permit higher-density development on key sites in the city to avoid further urban sprawl. And, although he knew Glenkerrin would face appeals to An Bord Pleanála, he still believed he was right to pay a premium for the site 'because it's in Ballsbridge and I thought worth it in terms of potential return'.

Still in his mid-forties, Grehan is well liked in the industry, where sources describe him as 'much more exciting than the others', 'great fun to have a few drinks with' and 'a real quality builder'. At the time of writing, he was bullish about Ballsbridge, insisting that the gamble didn't keep him awake at night: 'Not at all. I tendered for two sites on the same day – Ballsbridge was one, the other was €50 million for a site in Ealing Broadway. Any sites we bought were gilt-edged location sites. We've spread our risk – four major schemes in the UK, mainly in Canary Wharf and west London.' Although seasoned property experts characterized the Dunne and Grehan punts as 'absolute madness', many assumed that both men had received informal assurances from officials about their high-rise ambitions before bidding in telephone numbers. Grehan denied this: 'You do a square-foot price and calculate what you need to get on the site and you have a reasonable idea what density you'd get. Obviously, we were pushing the boundaries . . .'

Like many farmers' sons, Grehan had a multiplicity of skills, cutting silage since the age of 11 and becoming the reigning 'fixer' of the neighbourhood, a lad who could turn his hand to anything. He assumed that his future lay in farming. But a wise nun who acted as the Glen Vocational School's career guidance counsellor gently pointed out to him that he would be 37 or 38 by the time his siblings got through college and he would still be farming to keep the family. 'My own life would be "used up", she said, and I'd be stuck on the farm, where I wouldn't be giving myself a fair break at life. But if I went away for a few years, she said, maybe I could then come back to the farm if I loved it so much. I was dumbstruck. It was like someone had hit a switch. I came out hearing my own voice instead of my parents'.' The upshot was that he left school the following year, did an apprenticeship course in specialized welding and worked on the Alcan site in Aughinish, Co. Limerick, before hitting Dublin in 1984, in the depths of recession.

Reading the Useful Services section in the *Evening Herald*, he spotted a niche. 'It was the time when all the coloured bathroom suites were getting popular and I advertised a service to change the tiling to match. I also used the planning applications in the papers to drum up custom. I'd write to the house owners, putting myself forward "for some or all of the work involved", as I put it in the letters. Then I'd sit on the stairs of the flat at Beechwood Avenue and eat my tea there, waiting for the phone to ring.'

In 1985, he got a call from Park Developments, offering a contract for tiling for 500 houses; within 12 months, he had 22 tilers working for him. Logistics became more manageable when he became the first in the tiling sector to own a mobile phone. But, he recalls, 'margins were so tight, it was absolute torture.

You were getting a week's wages out of it, no more than that . . . They were very difficult times.' Then came what he calls 'a bit of a boom in 1987–88 and I gradually took over the tiling market, working for Cosgraves, Lark Homes, Shannon Homes, Berland Homes' – Seán Dunne's company. He was just 27 when he finally landed on Planet Developer himself, with the purchase of eight sites from Tony Murray of Lark Homes in Maynooth. 'I had the cash – £32,000 – and borrowed £60,000. My brother Danny was a bricklayer in England and I rang him and asked would he come home and be foreman. He did and took a share in the company. We built 80 houses there. That time, if you were making £3,000 to £4,000 pounds a house, you'd be doing well. We'd hoped to make £40,000 but we made £100,000 in the first phase. So we bought another 30 sites from Tony Murray, then another 40.'

He was inspired by developers who built to a high standard on well-located sites. 'It was Seán McKeon of Sheelin McSharry and Cosgrave Brothers that lit the candle for me. They had the stamp of quality.' But he admits wryly that he was responsible for some eyesores himself. 'I was naive when it came to architecture. The Glenroyal hotel and shopping centre [opened in Maynooth in 1995] are an example of that. They could have been so much better architecturally. I'd knock them [down] in the morning if I could.' Regrettably for him and the people of Maynooth, those early mistakes were made on his and their doorstep, on a prime site at the entrance to the old university town. Nonetheless, the Glenroyal is where he relaxes over a pint among old friends on a Friday night. Home is just a few miles away, in a rambling, turreted new-build house, with Geraldine, his very grounded, low-key wife and their young family. His brother Danny has built a house to his left. To his right is a vast new mansion, another monument to the boom, belonging to a local builder.

In many ways, Ray Grehan is the acceptable face of the younger generation of developers. He rarely seeks out publicity or bothers with the glitzy balls and lunches, but, unlike most of his older peers, he is happy enough to raise his head above the parapet on occasion and is clearly in favour of more transparency from the industry. In his down time, he loves to fly his helicopter, using it to travel up and down to Galway, to get to race meetings and take an overview of sites. Recently, he traded up from a four-seater to a €2 million seven-seater Squirrel. Then there is the 75-foot yacht down in Palma de Mallorca, plus 'about three racehorses' and the golf memberships at the K Club and Carton House. Like other developers in recent years, he has also involved himself in charity work, in his case in a project called The Big Rig, to provide clean drinking water to rural villages in Ethiopia. The logistics of finding the appropriate drill for the job clearly exercise him and no doubt there is also entertainment along the way; Tom Parlon, now director-general of the Construction Industry Federation, is his cooperations man on the Big Rig Team.

Grehan's expensive gamble in Ballsbridge was not the first time he had splurged on a site. In November 2004, his €85 million purchase of an 11-acre parcel of land fronting on the Stillorgan dual carriageway at Galloping Green set a new record for a residential development site in Dublin. Occupied for many years by Esso's Irish headquarters, the site had been bought in 2000 for £25 million by Quinlan Private, and carried a 'ready-to-go' planning permission for 478 apartments as well as a nursing home, offices and shops. The consortium of investors Derek Quinlan was acting for did very well from the deal, having seen the property more than double in value, though a war of attrition had to be fought to win an acceptable permission in the face of objections and appeals from well-heeled local residents and Dún Laoghaire-Rathdown's planners. Having paid €7.7 million per acre for the land, Grehan had to pull out all the stops to make this project pay; huge, tastefully designed billboards around the building site, fronting on to Stillorgan Road and Brewery Road, held out the prospect of an upmarket lifestyle at what Glenkerrin called 'The Grange', suffused with 'the spirit of gracious living'. The scheme of 478 apartments, with a sleek contemporary design by OMP Architects, also offered a New York-style concierge service.

Grehan, who was described as 'little known' at the time, specialized in acquiring sites where the principle of development was already established – as at Ballintyre Hall, a Victorian mansion on 24 acres opposite Superquinn on Ballinteer Avenue, which he bought for €51 million in 2003 and which came with permission for just over 400 new homes. Grehan managed to bump this up to more than 500 to make the scheme much more profitable.

It was a different story when Glenkerrin bought St Loman's Hospital in Palmerstown, a one-time TB sanitorium and later psychiatric care centre, from the Eastern Health Board in 2004 for €31 million. South Dublin County Council refused permission for 500 apartments and 70 houses on the 22-acre site, mainly because the number of flats was too high, and it seemed as if the scheme wouldn't fly. But An Bord Pleanála overturned this decision in February 2006, even though the planning inspector who dealt with the appeal agreed with the council's negative view. Cleverly, the scheme by architects McCrossan O'Rourke Manning was marketed as 'St Edmund's', borrowing from the name of another health board facility in the area (St Edmundsbury) to expunge its old associations.

Just two weeks after Grehan submitted his plans for 'No. 1 Ballsbridge', Seán Dunne finally lodged his planning application for 'One Berkeley Court' as the centrepiece of a major highrise development. Its towering vision was even more ambitious than earlier reports had flagged. The 32-storey tower mooted at the outset had grown by five floors to become more than twice the height of Liberty Hall, and it was to be flanked by seven other buildings ranging from 10 to 18 storeys along the street frontages, oversailing all of the post-1960 office blocks in the area, not to mention its grand Victorian houses. In terms of planning gain, what the scheme offered was mixed use – residential, hotel, retail, cultural, offices – and permeability, with no fewer than seven access points leading to an internal network of pedestrian routes, including two urban squares. There was a lot of open space – nearly 50 per cent of the site – but the plot ratio was also very high (almost six to one) because of the huge volume of development being proposed.

There was no getting away from the height and density issue. It was clear that everything around the site would be dwarfed by what was planned. Most of the focus, inevitably, was on 'One Berkeley Court', which would contain 182 luxury flats behind its multi-faceted, triple-skin façade. A curved street running parallel with Lansdowne Road would be lined with 'high-end' shops, presumably to confirm Ballsbridge as the 'new Knightsbridge' – although, as another leading property developer acidly observed, 'in the real Knightsbridge, you don't have 37-storey towers'. The disdainful look on the face of a local *grande dame* recoiling from the architectural model on view in the Berkeley Court Hotel, perfectly captured in an *Irish Times* front-page photograph, seemed to sum up what many people viscerally felt about Seán Dunne's vision.

A few days before lodging his planning application, Dunne paid a Canadian trust €53 million for a 1.15-acre site on Sir John Rogerson's Quay, next door to the Riverside IV office block which he later swapped for Hume House; it was a record price for a Docklands site. The expectation in property circles was that it would accommodate a substantial office block and could also be used to provide the required 'social and affordable' housing element of his Ballsbridge scheme, to keep it in the 'exclusive' category. If that happened, it would be fair to apportion around half of the purchase price for the Docklands site to the Jurys/ Berkeley Court redevelopment, bringing Dunne's total acquisition costs to just over €400 million. And that's without counting the €200 million he paid for his share of the AIB Bankcentre or the €130 million for Hume House.

The banks that had funded these deals denied that they were fuelling unrealistically high prices for land in Ballsbridge. 'In relation to the much-talked-about site acquisitions in Dublin 4, we believe that developers are taking the lion's share of risk and can afford to do so,' said Owen O'Neill, head of lending for Ireland with Anglo Irish Bank. Speaking at the Irish Property and

Facility Management Association's 'Vertical Boulevard' conference in October 2007, O'Neill said banks 'do not accept what developers and their advisers tell us as being gospel' and made decisions to provide funding 'based on our own development appraisals following independent advice and making our own assumptions' about factors such as location, demographics and transport infrastructure. Other 'key determinants' included a developer's track record and net worth, prevailing market conditions, pre-lets or pre-sales and overall 'sustainability'. And, while welcoming a new 'realism' in the market, O'Neill cautioned that this would make funding terms 'less palatable'.

Coincidentally, it was at this time that Seán Dunne finally took possession of Jurys and the Berkeley Court, two years after doing the deals to buy them. They were soon reborn as 'D4 Hotels', raising handy revenue from rooms and catering franchises – though Dunne's relationship with John Brennan, the distinguished hotelier he brought in to run the hotels, quickly went sour, with writs flying in both directions. Dunne's vehicle, Padholme, needed the turnover because it would have started paying millions of euro per annum in interest on bank loans. And with the once-burgeoning property market beginning to stall, the banks were getting edgy about their exposure – not just in Ballsbridge but everywhere. Padholme was required to give further security guarantees to cover its indebtedness to Ulster Bank, in the form of a composite charge over the entire issued share capital of JDPHC and BCPHC, the two unlimited companies involved in acquiring the hotel sites. 'From the outset, Ulster Bank has been entitled to a charge over the properties and the various companies which own the properties,' a spokesman for Dunne told the *Irish Times* in December 2007. 'The charges which were recently registered were administrative updates to maintain this position.'

Three months later, the *Irish Independent* reported that Dunne had negotiated to borrow a further €500 million from Irish and international banks, including Ulster Bank and London-based

Kaupthing Singer and Friedlander, to fund the development. 'Despite the slowdown in commercial and residential property markets and the clamping shut of credit markets, this new funding deal marks a pretty emphatic display of confidence by bankers in the high-profile and often controversial city building project,' the paper said. On the same day, Ulster Bank's chief economist Pat McArdle produced a gloomy forecast predicting that economic growth would slow down to just 2 per cent in 2008 and the number of new homes built would fall sharply to 45,000 because of continuing uncertainty in the housing market.

With Dunne's construction costs projected to exceed €1 billion, a lot of money was riding on his – and the banks' – big gamble. *Irish Times* Business Editor John McManus argued that the 'only logical reason' why Dunne and other developers had paid huge sums for sites in Ballsbridge was because they were 'certain' of winning approval for 'massive high-density development'; otherwise, they would be in trouble. 'And that might explain their optimism. Put crudely, Ireland's big property developers are too big to be allowed to fail,' he wrote. 'The Irish banking sector has a €100 billion exposure to developers and builders. The sort of blood bath that would ensue if a big developer got into trouble would cost the taxpayer billions to fix. Confronted with that sort of reality, it is possible to see Dunne getting his tower blocks and his peers getting whatever it is that they need. Manhattan in Ballsbridge may be just another Celtic Tiger chicken coming home to roost.' Indeed, Dunne himself warned Dublin City Council's planners in February 2008 that their decision on his planning application would have 'implications for the national economy as a whole'. An economic assessment of the scheme, which he commissioned, forecast that it would generate more than 4,000 jobs and contribute €313 million annually to Dublin's economy, while its shops would 'enhance the city's attraction and competitiveness as an international shopping destination'. The assessment even suggested that, unless permission was granted, Dublin would lose out to 'competing cities in Europe and the rest of the world'. In other words, turning Ballsbridge into the 'new Knightsbridge' was in the national interest.

What the planners were expected to do, in effect, was to overturn nearly two decades of planning policy in Dublin, in order to avert a bank collapse. And, while it was second nature for property developers to gamble on a prospect, it clearly was not one of the functions of the planning system to change the rules to favour high-rise schemes on particular sites, merely because high prices had been paid for them. The record shows that Ballsbridge had long been a target in the sights of property developers. Indeed, as the *Irish Times* observed in an editorial in June 2007, its leafy roads had been prized for their relatively high values since they were first laid out by the Pembroke Estate in the 19th century. 'The area first came under attack in the 1960s for office blocks and hotels, and it was in the wake of this wave – which continued until the 1980s – that the planners adopted a more restrictive approach to preserve as much as possible of Ballsbridge and redirect development to areas that really needed urban renewal, notably the inner city.'

Now, this discriminatory approach was being abandoned, even though Ballsbridge was not one of the areas identified as a potential high-rise location in Dublin City Council's policy document *Maximising the City's Potential: A Strategy for Intensification and Height*, released in January 2008. It identified more obvious locations for higher-density development, such as the areas around Connolly, Heuston and Tara Street railway stations as well as Docklands, Grangegorman and Phibsborough. Other areas seen as having potential for 'intensification' included Ballymun, Coolock, Dolphin's Barn, Drimnagh and Finglas. There was no mention of Ballsbridge anywhere in the document. Yet, within weeks of this policy being put on display for public consultation, the planners approved Ray Grehan's proposed redevelopment of the Veterinary College site, including its 15-storey centrepiece, clearly signalling their willingness to consider high-rise schemes in the heart of Dublin 4.

Seán Dunne's scheme was the big one, and senior planner Kieran Rose was enthralled by its bold-as-brass vision of an entirely new and different kind of Ballsbridge. 'In general this is a high-quality, carefully considered, innovative and creative scheme that will contribute significantly to the betterment of the local area and the city,' he wrote in his effusive report recommending that planning permission be granted. 'The decision to hold an international competition for the design of the scheme indicates an ambition for quality and creativity that is a model for other redevelopment schemes.' Significantly, he didn't mention the city council's draft policy document on intensification and height, published six weeks earlier, in which Ballsbridge was *not* among the many locations identified as suitable places for high-rise; all he could cite was an earlier (2000) study by London-based urban designers DEGW suggesting nearby Beggar's Bush as a potential high-rise location, and the contention by Dunne's planning consultants, RPS, that his Ballsbridge site would be 'superior' for this type of treatment.

In March 2008 the city management decided to approve Dunne's proposed development – minus the central 37-storey tower. (It didn't matter that the elected councillors would have thrown out the entire scheme, because development control is an executive function: the decision was made by city manager John Tierney, with the agreement of assistant city manager Michael Stubbs, who runs the planning department, and chief planning officer Dick Gleeson.) Rose, whose report would have influenced the decision, made it plain that an amended version of the central tower would get the green light. 'It is the strong view of the planning authority that a landmark building of architectural excellence is required at this location,' he wrote. Had it been up to him, the tower would have been approved; the only obstacle was 'the lack of sufficient policy support for a building of 37 storeys'. The 10-storey office block also had to be omitted, but merely because it was contrary to the Z1 residential zoning of the two hotel sites and the planners couldn't take the risk of asking a recalcitrant city council to rezone it. Apart from reducing the height of three apartment blocks on Lansdowne Road from 11 to 9 storeys, everything else was waved through, including an 18-storey tower on Shelbourne Road and a 15-storey embassy block which, Dermot Desmond warned in his letter of objection, would be a 'sitting duck' for terrorists.

The planning decision was driven by a misguided notion that in some way a high-rise cluster in Ballsbridge would secure Dublin's position as a 'dynamic, mixed-use, visually attractive, world-class city'. (Rose made the same point in defence of controversial redevelopment plans for the Clarence Hotel on Wellington Quay, which he hailed as having 'the realisable potential to deliver an iconic world-class hotel [that] would considerably enhance Dublin's competitiveness in actual terms and additionally in terms of the resulting imagery of Dublin as a forward-looking, dynamic and creative city'.) Rose accepted the architects' argument that creating a high-rise cluster 'will have a significant, positive and defining influence in identifying a "sense of place" for Balls-bridge', which he, like them, saw as having a 'national function' – exemplified by Lansdowne Road rugby ground, the RDS, the AIB headquarters and various embassies. 'Even the postal code has a place in the national consciousness,' he wrote. His report was also full of North American references, including a comparison between Dunne's proposed development and New York's Rockefeller Center, 'with its integrated composition of towers, a pedestrian mall, plaza and ice-skating rink'.

Rose's report noted pointedly that there had been a public debate in New York about the city's early skyscrapers: 'For some the new tall buildings symbolised the worst features of American life, "unbridled materialism" and disdain for tradition; for others the new buildings represented "the colossal energy and aspiring enterprise of American life . . . a symbol of a young and assertive nation with its best years still ahead".' It was clear on which side Rose himself would have stood in that debate. Acknowledging that there were also divided views in Dublin, his report said the 37-storey tower would come as a 'disturbing shock' to some, but for others: 'It will be exciting; in the words of Seamus Heaney, it could "catch the heart off guard and blow it open".' Citing yet another American source, Rose suggested that the 'cultural resistance' to apartment living in Ireland could be overcome in much the same way as it was in New York in the late 19th century when well-to-do families chose to live in apartments for their 'luxury and comfort'. He was particularly impressed by the average floor area of 140 square metres for the apartments on the Jurys/Berkeley Court sites: 'This is a quantum leap in spaciousness. In a sense, these apartment homes can be seen as the 21st-century equivalent to the large Victorian houses in Ballsbridge.' Certainly, none but the wealthy would be able to afford them; all of the 'social and affordable' housing was to be provided by Dunne on other sites in the area. (When he put in a planning application for just such a scheme on Church Avenue, Sandymount, it was vigorously opposed by several local politicians attuned to the prejudice of their middle-class constituents.) The developer was clearly delighted by the endorsement he got from the planners. His PR company, Fleishman-Hillard, issued a lengthy statement quoting chunks of Kieran Rose's 34-page planning report as proof that the planners were really on his side. It also noted that 583 of the 739 observations received by the city council were in favour of the development while 156 were against – and that, 'contrary to public perception', 174 residents of Dublin 4 'supported our plans and only 140 objected'. Letters of support included one from Monsignor Brendan Byrne, parish priest of Dunne's home town of Tullow, who suggested that the 37-storey tower was 'a great architectural beauty in itself' and would become a 'distinctive landmark' for Ballsbridge. Other friends from Carlow who wrote in support of the scheme included a local councillor, a solicitor and three estate agents.

Hot on the heels of the planners' decision, scale models of the proposed development, including a 1:500 model of the rejected tower, were put on display in the ex-Berkeley Court Hotel to drum up public support for it. The PR offensive also featured a one-to-one interview with Dunne on the *Marian Finucane Show*, in which the ebullient developer claimed to have 'lots of options' available for his 'superprime asset' if the current plans were not approved; these included keeping the hotels open, building an exclusively residential scheme, leaving the site vacant or 'turning it into a parking lot'. Neither did he think it was 'nuts' that property in Ballsbridge was dearer than in Paris. Though income from D4 Hotels wasn't covering Mountbrook's interest payments on its bank loans, the company's gearing was 'on the very conservative side . . . We have large borrowings, but we have large assets. We have 20 acres of land in the centre of Dublin . . .'

Seán Dunne was on a mission when he sat down that Saturday morning in March 2008 for his interview with Marian Finucane. Around the country, ears pricked in some amusement as the famously confrontational and litigious developer conducted a startlingly uncharacteristic, public love-in with Dublin city planners ('the unsung heroes of Ireland') as well as bankers and political parties of every hue (despite a long, very public association with Fianna Fáil grandees) while portraying himself as the poor, hard-working country-boy-made-good, anxious to facilitate continued access for other commoners to his gilded Ballsbridge acreage. Ulster Bank's Paul McDonnell was mentioned as the man who 'walked through the door of my office' at nine o'clock on a Friday night and produced a letter for €275 million to close the deal, 'just like that'. Having taken only a few days to assess the risk, by all accounts, the directors of Ulster Bank must have had mixed feelings about the views of other noted swashbucklers on Dunne's Ballsbridge venture. 'All I can say is, he's a brave man,' commented Jim Mansfield. 'I don't think he can make money on it,' said Owen O'Callaghan. Former supermarket mogul Ben Dunne (no relation) opined that it was 'loony stuff . . . Egos are dangerous things.' But Seán Dunne noted that: 'There was 2 per cent between the [top] four bids.' In other words, if he was being reckless, he was not alone.

Asked by Marian Finucane about his Fianna Fáil connections, he said he had never attended a Fianna Fáil meeting in his life. But why would he bother when he could have Bertie Ahern to himself on a private flight to Cardiff – courtesy of DCD builders – for the Heineken Cup final in 2002? The inclusion of Dunne and his wife, Gayle Killilea, in the coveted VIP seating plan for Ahern's historic address to the British houses of parliament at Westminster in May 2007, to mark the continued progress of the Good Friday agreement, also raised eyebrows, given the absence of such distinguished figures as former Taoiseach Albert Reynolds, who had played an important role in the peace process. The couple were also among the invited guests for Ahern's address to the US Congress in April 2008. Dunne built the expansive home near Naas, Co. Kildare, of former Finance Minister Charlie McCreevy, who, together with Ahern, was invited to Dunne's wedding party on the *Christina O* – although they both, perhaps wisely, declined to attend. Anto Kelly, a prominent member of Ógra Fianna Fáil, is his personal assistant, and former party fund-raiser Des Richardson is also said to be a close associate. According to an *Irish Times* report in April 2006, the guests at a lunch hosted by Dunne and Killilea at their home included 'half of the Cabinet'. And of course it was in the infamous Fianna Fáil tent at the Galway Races that Dunne first met Killilea or, as he told Marian Finucane, 'landed the jackpot'.

Part of Dunne's spin on the *Marian Finucane Show* was that by opting to apply for a mixed-use scheme on a site currently zoned as residential, he was aiming to preserve access to the heart of Ballsbridge for ordinary folk who could never hope to pay €2 million for one of his apartments. If the nay-sayers got their way and he was left with planning permission for apartments only, well: 'We leave the gates and the railings, so only the people who live there can ever cross that site again. And that would be the most economic option . . . In Ballsbridge, residential is higher yield.' Other developers would quibble with that, arguing that there is a limited market for high-end apartments, even in Dublin 4. In any event, 'The Dunner' had managed to insinuate the repellent image of a vast, smug, seven-acre fortress colonizing the old heart of Ballsbridge, replacing the social bonhomie of Jurys and the Berkeley Court. But of course, as he told Marian, the fusty old hotels made no sense either. 'The profitability of those hotels – stated to be highly profitable – combined was €6 million. On an asset of €380 million, that does not make sense . . . Better buildings that contribute more to the Irish economy make more sense,' he said. 'It's a prime, prime site. To get seven acres in the middle of Dublin, and to be able to think about doing something special, is a major attraction.' It was notable that his projected yields of €1,400 to €1,500 per square foot for apartments had fallen well below the average €2,000 per square foot widely thought to be the original target.

The indulgence shown by the planners towards high-rise schemes for the area ran counter to 20 years of planning policy designed to take the heat off Ballsbridge and encourage developers to build in the inner city and other areas needing renewal. Kieran Rose himself was senior planner for the south inner city, where the fruits of his excellent work can be seen in places like Cork Street and Dolphin's Barn. Michael Stubbs, assistant city manager in charge of planning, was another key figure in that area's rejuvenation. Now the planners – along with chief planning officer Dick Gleeson and city manager John Tierney – were prepared to roll out the red carpet for high-rise buildings in Ballsbridge, while denying that this had anything to do with the extravagant prices paid for sites. In the changed economic circumstances we are facing, particularly in the property sector, the consequences of such a 'policy' were clear: developers would gravitate towards high-value areas like Ballsbridge, leaving the parts of Dublin that really need renewal high and dry.

Even in the Digital Hub area of the Liberties, which Dublin City Council sought to brand as a new 'SoHo' (borrowing yet again from New York), developers were forced to scale back overly ambitious high-rise schemes: Cavan-based P. Elliott and Company's plans for a mixed-use development of offices, apartments, retail, restaurant and community facilities on the north side of Thomas Street were turned down by An Bord Pleanála in October 2007. Overturning Dublin City Council's approval for the scheme, which included a 16-storey tower, the board cited its 'unsatisfactory design and layout', saying this would cause 'undue overlooking and overshadowing' and detract from the setting of the 18th-century Guinness Windmill, which is a protected structure. This was a big blow to Elliott, which had paid the state around €64 million in cash and kind for the site, and its high-flying architects, HKR. With a contractual obligation to provide work space for digital media companies, Elliott came back in March 2008 with plans for a more modest development of two office blocks, five and eight storeys high, on the Thomas Street frontage and a half-promise that more would follow on roughly the same scale.

Manor Park Homebuilders (MPH), which had nearly won an exclusive contract in 2004 to develop the Digital Hub, was in an even worse pickle, having paid the state around €54 million – again in cash and kind – for a site of 2.5 acres on the south side of Thomas Street. Much more egregious than Elliott, MPH chose to ignore an architectural guide by the Office of Public Works (prepared when it was selling the two sites), which advocated mixed-use developments in buildings no higher than four to five storeys generally, punctuated by a number of narrow 'point blocks' eight to ten storeys high. Instead, it put forward plans for what the *Irish Times* described as a 'mini-Manhattan' of tower blocks rising to 53 storeys. Unveiled in June 2006, this astonishing scheme by de Blacam and Meagher Architects would have included a 33-storey digital media office block three metres higher that the Spire in O'Connell Street as well as a range of other high-rise buildings laid out around a central landscaped open space on a podium four storeys above street level. 'There's no reason why Dublin shouldn't have a skyline like that, with slender towers sticking up to great heights,' said Shane de Blacam. 'The history of architecture is about putting buildings on a hill' – a reference to the fact that Thomas Street is on a ridge. John Moran, MPH's development director, also defended the scheme, pointing out that the city council's planners had granted permission for a 12-storey tower in nearby School Street: 'So we're not the ones who broke the glass.'

But the planners baulked at the sheer scale of what was being proposed, and so did An Bord Pleanála. Noting that the site was 'located in the historic core of Dublin city' and fronted on to one of its oldest streets in a designated conservation area, the board referred to the council's policy of protecting the skyline of the inner city, in line with the criteria on building heights set out in a study conducted by design consultancy DEGW. It said MPH's scheme would contravene these policies because of the 'excessive height of the proposed buildings generally' and the 'unsatisfactory nature and form' of the podium, which would be 'significantly out of character with the area'. Thus chastened, the architects and their clients came back with revised plans, under which the tallest building was reduced to 26 storeys – and the council's planners were even dubious about that. In the end, following P. Elliott's example, MPH sought permission in March 2008 for 8,000 square metres of digital media office space in buildings no higher than eight storeys. Three months earlier, the company's founder, Joe Moran, and his family borrowed heavily to buy out DCC's 49 per cent stake in MPH for €181 million – a tribute to the success of their home-building business.

Back in Dublin 4, there was at least one precedent that was of little help to Seán Dunne and others with high-rise ambitions. In 2004, billionaire telecoms tycoon Denis O'Brien sought planning permission for a 26-storey residential tower on the former BizQuip site in Donnybrook, between the garda and fire stations. The glazed cylindrical tower, designed by de Blacam and Meagher as a landmark on the axis of Morehampton Road, was turned down by Dublin City Council, and An Bord Pleanála upheld this decision in March 2005. In its ruling, the appeals board said the 'excessive height and scale' of the proposed tower would 'result in an unduly prominent and overbearing form of development that would . . . detract from the established character, appearance and amenities' of a predominantly residential area. Even after O'Brien obtained a favourable decision from the council on plans to build a six-storey office block on the site in April 2007, this was overturned by An Bord Pleanála, which said it would constitute 'an incongruous and jarring element in the townscape' because of its 'height, mass, bulk and prominent location and contextual relationship to adjoining buildings'.

Not surprisingly, there was an avalanche of appeals over what was being planned for Ballsbridge – more than 20 in the case of Ray Grehan's scheme and an unprecedented 127 on Seán Dunne's. Unusually, well over half of these were in favour of the scheme (including one from the developer himself, seeking to reinstate his 37-storey tower and other elements of the scheme omitted by the planners); but the rest were vehemently opposed to it. The fact that so many individuals and residents' associations – admittedly in well-heeled Dublin 4 – were prepared to pay the required objection fee of €220 demonstrated the determination of citizens to overturn the city council planners' decisions. Like many others, An Taisce referred to the Dublin City Development Plan 2005–2011, which the elected members had formally acknowledged as 'the appropriate framewok for planning and development in the area' when they rejected the LAP for Ballsbridge in June 2007. In deciding to approve both Dunne's and Grehan's schemes, An Taisce said, the planners had 'totally disregarded the provisions of the Development Plan'. Not only did the two schemes 'materially contravene' the plan, they were also 'massively in excess of the plot ratio considered suitable' for these sites and would have 'seriously negative impacts on the architectural setting of Ballsbridge and its environs' as well as on the residential amenities in the area. The truth is that there was no substantive planning policy on which the decisions could be grounded.

What happened in Ballsbridge was planning in a vacuum or, more aptly, a bubble.

9. Breaking Away

The story is told that when Seán Mulryan was 20 and on an apprenticeship training course, he helped to build a little wall around a neighbour's new bungalow at Oran, Co. Roscommon. The neighbour took one appalled look at the result and spoke his mind, whereupon young Mulryan packed his tools and flounced off to Tallaght. And the rest, of course, is history.

'From the age of 18, I always knew I wanted to start my own business,' he told the *Sunday Telegraph* in 2006. 'It took a lot of hard work to get the money to do it. In the end, I started the company when I was 26.' The company was Ballymore Properties and the year was 1982, a time of political insanity, mass emigration, soaring interest rates and unsympathetic banks. For Mulryan, it meant seven-day working weeks and unrelenting stress. 'There were lots of times when I would pace the floorboards at night because we were in a difficult financial situation and, at that time, the economy was bad and the market very difficult.' It is said that to finance his first development, he and his wife Bernie (a local girl from Cloonfad) sold their home and moved into rented accommodation, as well as trading in their cars for cheaper models. But that was then . . .

Now, Mulryan is one of the most prominent Irish developers in Britain – and one of the handful of Irish developers and investors whose international ventures are more significant than their interests back home. In 2004, Ballymore Properties was marketing the 29-storey Ontario Tower, at New Providence Wharf, in London's Docklands as the city's tallest residential building. It has since broken this record with Pan Peninsula – two towers of 40 and 50 storeys containing more than 700 apartments. Within walking distance of Canary Wharf, both developments were designed for Mulryan by international architects Skidmore, Owings and Merrill

(SOM). Ontario Tower has an iconic quality, with its neon-lit tilted elliptical top, and the 260 apartments share a health spa, gym and swimming pool with the adjoining eight-storey Radisson Hotel. Pan Peninsula will be even more opulent, with a private cinema, 24-hour concierge, a holistic fitness centre, a 'signature restaurant' on the waterside and a cocktail bar on the 50th floor for residents and guests. It also complies with British planning policy to make maximum use of 'brownfield sites', rather than building in green fields as we do in Ireland; if all of its 700 apartments had been two-storey houses, they would cover 50 acres.

When sales opened for Pan Peninsula in November 2005, viewers were taken out by motor launch to the marketing suite – a glass box in Millwall Dock with full-scale show flats. Nearly 200 apartments were booked by the end of the day at prices ranging from £230,000 to £1.6 million, mainly by bonus-rich bankers and lawyers seeking city pads. Small studios of 30 square metres – nothing more than a pied-à-terre, however cleverly designed – were fetching £230,000. A year later, the sale of a vast 2,400-square-metre penthouse on the 50th floor for £7 million broke records for the Docklands area, putting it on a par with more exclusive parts of London. 'The place to live above all others' was the marketing slogan for this scheme, and its scale dwarfs all the toytown stuff built on the Isle of Dogs in the late 1980s. The final phase of the development at New Providence Wharf is the 42-storey Quebec Tower, containing 300 apartments that will be 60 per cent more energy efficient than those built 10 years earlier – with shops at ground level.

Mulryan's personal worth is said to be around €350 million and his Ballymore group of companies reckoned to have some €20 billion in assets. Now, instead of two old bangers, he and his wife have a pair of Sikorsky helicopters (which by all accounts he uses like a bus service) and a private jet at their disposal, as well as the services of a full-time chauffeur when they must resort to the roads. It takes about five minutes to fly Mulryan by helicopter from his stunningly restored home at the 250-acre Ardenode Stud – full of art, sculpture and thoroughbreds – in Ballymore Eustace to his equally exquisite offices in 18th-century Fonthill House, Lucan. He also has a suite of offices near the Shelbourne Hotel, in Huguenot House. The Sikorsky is just as likely to take him to London, where he spends much of his working life near the most potent source of his wealth: vast swathes of the east London docklands that he bought after the 1990s British property crash. (Mulryan speaks modestly of 'lucky timing'.)

Mulryan was personally involved in the campaign to bag the 2012 Olympic Games for London, donating nearly £1 million to the organizers and another £250,000 for the Trafalgar Square celebrations that greeted its success in July 2005. This was not an entirely disinterested gesture; as the second-largest landowner in the Docklands, close to where the Olympics will be staged, Ballymore stands to benefit. The company's land bank would have the scope to provide up to 15,000 apartments as well as commercial, retail and leisure facilities before the games get under way. As a result of his involvement in the Olympic campaign, Mulryan has been a visitor to 10 Downing Street and counts such luminaries as Sebastian Coe among his friends. The story is told that, on his Downing Street visit, he was met by Gordon Brown, who asked him what the odds were that London would get the Olympics. Mulryan said he was in touch with consultants in Ireland, and their view was that, while it wasn't looking too great, things could shift very fast. The 'consultant' turned out to be bookmakers Paddy Power.

Industry observers are not surprised that the man reared as one of a family of seven in a little thatched cottage near Castlerea, and who did not receive a third-level education, has conquered the British establishment. 'He has handled the transition from small builder to international property developer in an almost seamless way. He has style and a genuine interest in quality,' says someone who tends to see developers with a jaundiced eye. He has made no secret of his closeness to Fianna Fáil or his long-time friendship with Charlie McCreevy. Former Fianna Fáil TD Marian McGennis has been listed among the beneficiaries of his political donations, and Mulryan was a guest at the wedding of the daughter of former senator and quintessential Fianna Fáil insider Eddie Bohan. It was revealed at the Planning Tribunal that Ballymore made payments totalling £50,000 to the late Liam Lawlor between 1994 and 1998.

Mulryan is invariably described as generous to charities and to those down on their luck; modest, gentle and even understated, despite hiring Debbie Harry of Blondie to perform at his 50th birthday, a champagne-only bash for 400 guests in a marquee of glass, and having Bono as an overnight guest (on a settle bed) at the old restored thatched cottage in Oran, with no modern comforts other than underfloor heating. He sponsors several county GAA teams and is believed to have a stake in Sunderland football club, although he is not a named member of the Irish consortium that owns the club. His great passion is horse racing; in 2006 he told the *Daily Telegraph* that he owns 'somewhere between fifty and a hundred' racehorses.

We can no longer even guess what he's worth because Ballymore Properties switched to unlimited liability status in 2005, and the last publicly available accounts are for the year ending March 2004. In that year, as Colm Keena reported in October 2007, 'turnover was €205 million, compared to €65.8 million a year earlier and €134 million in 2002. Approximately two-thirds of turnover was in the UK, and one-third was in the Republic. Pre-tax profits were €18.3 million, up from €3.5 million in 2003. Net assets were €126.8 million. Stock, including development properties and work in progress, was €509 million. The accounts show that stock is one item that was growing steadily upwards. The 2003 figure was €352 million and the 2002 figure €173 million.' Mulryan's UK holding company, Ballymore Properties Holdings Ltd (which is still required to file accounts), had a turnover of £62 million sterling in the year to March 2006, down from £136.8 million the previous year, and net assets of £90 million. The group owed £50 million to other group companies and £328 million to its bankers – AIB, Anglo Irish Bank, Fortis

Bank, Irish Nationwide, Württembergische Hypothekenbank and Royal Bank of Scotland. The accounts also state the group made charitable contributions of £468,780.

Although London is the epicentre of Ballymore's activities, the company is also active on the Continent. The first phase of its Eurovea International Trade Centre in Bratislava, involving an investment of €270 million, will provide the Slovak capital with its largest retail, leisure and entertainment complex as well as 23,000 square metres of offices, 250 apartments and a five-star Sheraton Hotel with over 200 bedrooms. Based largely on its track record in London's Docklands, Ballymore won the prize of developing Eurovea on the site of Bratislava's redundant riverside port on the Danube, and the 36-acre site is being raised by two metres to protect it against future flooding. Irish architectural firm Murray O'Laoire is involved in designing the complex, along with SOM, Bose International and Respekt, and the aim is to create a whole new city quarter between Bratislava's historic core and its emerging central business district. Ballymore is even building a metro station on the site, with no guarantee that a metro system will actually materialize, and there will also be hydrofoil services to Eurovea from Budapest and Vienna.

Ballymore paid more than €25 million in 2004 for a parcel of properties on Wenceslas Square in the centre of Prague, including several listed buildings, and this holding has since been expanded for a scheme of offices, apartments and shops on a new pedestrian street linking up with Na Prikope. One very particular project involves the conversion of a major historic building in the city centre into the Kempinski Residences, offering 75 apartments with five-star services to business executives, on long- or short-term rentals. In Budapest, Ballymore has its sights on developing another shopping centre, office complex, leisure facilities and housing, to be built on a large site close to the city's main railway station and parliament.

In September 2007, Mulryan bought Kudamm Karree, an established complex of shops, restaurants, offices and apartments occupying nearly five acres between Kurfürstendamm and Uhlandstrasse in the centre of Berlin, from Fortress Capital for €155 million. He described it as a 'stunning location in the very heart of one of the great cities of the world', which Ballymore would 'further develop and enhance'. What the acquisition demonstrated, he said, was 'our global focus on large-scale, mixed-use developments in prime locations'.

Ballymore has been involved in major commercial developments in Ireland, notably the Whitewater shopping centre in Newbridge, Co. Kildare (in partnership with Seán Dunne), as well as huge housing schemes in Greystones, Co. Wicklow, and Pelletstown, where it has worked closely with Joe O'Reilly's Castlethorn group. Whitewater was conceived in 2000 as a 'mass market fashion centre' that would appeal to shoppers in a wide catchment area, from Meath to Waterford, in competition with Blanchardstown, Liffey Valley and The Square in Tallaght. Opened in April 2006, the centre contains 32,000 square metres of retail space, with Debenhams, Marks & Spencer and H&M as the anchor tenants. It also has a food court that seats 500 and parking for 1,700 cars, but no sign of a promised multiplex cinema, much to the anger of local people.

Mulryan and Dunne also got together to pursue plans for up to 1,500 apartments and houses on a 108-acre site at Charlesland, at the southern end of Greystones. To open up the area for new housing, they joined with other developers in making an offer to build an interchange on the N11 at Kilpedder and a new bypass for Delgany. Their vehicle, Zapi Properties, provided a 20-acre site for playing fields and, last December, agreed to provide sites for a range of community facilities, including a school, garda station and enterprise centre, in return for Wicklow County Council rezoning part of the Charlesland site for yet more housing and a money-spinning district shopping centre. In Bray, Ballymore has been markedly slow in developing another shopping centre and multi-storey car park on Florence Road. Though it got full planning permission to go ahead in 1998, the acquisition of adjoining properties meant lodging revised plans for the 9,000-square-metre Florentine Centre, and these were finally approved in April 2007; it is now to be scaled down due to the recession.

Meanwhile, Ballymore is working side by side with Castlethorn to develop what planners hope will be exemplary housing schemes with a good mix of amenities and community facilities at Pelletstown, an elongated development area near Ashtown with a commuter rail station at each end. Mulryan is also active in and around the former Baldoyle racecourse site in north Dublin. Veteran property developer John Byrne had assembled some 500 acres in the area, but failed to get it rezoned and then sold an option on the land to Pennine Holdings, in which lobbyist Frank Dunlop had an interest; Pennine later sold it to Mulryan for £1 million. Mulryan bought the land for around £30 million in the mid-1990s, and managed to get it rezoned for housing, on the basis that the DART had been extended to Malahide and the area was now well served by public transport. In 2004, he sold a 50 per cent stake to Menolly Homes for €95 million. Ballymore also sought to persuade South Dublin County Council to rezone almost 100 acres of land at St Edmundsbury, near Lucan, for a major housing scheme under which 70 per cent of the 1,600 units would qualify as 'affordable housing' and, in return, the company would transfer 184 acres to the council for inclusion in the Liffey Valley linear park. But the Affordable Homes Partnership, a government-sponsored quango, withdrew its support for this scheme in April 2008 after being informed by Ballymore that it had failed to win favour with most of the councillors.

Mulryan's London interests are not confined to Docklands. Ballymore is undertaking the restoration of Spitalfields Market, a 1.5-acre covered space that was once going to be flattened by British Land, as a bustling mixed-retail attraction similar in style to Covent Garden. Much bigger schemes, with Foster + Partners as master planners, include the prospect of building some 3,000 apartments on 20 acres of land in Vauxhall, on the south bank of the Thames, and the redevelopment of Bishopsgate goods yard in the City for a cluster of high-rise office buildings, with a landmark tower up to 200 metres high. In Manchester, Ballymore is planning to build Europe's tallest apartment block on a site adjoining Piccadilly Station and Ashton Canal Basin, having acquired a 95 per cent stake in this ambitious project in September 2007. The 60-storey Piccadilly Tower, designed by architects Woods Bagot, would be flanked by two other buildings in a major mixed-use development comprising nearly 700 apartments, a hotel and retail units at street level.

The scale of what Mulryan is building or planning in London Docklands is quite staggering: projects in the pipeline include Baltimore Wharf, another major residential development currently under construction at Millwall Dock, and Arrowhead Quay, two SOM-designed office blocks of 16 and 24 storeys in the Millennium Quarter near Canary Wharf. The company is also active in Birmingham, where its Snow Hill scheme in the heart of the city will include 55,000 square metres of offices, a 44-storey tower containing 332 apartments and a 170-bedroom Westin Hotel with bars, restaurants and retail units laid out around five new public spaces. An 11-acre brownfield site on Leamouth Peninsula, where the River Lea meets the Thames, is to be transformed into a 'thriving, fine-grained, arts-inspired riverside community' with 1,837 new homes, a primary school for 300 pupils, arts and community centres, and 'flexible workspace for creative industries', all designed by SOM. Described as 'one of the most exciting regeneration opportunities in east London', this brave new world will also include crèches, shops, restaurants, cafés, landscaped plazas, communal gardens, a waterfront promenade and a dramatic pedestrian/cycle bridge linking the peninsula with Canning Town. Not far away, Ballymore owns four sites around the Royal Docks, including Minoco Wharf (beside the Thames Barrier) where it is building 4,000 new homes as well as more than 20,000 square metres of offices and retail and leisure facilities, anchored by a new London marina. Due for completion in 2009, it has been described by agents as 'surely one of London's most exciting pre-Olympic developments'. And in line with its 'Sustainable Ballymore' programme, the scheme will have its own combined heat and power (CHP) plant as well as taking out all excavated materials by boat and using dock water for heating and cooling systems.

The Isle of Dogs, where Ballymore has its London offices, is another major focus of development activity. In 2005, when British Waterways sought partners to develop a 17.5-acre site at nearby Wood Wharf, once part of West India Docks, the successful bidder was a joint venture formed by Ballymore and Canary Wharf Group. An earlier master plan approved by Tower Hamlets Borough Council envisaged a mixed-use scheme of 325,000 square metres of office space, rising to 35 storeys, and 1,500 apartments. But the development consortium came back in November 2007 with a revised master plan by Rogers Stirk Harbour + Partners for a higher-density scheme with at least two iconic towers, one comprising offices and the other residential, as well as a glazed 'high street' lined with bars, restaurants, cafés and retail units. According to Damian Wisniewski, chief operating officer of the Wood Wharf Partnership, this £4 billion development 'has the potential to deliver thousands of new jobs, some of the best-located and designed affordable housing in the country and a world-class waterfront'.

Also on the Isle of Dogs, Dublin-born architect Angela Brady and her partner Robin Mallalieu have designed an 'exemplary' affordable housing scheme for Ballymore at Mastmaker Road. It will provide nearly 200 new homes, with a range of environmental features including solar panels, heat pumps, rainwater recycling and façades designed to minimize heat loss as well as amenity spaces, wildlife habitats and even a five-a-side football pitch on the roof of its community centre. Similar environmental concerns are evident in Ballymore's plans for a 12-acre site in Brentford, west London, between the area's high street and the Grand Union Canal. The scheme prepared by BDP Architects for what Ballymore calls 'Brent Waterside' includes more than 1,000 new homes, along with shops, restaurants, cafés and leisure facilities. It will replace Brentford's canal boatyard site, which Mulryan's vehicle, Geronimo Ltd, bought in 2006 for its canalside location, demonstrating once again that he is 'addicted to water'. But with property values falling both in Ireland and Britain, the time came to take stock, and even retrench. For 12 years, Ballymore had been a major sponsor of the Irish National Hunt Festival at Punchestown, close to Mulryan's Ardenode Stud, and the company marked its 25th anniversary by adding a new handicap hurdle with a prize fund of €220,000. However, with 50 of its own staff being laid off as the recession began to bite, it cancelled a 500-seat celebratory lunch at the Irish Grand National in March 2008; one of those laid off was the economist Dr Peter Bacon, Ballymore's director for Europe.

The most sensational property coup of the Celtic Tiger era was the acquisition, for £750 million, of the Savoy Hotel group in London by a syndicate of wealthy Irish investors led by former tax inspector Derek Quinlan. Almost unbelievably, and in one fell swoop, such totems of the British Establishment as Claridge's, the Connaught and the Savoy itself fell into Irish hands; the country that once supplied the navvies for Britain's building industry had now taken over some of its most prestigious bricks and mortar. The Irish group had fought off competition from one of the world's richest oil sheikhs, Prince Al-Waleed bin Talal of Saudi Arabia, to snatch this glittering prize, which also included Simpson's in the Strand, a London landmark where the best of British food has been served from silver-domed trolleys since 1828. When news of the deal broke in April 2004, Rory Purcell, the Savoy Group's Irish-born engineer, had the tricolour run up on the hotels' flagpoles. 'It was put up without my knowledge,' Quinlan himself later told *Prospect* magazine. 'But I cried. My poor father, who was in the Irish Army, would have loved to have seen this.'

Quinlan managed to arrange funding for the acquisition in just three weeks, although the amount of bank debt reportedly left him 'leveraged up to his eyeballs', at least initially. It also earned him the title 'Property Personality of the Year' at the annual Irish Property Awards. Just over six months later, his Quinlan Private syndicate offloaded the Savoy and Simpson's to billionaire Prince Al-Waleed for £230 million, thereby making an almost immediate return of about £30 million on its investment, and leaving the syndicate still in control of the Berkeley, Claridge's and the Connaught – all flagships at the super-luxury end of London's buoyant hotel market. The full membership of the syndicate has never been revealed, but it is known to include property developer Paddy McKillen. Derek Quinlan was no stranger to hotels either, having put together another syndicate of wealthy investors to purchase the vulgar-plush Four Seasons Hotel in Ballsbridge in 2000 – amazingly, for less than it cost to build. The Nollaig Partnership, which included AIB chairman Dermot Gleeson and property developer Mark Kavanagh, was able to use mouth-watering state incentives for hotels to write off 100 per cent of its €76 million capital cost against income tax. Quinlan also led a syndicate that invested as much again in renovating the spectacular Secessionist-style Gresham Palace in Budapest as a five-star hotel, lining up the Toronto-based Four Seasons group to run it; located right in front of the Chain Bridge over the Danube and with panoramic views from its upper floors, the hotel has been rated as one of the best in Europe.

In 2007, Quinlan Private acquired the Jurys Inn chain of 200 budget hotels in Ireland and Britain for £1.16 billion, making P. V. Doyle's family even richer, as well as a 44 per cent stake in the Marriott Group's 47 hotels in the UK, in partnership with Israeli investor Igal Ahouvi; this deal was worth an estimated €1.6 million. QP has ambitious plans to expand the Jurys Inn chain, particularly in central and eastern Europe, with plans to build it up to 75 hotels within five years.

Back in London, Quinlan's newly formed Maybourne Hotel Group, in which Paddy McKillen has a 40 per cent stake, was carrying out a splendid refurbishment of the Connaught and planning a major extension to the rear incorporating 33 rooms, a swimming pool and health spa, at an overall cost of £80 million. In November 2007, the group announced that it would invest £250 million in renovating Claridge's and the Berkeley. For

Claridge's, this will involve the addition of two floors incorporating 40 new guest rooms and suites – replacing an ugly accretion of air-conditioning units and other plant at roof level – as well as a gym, health spa, swimming pool, conference facilities and shops, all designed by London architect Michael Blair, who was also responsible for the Connaught. In both cases, Blair is working with the fabric of these listed buildings, renovating and embellishing them in a sympathetic way.

This contrasts with the plans for the Clarence Hotel on Wellington Quay in Dublin, in which McKillen and Quinlan are partnering U2's Bono and The Edge to transform it into a much larger, super-luxury establishment. The plan of starchitect Norman Foster is to demolish all but the quayfront façades of a group of protected structures and replace the lot with a contemporary hotel oversailed by an elliptical flying saucer-style roof. Maybourne wouldn't have got away with that in London, which probably explains why Richard Rogers could only be let loose on the Berkeley, a much more recent hotel dating from 1972.

By 2005, Ireland had overtaken the US as the largest foreign investor in British commercial property, accounting for almost 22 per cent of the total inflow of £12.3 billion that year, according to chartered surveyors DTZ. 'The lion's share of overseas investment is dominated by five sources: Irish, US, Middle East, German and Dutch capital,' its *Money into Property* report for the year said. 'Irish investors represented the largest single source of cross-border capital into the UK with more than £2.7 billion of purchases in 2005; this figure mirrors the levels achieved in 2004, which stood at £2.8 billion.' In a breathless April 2005 report on 'the Celtic reconquest', the *Economist* highlighted Quinlan's high-profile UK and continental acquisitions, the £186 million purchase of the Belfry golf course and hotel in the West Midlands by the Co. Cavan-based entrepreneur Seán Quinn, and the purchase of Unilever's London headquarters by an investment vehicle backed by John Magnier and J. P. McManus, two Irish tycoons best known for their Coolmore racehorse stud.

Quinlan Private was reported to be managing assets worth

more than €11 billion in Britain, mainland Europe and the US by 2007. In Britain alone, the company's investments would have accounted for a large proportion of the €11 billion invested by Irish people in commercial property there between 2001 and 2006, according to an estimate by leading estate agents Savills. Another €4 billion of Irish money was invested in property elsewhere in the world during that period. To highlight this dramatic flight of capital from Ireland (and in the hope of persuading the government to make it more attractive to invest at home) the Construction Industry Federation noted in November 2007 that €3 out of every €4 invested by Irish people in commercial property was going abroad.

By then, however, there were clear signs of a slowdown in the UK commercial property market, with analysts warning that the value of office, industrial and retail investments could fall by as much as 11 per cent in 2008, but Derek Quinlan remained upbeat about London's long-term prospects. In May 2007, in partnership with Glenn Maud, a low-profile British investor, Quinlan bid for the HSBC office tower on Canada Square in Canary Wharf, but the pair were pipped at the post by Spanish group Metrovacesa, which paid a whopping £1.09 billion for the building; in terms of value, it was the largest property transaction in British history. Just a few months later, Royal Bank of Scotland accepted the partnership's offer of £1 billion for a 42-storey office block on Canada Square, occupied by Citicorp. This time, it was a personal investment by the man who has been dubbed the Sheikh of Claridge's; it had to be, because when he tried to round up other investors, nobody responded. Being the reticent man that he is, Quinlan didn't disclose how much of his £500 million share in the investment was equity and how much was debt, but he may have to sell other assets if he wants to hold on to the Citicorp building. The bank would certainly have been regarded as a blue chip tenant – at least until April 2008, when it posted a whopping loss of over $5 billion for the previous three months.

In July 2007, the same month as the Citicorp deal, Quinlan Private got together with a German property company, FOM

Real Estate GmbH, to buy a completed office and hotel complex on Bleichstrasse in the centre of Frankfurt for the relatively trifling price of €60 million. Over 40 per cent of its 7,300 square metres of office space had already been let, and one of Quinlan's partners, accountant Thomas Dowd, said: 'We believe the asset represents a good opportunity to acquire well-located office space in the recovering Frankfurt office market. As the property is increasingly let, it will return a very attractive yield for our investor group.' A week later, the company and Norwegian shipping and real estate firm Borgestad more than doubled their money by selling a shopping centre they had just jointly developed in the southern Polish city of Gliwice for €128 million to Deka Immobilien. But the new German owners retained Quinlan Private Golub, a joint venture with Chicago-based Golub and Company, to run the huge Forum Centre, which has 43,000 square metres of retail space anchored by a Carrefour hypermarket. According to Golub's website, it has 'developed, owned or managed more than 30 million square feet of commercial space and 50,000 multifamily units within the United States and abroad, with total value exceeding $4 billion'. Golub first ventured into central and eastern Europe in 1989, 'focusing on markets that were part of the soon-to-collapse Soviet bloc' in partnership with GE Capital to develop offices in Poland, the Czech Republic, Hungary and Russia. In early 2006, GE Capital was replaced by Quinlan Private, which Golub hails for its 'real estate experience in western and eastern Europe, strength in originating, structuring and financing a diversified portfolio of prime assets, and established partnerships with international banking groups for the syndication and placement of private equity'.

Derek Quinlan was born in 1948. His father was an army sergeant from Kerry who managed to send young Derek to Blackrock College, where he played second row on the school's rugby team – it's still one of his passions – before going on to study commerce at UCD. After training as an accountant with Coopers and Lybrand, he became a tax inspector in the investigations branch of the Revenue Commissioners at a time when it had few enough powers to probe the affairs of Ireland's tax cheats. He turned the experience to his advantage back in the private sector, setting up a tax advisory firm with colleague Kieran Ryan from accountants John Wood in the mid-1980s. They started out counselling wealthy people on how to invest their money in tax-efficient ways – for example, by availing themselves of government incentives for the construction of hotels or multi-storey car parks. But Quinlan wasn't content merely to provide advice, and he set up his own operation in 1989; the real game in town, as he saw it, was to assemble syndicates of high-net-worth individuals – 'Hinwis' – for property deals and become a big player himself.

His new vehicle, Quinlan Private, took off during the boom years as the number of Irish millionaires grew almost exponentially and there simply weren't enough investment opportunities at home. According to a 2005 profile in *Property Week*, Quinlan 'is described as a man of few words "who takes your money, goes off and doubles it"'. At the height of the boom, he used to boast that he had a core group of 50 investors on whose behalf he could write a cheque for €10 million apiece without prior authorization, because he had made so much money for them in previous deals. The only downside, clients complain, is that 'once you put your money in, it can be tempting not to take it out again. Derek will always have another investment opportunity up his sleeve to put it in.'

Quinlan Private was typically taking 15 per cent of the value of each transaction, to cover its own expenses and make handsome profits. However, as *Property Week*'s Deirdre Hipwell discovered, Quinlan 'does not fit the brash, go-getting stereotype of the new breed of Irish property investor. People who know him say he is a cultured and generous man; that he enjoys the company of women "but is not a womaniser"; and that he never swears nor maliciously gossips, citing the adage that "it's a long road and you never know when you are going to meet people again".' His clothes are tailor made, he collects classic Irish art, and he is 'a bit of a gastronome', dining at the two Michelin-star Patrick

Guilbaud restaurant in Dublin as well as being partial to a good barbecue in the summer.

A lot of the work done by Quinlan Private goes into sourcing potential deals and undertaking due diligence on any potential investment property as well as wider demographic and market research on the country or area where it's located. And the fact that QP always puts its own money in whatever project it is placing is a source of confidence to other investors. So it is little wonder that so many of Ireland's new rich, including *Riverdance* originators Moya Doherty and John McColgan, have beaten a path to its opulent offices on Raglan Road in Ballsbridge. 'The stately building is home to 40 staff,' *Property Week* reported. 'In the private car park, only the latest Mercedes and BMWs are to be seen. The interior reflects a more contemporary side of Quinlan with its hardwood floors, modern art, and spacious hallways and boardrooms. Quinlan runs a tight ship and not much seems to happen without his say-so.' His two principal partners, accountant Thomas Dowd and solicitor Peter Donnelly, are instrumental in Quinlan Private's self-professed 'efficient deal structuring'. They have since been joined by Corkman Olan Cremin, formerly head of private banking at Irish Intercontinental Bank; he became QP's chief executive officer in July 2005, with a mandate to 'drive the growth and further direction of the business in line with ambitious expansion plans'. Reflecting its global reach, the company also has offices on Upper Brook Street in London's Mayfair and East 64th Street in New York (near a town house which Quinlan himself bought for the show-stopping price of €22 million) as well as staff in Budapest, Prague and other cities in central and eastern Europe where deals are being done or developments under way.

It is a measure of how times have changed that Derek Quinlan's first investment – an ice-cream outlet in The Square shopping centre in Tallaght, of all things – has mushroomed into a complex, multifaceted international business with four divisions: Quinlan Private Capital, Quinlan Private Client Services, Quinlan Asset Management and Quinlan Private Golub – managing an ever-growing portfolio. Assets include the freehold title to all of the buildings on an island block of nearly three and a half acres in Knightsbridge 'incorporating the entire prime retail frontage between the world-famous department stores of Harrods and Harvey Nichols', as the company's website says. The freehold was acquired in May 2005 for £530 million, with Abu Dhabi's royal family among the disappointed underbidders. Exactly a year later, another consortium put together by QP paid more than €300 million for the Diagonal Mar shopping centre in Barcelona, comprising 87,000 square metres of retail space on three levels; it was 'the largest ever single property transaction in Spain'. Also in 2006, the company paid €60 million for a 50 per cent stake in Palac Flora, a shopping centre and office complex in the affluent Vinohrady district of Prague, and €172.5 million for the bustling Neumarkt Galerie, on Cologne's main shopping street. It has also developed the first major shopping centre in the Czech city of Most and acquired a prime shopping and office property on Munich's Maximilianstrasse, which it describes as 'the premier luxury retail street in Germany', for €270 million. It's certainly a long way from Tallaght.

Central and eastern Europe have accounted for at least 40 per cent of QP's deals, at least in terms of number. Bulgaria's first international-style shopping centre, the Mall of Sofia, opened its doors with great fanfare in June 2006. A year before the opening, QP in partnership with GE Real Estate had acquired a 50 per cent stake from its Israeli developers for €37 million and later bought them out altogether, to reap a rent roll from 130 shops, an office block and a 12-screen multiplex cinema that boasted the first 3D-IMAX theatre in south-eastern Europe. The QP–GE joint venture spent nearly €100 million in June 2007 to buy the Mall of Plovdiv, the country's second largest city, from the same Israeli developers, CCI and Aviv-Osif, and has new shopping centres under construction all over Bulgaria.

QP made a profit of €34 million in September 2007 when it sold the Charles Square Centre office and shopping complex in Prague to German property group Commerz Grundbesitz for

€90 million, having bought it in 2003 for just €56 million. Other investments include the Four Seasons and Yasmin hotels in Prague, two office blocks in the Warsaw Financial Centre, and residential developments such as Oakland Park near Warsaw and Sunny Hill in Prague, aimed at expatriates and the indigenous 'new rich'. And then there's Lake Balaton, the largest inland lake in Europe, where QP has got into bed with Hungarian real estate company SCD on a €450 million plan to develop hotel-spa resorts, marinas and 'premium' holiday camps, all aimed at reviving Balaton's flagging fortunes. SCD got its hands on 23 properties around the lake in 2005 when public campsites dating from the communist era were offered for sale by the Hungarian government as part of its privatization programme. Totalling 427 acres, the scale of this development opportunity was too much for SCD to undertake on its own, so QP was brought in as a partner in November 2007, with its Golub division acting as project manager. The first phase, with an estimated price tag of €53 million, is to include a luxury hotel dedicated to wine and gastronomy, a 'beauty hotel', and the refurbishment of a run-down camping and holiday resort – some or all of which may qualify for aid under the EU's tourism programme.

In April 2006, QP set a new world record when it sold the Four Seasons Hotel in Milan to Italian tycoon Giuseppe Statuto for €220 million just two years after acquiring it, at a profit of €43 million. It wasn't the profit that made this a record, but the sale price, which put a value of €1.86 million on each of the hotel's 218 rooms. Towards the end of the same year, QP bought Eircom's new headquarters, then under construction near Heuston Station, for over €190 million in a sale-and-leaseback deal with the telecom company's subsidiary, Osprey Property Ltd. Eircom, which had just been taken over by Australian investment fund Babcock and Brown, was expected to invest the capital sum in developing Ireland's relatively limited broadband network. Another acquisition in 2006 was the Irish property portfolio of Brussels-based KBC Asset Management for €105 million – €12 million more than the guide price quoted by Jones Lang LaSalle, which described it as 'ideal for an individual or syndicate looking to acquire a ready-made portfolio of prime properties' with an annual rent roll of €4.4 million. The package included Oldbrook House, an ugly but well-performing office block on Pembroke Road, three other office buildings in Lower Mount Street (part-let to Fianna Fáil), Donnybrook Main Street and East Point business park, as well as a retail building occupied by Argos at Queen's Old Castle on Patrick Street in Cork and the Hitachi warehouse on Clonshaugh Industrial Estate near Dublin Airport. In the US, Quinlan Private Golub paid $100 million for a 30-storey office block on West Washington Street in downtown Chicago, closing the deal – in typical Quinlan style – within a month of shaking hands on it.

Dermot Desmond has also spread his wings, even as far as Barbados, where he jointly owns the exclusive Sandy Lane resort along with bookmaker and fellow tycoon J. P. McManus; it was voted runner-up 'Best Caribbean Spa' in a *Condé Nast Traveller* poll in February 2008. But his biggest single coup was the sale of London City Airport for £750 million in October 2006. Built by Mowlem and opened in 1987, it was bought by the billionaire financier less than 10 years later for not much more than £25 million. Since then, the once-struggling airport has quadrupled passenger numbers and aircraft movements, particularly private jets; Desmond was clever enough to see that an airport in close proximity to Canary Wharf was bound to grow by leaps and bounds, in line with the old property adage 'location, location, location'.

Developer David Arnold has also been buying property in London, through D2 Private – a boutique version of Quinlan Private's emporium of riches – including a pair of office blocks in Mayfair for nearly €88 million in 2006. Other Irish investors in the British capital include Dublin solicitor Brian O'Donnell and his wife, Dr Mary Patricia O'Donnell, who spent £250 million on office blocks in the vicinity of Canary Wharf. Also active in the same area is Glenkerrin's Ray Grehan, whose most recent acquisition (for £32 million) was a site close to the Hilton Docklands Hotel, which is owned by Sloane Capital, the investment vehicle for horse racing duo J. P. McManus and John Magnier, along with Aidan Brooks, a young Limerick developer. It was Sloane Capital that ...elled out £170 million for Unilever House, on Victoria Embankment, in a sale-and-leaseback deal with the multinational conglomerate in September 2004. As the *Irish Times*'s Barry O'Halloran reported in January 2005, Magnier and McManus are also among the 140 Irish shareholders in Barchester, the biggest private nursing home chain in Britain, with over 10,000 beds in 163 locations throughout the country; another is their long-time buddy Dermot Desmond.

In 2004, when the flood of new Irish money into London started to be widely noticed, Mick Whelan of Maplewood Homes paid £160 million for Victoria House, a newly refurbished office block on Bloomsbury Square, mostly let to the UK Competition Authority. He came back again a year later with another £160 million to buy 70 Gracechurch Street, in the City, a modern office block let to XL Capital, with Marks & Spencer on the ground floor; the vendors were a group of investors including Manchester United boss Alex Ferguson. Another Irish consortium fronted by KPMG Corporate Finance bought CAA House on Kingsway, headquarters of Britain's Civil Aviation Authority, for just under £100 million. At one stage, it looked as if the iconic Lloyds Building in the City would also fall into Irish hands, but a deal fronted by Garrett Kelleher to buy the block for £236 million fell through after faults were found in its fabric. In the same year, Paddy McKillen's Clarendon Properties, in partnership with a group of private investors assembled by Anglo Irish Bank, bought the Royal Opera House's portfolio of 16 shops in Covent Garden for €114 million. Clarendon, a joint venture by Belfast-born McKillen with former Power Securities chief Tony Leonard, owns the Powerscourt Centre in Dublin and the Savoy Centre in Cork. In 2006, it bought an office building on Boston's Franklin Street for €134 million, adding to holdings in the city that already included another block on State Street and the

Borders bookstore. The Anglo Irish-Clarendon group made a profit of €70 million in March 2007 when they sold on the Royal Opera House portfolio to property investment company Capital and Counties for €188 million.

It was quite a coup for Paddy McKillen, a native of Belfast who started working as a teenager in DC Exhausts (the family business) before branching out on his own or in partnership to pursue such diverse money-spinners as Apollo One discount stores, Beshoff's fish 'n' chips shops, Captain America's restaurants, Champion Sports, Tower Records and Wagamama. He got into property development in the late 1980s, with Johnny Ronan as his partner, and their joint ventures included the Peppercanister office block on Mount Street Crescent, the Treasury Building on Grand Canal Street and the Temple Bar Hotel. But McKillen's biggest scheme in Dublin was the Jervis Centre, which he developed in partnership with Pádraig Drayne through Stamshaw Ltd; with its car park cheaply stacked on the upper levels to avoid having to excavate below, this retailing machine was an immediate success when it opened in 1996 with an offering of British chain stores such as Argos, Boots, Dixons and Debenhams. 'It was either extremely lucky timing or a well-thought-out, forward-seeing move – but it was probably a bit of both,' according to Aidan O'Hogan, of Hamilton Osborne King. 'When the centre was being built, McKillen often showed up unexpectedly to see how work was progressing. One night he appeared at 3 a.m. to watch concrete being poured at the site,' Neil Callanan reported in the *Sunday Business Post*, quoting a source as saying that McKillen 'nearly killed himself' doing the Jervis Centre. But then, as another said, 'if you wanted to caricature him it would be as a non-drinker who has a reputation for working 24/7' and 'gets a kick' out of making money. By 2005, his stake in the centre was valued at more than €225 million.

McKillen had picked up the the three-acre Jervis Street Hospital site for less than £5 million in 1994, and secured some £60 million in development funding from a consortium of banks, including Anglo Irish, ICC and IIB; by 2000, the annual rent roll from some 330,000 square feet of retail space in the Jervis Centre was £6.5 million. McKillen got another bargain in 1997 when he bought a run-down terrace of early-19-century buildings on South Ann Street for £4 million, in partnership with solicitor Ivor Fitzpatrick; it included McGonagle's, which had been a thriving music venue for many years. Their company, Briarglen Ltd, originally intended to develop a 'boutique' hotel on the site, but there was a glut of hotel space under construction at the time – fuelled by lucrative tax incentives – so the pair decided to go for an upmarket retail scheme instead. An impressive double-height basement was let to restaurateur Patrick Guilbaud's son Charles, who set it up as a trendy brasserie called Venu (it was the last interior to be designed by the late Arthur Gibney), while the street level is anchored by fashion retailers Guess and Hackett as well as an Aveda beauty salon run by Whetstone.

McKillen was the first Irish developer to discover Vietnam. He owns several investment properties and development sites in Ho Chi Minh City (formerly Saigon), where he now spends quite a lot of his time. Other developers have been more wary of Vietnam, believing that it has been slow to underpin foreign investment in property with a cast-iron legal framework. Like his old pal Johnny Ronan, McKillen owns buildings in Paris as well as in London, where he paid £25 million for a retail investment on the less tawdry stretch of Oxford Street in 2004. Four years later, the Cosgrave Property Group followed his lead by paying almost £44 million for the nearby Zara shop adjoining Jubilee House, which it already owned, to create a land bank of just over an acre east of Oxford Circus. In 2007, the company shelled out a lot more – £86.5 million – for additional retail premises on Oxford Street, housing River Island. Blackrock International Land, a plc established by fruit importers Fyffes, has also been acquiring assets in Britain, mostly in joint ventures with other property companies, including office blocks in Milton Keynes, industrial buildings in Bristol, Basingstoke and Southampton, development sites in Edinburgh, Glasgow and London, and investment properties in Belgium and the Netherlands. Owen

O'Callaghan also turned up in London, buying a site on the fringe of his Liffey Valley partner's Grosvenor Estate in Mayfair and developing a smallish office block for £7 million.

The most deliciously ironic Irish acquisition in the British capital was surely the Conservative Party's headquarters on Smith Square. God knows what Tory 'grandees' thought when they heard the news in February 2007 that the building they once lorded over had fallen into the hands of a man from Buncrana, Co. Donegal. Harcourt Developments, controlled by Pat Doherty, had bought the 1920s building for just over £30 million. 'There is a kind of little buzz about it. You think, "Isn't it amusing?" There is a little touch of irony,' crowed one of his fellow directors, former broadcaster Mike Murphy, on RTÉ radio. 'It has to be said that the Conservative Party didn't come with it – they have left.' Indeed, the party had been trying to find a buyer for the property since 2004, after moving to modern offices in Victoria Street, and the deal with Harcourt meant that the Tories freed themselves from a burden of debt. Lord (Cecil) Parkinson, former chairman of the party, recalled that 'a distinctly shabby feel' was cultivated by the then treasurer Lord McAlpine to encourage donors to be generous. 'McAlpine had a huge hole in the carpet when you went into his room. A benefactor offered to give him a new carpet. But McAlpine said: "Over my dead body. That hole is worth thousands",' the *Daily Telegraph* reported. Just over a year later, Harcourt sold the original building for £25 million, but retained the adjoining office block, which it had acquired as part of the deal. Pat Doherty had his own connections with the British establishment: one of Harcourt's directors (in a non-executive capacity) is Andrew Parker Bowles, former husband of Camilla, Duchess of Cornwall. As John Burns revealed in the *Sunday Times*, Parker Bowles and Doherty also share the distinction of having had their portraits painted by veteran artist Lucian Freud, who titled his respective pictures of them 'The Brigadier' (with Parker Bowles in full regalia as a brigadier general) and 'Man from Donegal'.

Harcourt Developments moved on, and Pat Doherty had other

irons in the fire, mainly overseas. 'We decided a couple of years ago to start spreading our interests because the boom here is not going to last for ever,' Murphy told the *Sunday Business Post* in 2006. 'The recent auction results show that there is somewhat of a cooling . . . a little bit of a slowdown coming.' He has a stake in Harcourt and a keen interest in what the company is doing. 'We have built up a significant land bank in Britain. We are about to start a business park in Riga in Latvia and we are building a hotel in Montenegro,' he said. But that wasn't all. Harcourt was also building a financial services centre in the Channel Islands and a golf resort in the Bahamas, had 600 acres of beachfront land in Tobago and was leading the Titanic Quarter urban regeneration project in Belfast. Murphy couldn't be drawn on what all of this might be worth. 'There isn't a figure, but we are talking about a hell of a lot of money . . . You need to be very good friends with the banks, let's put it like that.'

Although Doherty was ranked in 32nd place on the *Sunday Times* list of Ireland's richest people in 2006, with an estimated net worth of €338 million, Harcourt's accounts for the year showed that, while the value of its investments increased to €281 million, bank debts rose to more than €345 million and the company owed other creditors a further €36 million. Its biggest scheme at home is Park West, between Cherry Orchard and the M50/N7 interchange, where Doherty bought 150 acres of land in the early 1990s when land prices were relatively low. He later added substantially to Harcourt's holding in the area with acquisitions including the former Semperit tyre factory and 100 acres adjoining the City West business park, snatched from under the noses of its developers, Davy Hickey Properties. What set Park West alight in its early years of development was an 'enterprise zone' designation by Ruairí Quinn, then Minister for Finance, which meant that investors were able to write off 100 per cent of the capital costs against their tax liabilities. As a result, the first phase raked in £100 million for Harcourt even before it was launched by Taoiseach Bertie Ahern in October 1999 as the future 'nerve centre of the IT industry in Ireland'. But predictions that 25,000 people would be employed there by 2003 proved very wide of the mark; it barely reached 7,000. As the market for out-of-town office space took a nosedive, Doherty switched to building hundreds of apartments – and made more money selling them.

Harcourt put a lot of effort into landscaping and public art at Park West, under the patronage of Mike Murphy, who used to present RTÉ's *Arts Show*. Specially commissioned sculptures include works by Orla de Brí, Ronan Halpin, Patrick Coughlin and, most dramatically, Angela Conner, whose *Wave* is reputedly the tallest mobile sculpture in Europe. Much less evident is the artistic, or even architectural, input into other parts of Harcourt's extensive property portfolio in Ireland, which includes the shopping centres in Donaghmede, Dundalk, Galway, Portlaoise and Letterkenny, Co. Donegal, where Pat Doherty has a holiday home overlooking Lough Swilly. Other interests include the Parkway shopping centre in Limerick, which he bought in 2006 for over €50 million, the Carlton Redcastle Spa Hotel near Moville, on the Inishowen peninsula, and the Lough Swilly Bus Company.

Harcourt gained its foothold in Belfast's Titanic Quarter by bidding £46 million for the development rights in 2003 – way above what local developers were prepared to tender. 'No one locally had bid more than £25 million. Everyone thought at the time they had paid far too much. Now it looks like a real bargain,' a rival developer told the *Financial Times* four years later. Described by the *Irish Times* as 'the biggest property development ever undertaken in Northern Ireland', with an end value exceeding £1 billion, it covers an area of 185 acres in the city's former shipyards and was expected to take up to 20 years to complete when planning permission for the first phase was granted in 2005. This will provide nearly 14,000 square metres of office space, 460 apartments and a 120-bedroom hotel on Queen's Island, where the *Titanic* itself was built by Harland and Wolff.

Other opportunities beckoned much further afield. In October 2006, Mike Murphy revealed that Harcourt was planning a $1 billion development on a 16-acre site in Las Vegas, to be called

Sullivan Square. 'This is not for tourists,' he told the *Sunday Business Post*. 'This is not a casino. This is for people who are moving to Las Vegas. It is for residents, so we believe it will appeal.' (That was long before Nevada was named by the BBC in June 2008 as 'America's foreclosure capital'.) Six months later, Doherty bid successfully for the rights to develop the Royal Oasis golf resort and casino in the Bahamas, much to the delight of its then prime minister, Perry Christie. The 427-acre resort near Freeport, Grand Bahama, had been devastated by Hurricane Frances in September 2004, and David Buddemeyer's Driftwood Group had simply walked away, 'leaving massive liabilities behind them and no assets to settle them or their severance obligations to their employees', as Christie told an election rally in April 2007. Doherty had to negotiate with New York investment bank Lehman Brothers, which held a big mortgage on the property, and then find new operators, finally doing a deal in February 2008 with Foxwoods, which claims that its casino in Ledyard, Connecticut, is the largest in the world. Harcourt also had good credentials in the Bahamas, where it was already developing a gated high-rise condominium scheme called Suffolk Court, in Freeport, and everyone knew about its five-star Carlisle Bay resort on the Caribbean island of Antigua; apparently, it was while on holiday there with his second wife, Rosemary, that Andrew Parker Bowles got a phone call from Camilla telling him she was finally going to marry Prince Charles.

Also spreading his wings is Menolly's Séamus Ross, who paid more than €30 million in January 2006 for a nine-acre site on the bank of the Vistula in Warsaw, occupied by a disused coal-fired power station. The €200 million development is to include up to 800 apartments, 15,000 square metres of office and retail space, and a 160-bedroom hotel. His old pal and fellow Longfordman Mick Whelan was even more adventurous, with plans by his family investment company, Moritz, to invest €500 million in the development of 10 shopping malls in Romania through a local consortium called Mivan. Branded as Tiago Malls, each of these mini shopping centres is to contain 25–30,000 square metres of retail space, and Mivan aims to have them all completed by 2010.

South Africa has also attracted new Irish money, which is not surprising given that Cape Town receives some 40,000 visitors from Ireland every year, mainly for mid-winter breaks. Seán Dunne has left his mark with the four-star Lagoon Beach resort at Milnerton, on the Cape's 'gold coast', with views of Table Mountain. Completed in 2005, the 250-room hotel has two swimming pools, a health spa and an 'original Irish pub'. Dunne hosted breakfast at his Shrewsbury Road home for Nelson Mandela during his last visit to Ireland and also mucked in with more than 300 Irish volunteers (including Anglo Irish Bank chairman Seán Fitzpatrick) to build new homes for shack-dwellers in the Cape Flats, under the leadership of Dublin developer-turned-philantropist Niall Mellon. Cork-based Howard Holdings, run by soft-spoken Frank Gormley, has also been drawn to Cape Town, where its Eurocape Investments offshoot is developing 180 apartments at Mandela Rhodes Place, just off Parliament Square. Gormley was 'slightly bemused by some of the negative reactions to the project' when it was first launched, South Africa's *Property* magazine reported in April 2008. 'People told me no one would want to live in the city centre because of the crime,' he says. 'I walk around here all the time, night and day.' And the proof of the pudding is that most of the apartments have already been sold – and Eurocape is also planning to invest in the heart of Johannesburg, where the crime problem is much worse.

But no Irish developer has such soaring international ambitions as Garrett Kelleher. Because what he's planning to build, since he acquired 'the best piece of dirt in Chicago' (a site of just over two acres on Lake Shore Drive), would be the tallest building in North America. The proposed Chicago Spire, with its 150 storeys of luxury apartments priced from $750,000 for studios at the lower levels to over $40 million for duplex penthouses with panoramic views over the city and Lake Michigan, would be nearly twice as high as the twin towers felled on September 11th,

2001. 'When completed, it will be home to 1,194 individual residences along with a range of amenities that will rival any in the world including health and fitness facilities, children and teen areas, cinema and private dining facilities, business centre, retail and restaurant services as well as a library, wine cellar and humidor [for Cuban cigars, presumably],' according to a March 2008 statement from Kelleher's company, Shelbourne Development.

Savills, the agents selling London's most extravagantly expensive apartment blocks, Candy & Candy's One Hyde Park, were engaged to market the Chicago Spire apartments 'in every major capital in the world'. The main reason for this international campaign was that overseas investors were more likely to find the prices attractive due to the plunging value of the once-mighty US dollar. Certainly, Kelleher could not rely on the depressed market in Chicago: in mid-2007, there was such a glut of condominium units in the city that even Donald Trump had scaled down his Trump International Hotel and Tower just a few blocks away. Trump, who once cornered the market for chutzpah, still had 200 condos left to sell and the last thing he needed was competition from a much more dramatic and better located skyscraper. 'In this climate, I would not want to build that building. Nor would I want to live in that building,' he said dismissively of Kelleher's project, suggesting that it could become a terrorist target. But one blogger probably hit the nail on the head: 'Donald Trump is such a little baby. He can't stand the idea of another skyscraper overpowering his new skyscraper.'

Kelleher himself was no stranger to Chicago. Son of a dentist, he had first come to the US as a teenager to play competitive tennis; he later attended Trinity College, Dublin, where he was on the tennis team. When he returned to Chicago in the mid-1980s, he worked in the contract painting business and later as a property developer renovating old buildings as loft-style apartments. After returning to Dublin in 1996 to set up Shelbourne Development and cash in on the Irish boom, he has gone from strength to strength, with projects such as the former *Irish Press* offices on

Burgh Quay, the former Virgin Megastore on Aston Quay and the former Department of Justice offices on St Stephen's Green as well as investments in Brussels, Paris and London. One of its buildings in Dublin is the ghastly Apollo House office block on Tara Street; it has a joint-venture agreement with the Office of Public Works to replace it and the even more ghastly Hawkins House with something that's bound to be much better.

In Chicago, Kelleher knew Christopher Carley, president of the Fordham real estate company, which specialized in luxury condominium schemes in and around The Loop, and would have heard news of his astonishing proposal to build a slender spiralling 'supertall' tower by Santiago Calatrava at the confluence of the Chigago River and Lake Michigan. First announced in July 2005, this was a refinement of the Spanish starchitect's 54-storey Turning Torso tower in Malmö – but much taller and twistier. The Chicago tower, then called the Fordham Spire, was to be 115 storeys high, topped by a spire that was likened to 'a giant candle fit for a cake'. The overall height of 2,000 feet (606 metres) would outstrip both the Sears Tower – Chicago's tallest, at 1,450 feet (439 meters) – and New York's planned Freedom Tower on the World Trade Center site, which Daniel Libeskind insisted should have the historically resonant height of 1,776 feet (538 metres). The Fordham Spire was also intended to beat Taipei 101 in Taiwan, the current world record holder at 1,670 feet (506 metres), although Carley realized there would be no chance of besting SOM's Burj Tower in Dubai, then under construction, which aimed to be the highest no matter what.

'Chicago was America's birthplace for modern architecture, nurturing the genius of Louis Sullivan, Daniel Burnham, Frank Lloyd Wright and Mies van der Rohe,' he said at the launch. 'We want to carry that tradition into the 21st century and give our city a masterpiece by one of today's indisputable geniuses.' Chicagoans were thrilled by Calatrava's scheme; for nearly a decade, they had been bristling over no longer having the world's tallest building, since the construction of the Petronas Towers in Kuala Lumpur in 1996. But previous plans to reclaim this prize had foundered because the putative developers couldn't raise the money – and Carley ran into the same difficulties within a matter of months, forcing him to cut his losses by selling the site at 400 North Lake Shore Drive.

That's when Garrett Kelleher entered the picture, and he was so smitten by Carley's bold vision that he immediately bought the site, aided by the ever-accommodating Anglo Irish Bank. As he told a public meeting at the Daley Bicentennial Plaza in January 2007, 'I was over here on other business and the opportunity arose to buy this site. I looked at it on a Wednesday, and we closed it the following Thursday. Did no due diligence on the site whatsoever. I decided the site spoke for itself.'

A large and mostly enthusiastic crowd had turned up to hear him present the project which, even by then, had been substantially changed. The hotel element originally envisaged by Carley had gone and the tower was now to contain just luxury condos. What's more, the candle-like spire had been omitted and the number of storeys increased to 150, which made the building much more chunky; instead of tapering towards the pinnacle of 2,000 feet, the latest version had a flat top, which made it look more like a liquorice twizzler than a graceful spire. And, while planning permission had been granted for what Carley had in mind, Kelleher and his team were still in discussions with the planners about the proposed revisions.

'Donald Trump step aside. Garrett Kelleher may be the most confident developer on the face of the Earth,' wrote Chicago architecture watchdog Lynn Becker in a blog on the public meeting. 'Kelleher, chairman of Dublin's Shelbourne Development, talked like a man who has Chicago's Department of Planning in his back pocket. "The plan is to get on site as soon as possible," he told the crowd. "The plan is to order caissons within weeks." This despite the fact that the final project hasn't even been formally presented.' It also emerged that there was no firm estimate of how much it would cost to build, not even a ballpark figure, and that Kelleher intended to start constructing the foundations 'without any pre-sales', as he said himself, and, apparently, without any serious research of the local market; it was seen instead as a 'global product'. But what exercised Blair Kamin, the *Chicago Tribune* architecture critic, was that people had not been shown perspective images or renderings of the latest version of the scheme. This led to what Becker called a 'politely testy exchange' between him and Kelleher, at the end of which the Irish developer said, 'We're just getting on with it . . . We're not really being led by media or journalists.'

The very next evening, however, Kelleher invited Kamin to join him and Calatrava 'for a discussion of the project's evolution', as Becker reported, with the architect pulling a small brown snail shell from his pocket to show how (as Kamin wrote) its 'whirring, rhythmically complex, softly coiling shape' was his inspiration for the top of the tower. Thus, in the final version, a tapering profile was reinstated, to general public approval. Chicagoans also liked Calatrava's evocation of his spire as 'an imaginary smoke spiral coming from a campfire near the Chicago River lit by Native Americans indigenous to the area', though most people likened it rather more prosaically to a giant drill-bit, which is not a wildly inappropriate metaphor. Either way, its designer said without any hint of humility that his spire 'will become the centrepiece of the cityscape and part of Chicago's identity'. Such hyperbole was music to the ears of Mayor Richard J. Daley Jnr., who gave the project his personal support, endorsing it as 'environmentally friendly'; a lengthy entry in Wikipedia notes that the Chicago Spire's 'sustainable engineering practices' would include rainwater recycling, intelligent building management systems, the use of river water for cooling and even 'ornithologically sensitive glass' to protect migratory birds. Its unique selling point was that it would be the world's tallest residential tower – important in Chicago, where the second-city mentality is quite similar to Cork's – and the whole project was shown off in a dramatic 'fly-around' video, with excerpts from Dvorak's New World Symphony as its soundtrack.

Kelleher's pledge of $6 million towards the development of DuSable Park, in front of the tower, also helped smooth its passage through the various planning and zoning hoops. And so, after he had made a full public presentation of the project to residents of Streeterville in the immediate vicinity, the final design was approved by Chicago City Council in May 2007. Just six weeks later, the developer showed his mettle by moving construction equipment on to the site in preparation for drilling more than 30 concrete and steel caissons deep into the bedrock to support the structure that would rise above a six-storey underground car park.

Blair Kamin of the *Chicago Tribune* was disappointed to learn that the 'shag-a-delic, Austin Powers-like studio apartments' (officially called 'gallery units') had been selling so well that more were to be added to the mix. He also flagged a front-page story in the previous day's *New York Times* reporting that the US economic slump was likely to delay key parts of the Frank Gehry-designed, $4 billion Atlantic Yards project in Brooklyn, saying this was sure to cause a shudder among property developers elsewhere. 'The news comes as people in Chicago architecture and real estate circles speculate on whether developer Garrett Kelleher, who has already started building the foundations of the Santiago Calatrava-designed Chicago Spire, will be able to complete the project.' As Lynn Becker put it, 'There's no disputing that Kelleher has guts, but the question for the city remains: For a billion-dollar project, is it enough to be a faith-based initiative?'

The Chicago Spire international roadshow was supposed to start in September 2007 but didn't get under way until January 2008 with a glittering Dublin launch in Fitzwilliam Square attended by Hollywood star couple Liam Neeson and Natasha Richardson. A vast marquee had been erected in the middle of the square for the party, to which 500 movers and shakers had been invited; inevitably, they included several developers curious to find out what all the fuss was about. Calatrava himself was present, immaculately dressed as usual and exuding enthusiasm, brilliance and charm; he was the real star of the show. More than 1,000 people visited the four-day exhibition and it was extended for two weeks 'due to this unprecedented level of interest', according to Shelbourne. 'Our sales team has been busy writing contracts every day,' said Dominic Grace, head of residential development at Savills and leader of the global sales campaign. It was the same story in Singapore, where more than 800 visitors attended the first Asian launch in March at a two-day event in the Four Seasons Hotel. 'The response to the Chicago Spire was overwhelming,' said Michael Ng, local managing director of Savills. 'Our sales team was busy signing deals throughout the exhibition.' Again, apartments were said to have sold 'briskly', aided by the strength of the Singapore dollar against the weak US currency. Savills would not disclose any figures, but sources told the *Straits Sunday Times* that 'about 30 units were sold, mostly one- and two-bedroom flats that averaged $1 million each'. Not much, in other words. Next stops for the roadshow were Kuala Lumpur, Hong Kong, Shanghai, Moscow and Johannesburg, and a number of destinations in Europe.

Chicago is not New York and has been described as the most American of US cities. The notion that Hinwis in other parts of the world would queue up to buy luxury apartments there was probably fanciful. Having kept mum about sales figures for nearly six months, Shelbourne announced in June that 352 units – less than 30 per cent of the total – had been sold.

There were much less risky ways for Irish people to invest some of the loot they had made from the boom. Fermanagh-born Seán Quinn, who has amassed a vast fortune from making cement and concrete products, glass and plastics, as well as selling insurance and running a chain of hotels and pubs in Ireland, had more money to spend than most. Quinn hit the headlines in January 2004 when he paid €145 million for the Hilton and Ibis hotels in Prague; it was the biggest single property deal in Czech history. A spokesman for the Quinn Group indicated that it would be ploughing a total of €1 billion into similar investments outside the state: 'Our view at this point in time is that there is more value to be found abroad,' he told Barry O'Halloran of the *Irish Times*, in an obvious reference to Ireland's overheated property market. In 2006, the Prague Hilton – a huge tinted glass box by the Vltava River – underwent a €50 million refurbishment, which included the addition of a conference hall with a capacity of 1,400.

By then, Seán Quinn had been named by *Forbes* magazine as one of the 300 richest people in the world, with an estimated net worth of €2 billion. The weathiest man in Ireland by a long shot, he had started out in 1973 with a sand and gravel business, as he recalled in a very rare public appearance at a conference at the Slieve Russell Hotel in March 2007; his remarks were recorded by Tom Lyons, the business editor of Newstalk Radio, and published by the *Sunday Business Post*. 'I only had two hundred quid, so I had to be very careful with what I did with it,' he said. 'I wasn't able to do very much with it, and the banks weren't overly keen to give me too much money. So we just had to flooter about with bits of lorries and secure the deeds of the farm to get a few pound from the bank,' Quinn told his audience. 'I suppose I was always very greedy. Whatever we had, I was never happy with what we had. And I was always looking for new opportunities. If it was sand and gravel, it was blocks and ready-mix; if it was blocks and ready-mix, it was roof tiles and the floor.' He started buying pubs in Dublin because every time he came to town the pubs were always full and he said to himself, 'This has to be a simple business because they're charging a ransom for the beer; they get paid for the beer before they pay Guinness . . .'

Now Seán Quinn is investing a lot of his wealth abroad: 'Two-thirds of the money is probably going to go into developing in eastern Europe and India, and probably one-third of it into expanding the Quinn Group,' he said. His acquisitions have been quite breathtaking in their scale and geographical spread. Apart from The Belfry in Warwickshire, with its three golf courses on 550 acres, they include the Crowne Plaza Hotel in Cambridge, the Holiday Inn in Nottingham, the Sofia Hilton, the Krakow Sheraton, the Leonardo business centre and Ukraina shopping mall in Kiev, the 20-storey Kutuzoff office block and Caspiy shopping centre in Moscow, and the Prestige shopping mall in Bahçeşehir, on the outskirts of Istanbul. In addition, according to its own website, the Quinn Group is developing a chemical plant in Leipzig, a glass factory in Cheshire, a vast logistics and warehousing park on the outskirts of Kazan, 800 km east of Moscow, and DIY superstores for StroiArsenal in 10 Russian regional cities, starting with Yekaterinburg.

'We always followed the bigger return,' the man at the helm of this peculiarly Irish conglomerate told his captivated audience at the Slieve Russell conference. 'Some people go for a safe return – we go for a bigger return. We don't like the 3, 4 or 5 per cent returns. Any of the properties we ever bought, we only bought them on the basis that we'd receive a 10 per cent return, with one or two exceptions. In Prague, Bulgaria, Poland, Russia, wherever we went, we always got those double figures . . . We've a team of people out in India now and we have about 40 people altogether involved in property development in eastern Europe, Russia and India. There are fantastic opportunities there . . . the growth there is unbelievable.'

He also explained that the properties in central and eastern Europe are not part of the Quinn Group, but personal investments by him and the members of his family. 'The company has become extremely wealthy and my family has become extremely wealthy. What we are trying to do now is to involve our management and staff in different schemes, and in some of our property investment in China, India and Russia. I don't think it's good if it all goes to the Quinn family. We were too greedy for too long, and we are still too greedy. But the intention would be over the next few years to leverage a lot of profits towards our management and staff. That's my final ambition in the business world.'

It isn't just Irish millionaires and billionaires who are investing their money overseas – ordinary people are also doing it, though in smaller numbers since the onset of the global credit crunch and the Irish recession. Mostly, they were buying Noddyland villas or holiday apartments on the Spanish *costas*, but the shrewder investors were looking to central Europe. When the Bertie Boom was in full swing, an expat real estate company called Lexxus, which specializes in finding suitable investments in this region, was arranging up to 250 deals a year for Irish people looking for property in the Czech Republic. 'Most of the investments are being made by individuals or small syndicates, who are buying apartments in Prague by remortgaging their Irish homes,' as Jamie Smyth reported in the *Irish Times* in 2004. 'The classic profile of an investor is someone between the ages of 35 and 55 who has made a bit of money and who does not want to put more money into the Irish market.'

What drew them to central Europe was the the prospect of capital growth rates of 15–20 per cent, fuelled by expectations of an EU-driven property boom as well as the relative affordability of apartments compared to Dublin. 'KeyInvest, a Polish-based property investment company founded by Irishman Pádraig Coll, will have invested €200 million in Poland by mid-2004, much of which has been invested by high-net-worth individuals and syndicates from the Republic,' Smyth wrote. 'People who previously invested in Britain are now looking for good yields in Poland, where there are a lot of good-quality offices available,' Coll told him. 'Good-quality apartments in Poland also cost a quarter of the price of a Dublin apartment.' Other factors included easier access to finance at low interest rates and the opening up of new air services between Ireland and central European countries – partly due to the influx of Poles, in particular, working in Ireland and taking regular trips home to visit relatives. At the time, Czech banks were offering mortgage rates of under 3 per cent while Irish investors could also raise low-interest loans from AIB's Polish bank, Bank Zachodni WBK, which also set up a Polonia Property Fund targeted at Irish Hinwis. Everyone was on the pig's back, or at least so it seemed at the time.

Four years on, alarm bells were ringing, none more ominously than the International Monetary Fund's prediction in April 2008 that the banking crisis sparked off by uncontrolled 'sub-prime' lending in the US could end up costing the global economy almost \$1 trillion – or \$145 for every man, woman and child on the face of the Earth. Most of the world's men, women and children had nothing to do with causing the crisis, which was brought about by banks, hedge funds and dealers in financial derivatives who failed to recognize the risk in the proliferation of financial products based on high-risk loans.

Many of the more grandiose schemes being planned by Irish developers in Britain and elsewhere are likely to be postponed until the economic outlook improves; some may be dropped altogether. Those who have invested in China, notably Treasury Holdings, took comfort from the fact that the IMF still expected its economy to continue growing by more than 9 per cent annually in 2008 and 2009 – even after years of spectacular growth – while India's was likely to exceed 8 per cent annually in the same period. Thus, as Paul Tansey noted in the *Irish Times* in April 2008, while western economies had been 'battered and bruised by a series of shocks and surprises the emerging economies are powering ahead'.

Epilogue: Bust

There was an end-of-empire feel about Donal Caulfield's party on a Monday night in April 2007 to launch Belmayne, the developer's 2,200-unit scheme on Malahide Road, in north Dublin. Rival developers turned out in numbers at Belmayne's futuristic marketing suite, where TV garden designer Diarmuid Gavin, flouncy interiors consultant Laurence Llewelyn-Bowen and a slew of scantily clad young women rubbed shoulders with property journalists and gossip columnists. Former Liverpool footballer Jamie Redknapp and his wife Louise provided the minor celebrity glitz, champagne flowed late into the night and many pondered Caulfield's full-colour, full-on, racy marketing strategy in a – whisper it – shaky market.

The highly provocative media campaign created by multinational advertising agency McCann Erickson had become a major talking point, involving such steamy antics as a couple lying astride one another on top of a kitchen island unit, and another with two young ones lounging on a bed, minimally clad, with a male hoving into view behind them. Truly, the days of the tastefully drawn artist's impression to sell property were over. Then again, so were the nights when panicky young couples had to queue in their sleeping bags and throw themselves at the mercy of smug young agents for the privilege of chaining themselves to a property bubble.

Now a property developer had to do what a property developer had to do: try harder. And Caulfield, a likeable, UCD-educated civil engineer and former captain of the under-21 Wexford Gaelic football team, was doing just that. In his diamanté-studded Roberto Cavalli beanie, Versace jeans, *Matrix*-style coat and shades – worn indoors and out – he was bling incarnate, light years from the traditional country developer. So, naturally, there would be no Portakabins masquerading as marketing suites at Belmayne. The 'information centre' alone cost €2 million to build, the 10 olive trees planted around it contributing €60,000 to the bill. The coffee dock, smart sofas and *Star Trek*-style computer-generated images were an invitation to linger and sample a 'lifestyle' for sale, one graced with the interior designs of Llewelyn-Bowen, gardens by Gavin and a flashy chauffeur-driven Chrysler Voyager to ferry viewers the short distance to the show apartment.

It would be easy to dismiss Caulfield – a former European kick-boxing champion with a former Miss-Universe-entrant-turned-civil-engineer for a fiancée, who drives a red Ferrari and paid many millions for the Belmayne site while still in his thirties – as a flash git. In fact, he is one of the most straight-talking men in the business, his wild oats well and truly sown. In conversation, he returns repeatedly to the importance of 'first principles' – strong design, sustainable developments, schools and parks – and regards more experienced developers such as Joe O'Reilly, Gerry Gannon and Garrett Kelleher very highly. 'But they're in a different league. They have 15 years on our company, the guys who bought the land in 1998/99 when I was kick-boxing. The older developers have hundreds of millions of liquidity as a result of their developments. Our generation is going to have a harder time. Now we will really have to work first principles to survive.' He has tried to spread his risk, with developments in Poland, the Canaries, London, Madrid and Ibiza. 'In terms of GDV [Gross Development Value, or total sales value] I'm about half here and half abroad. On GDV, you're always aiming to make 10 to 20 per cent margins. Some would have been on 30 to 60 per cent of GDV. We have to be more realistic now. You have to work at it ...' So the big glitzy marketing push at Belmayne was not a bit over the top, then? 'To shift 330 units in this market will take two to two and a half years and you'd spend €2 million in advertising, marketing and show-off costs. That half-million euro hoarding is our main medium of advertising. The fact is that most people buy in their own area. If you're a northsider, you'll usually stay a northsider and 90 per cent of first-time buyers here actually live within a five-kilometre radius of us. So for two years, they won't be able to avoid seeing that hoarding in front of them.'

Meanwhile, Caulfield admits, he is sitting on several hundred million euro in loans and didn't see the slump coming. 'Development is not a business for the faint-hearted. When I bought the Belmayne site, I thought I'd sell to first-time buyers, that there would be inward investment and continuous growth and the east European immigrants would keep coming. We thought the €330,000 buyers would always be there because it's affordable. What we're looking at now is 10 to 12 per cent less in sale prices and a probable 30–35 per cent drop in projected profits. I would probably have paid less for the site if I'd foreseen this.'

In the information centre, the bizarre mélange of new and traditional is illustrated by one of his 'gorgeous girls' wall posters framed by curtains on either side. The purpose of the curtains becomes evident on alternative Sundays, when they are closed over the steamy poster and become the backdrop to a Mass altar, for the new Belmayne inhabitants.

While the first batch of apartments booked are closing now and helping to alleviate that massive debt, he anticipates a crunch in about 18 months' time, when the absence of first-time buyers in early to mid-2008 will expose the more vulnerable developers. 'That's when the banks will start looking for interest. So we *have* to keep selling and that means 80 per cent of our sales are to investors now.' So these are worrying times? 'It gets you out of bed in the morning. Definitely. It's not just about having a legacy to show your children,' he said, speaking at a time when his financée, Louise Doheny, was expecting their first child. 'It's your own pride.'

Caulfield is a classic developer, never content to pull off a spectacularly lucrative deal and become a lotus-eater. After an undistinguished start as an engineer, and a few years of kickboxing his way around the world, mainly making money by betting on himself, he went to work with Michael Cotter's Park Developments, where he managed the set-up of the industrial-commercial division. At 28, he was driving a Porsche – 'I was getting well paid' – and was buying and selling units for himself. He left Park because he didn't want to be an employee any more and went into business with Leo Meenagh, the owner of a construction company, LM Developments Ltd, on a 50–50 profit-share basis. Their first major project together was the development and construction of 900 units and a shopping centre in Cityside in north Finglas. At the height of the boom, the company employed up to 1,200 people. That first foray into development for Caulfield was achieved with the cooperation of a patient landowner, a silent partner who was prepared to wait four years for the development to materialize before he took his gains. 'So a million quid was all I needed to start. Once I had the contracts signed, and with my Cotter background, the banks gave us the go-ahead for finance. We were very lucky. We all made a good return on our money, up to 50 per cent cash return.'

Four years after leaving Park, he was able to buy a jet for the business. 'It's not so much about owning the jet. It's about having the money to give you the freedom to do what you want, to *say* what you want. The more money people have, the more free they are, if they have the right psyche. Having a jet means you're not queueing up for an hour in Dublin or London airports. Money is pure and utter freedom. If you want to wear shades inside, which I often do, I don't care what people say about me. My da, Joseph, used to say that money was freedom. But he had five kids, he was a great goer, a great small builder, but he couldn't risk it because he had five kids.'

In those hedonistic early days, Caulfield's taste for luxury was impressive. 'I'm happy to admit that when I first started seeing returns, I might have got carried away. I was into clothes, holidays, cars. I was a Versace fan, a shopaholic,' he said wryly. 'Every second weekend, I was in Marbella, Paris, Rome. I lived in the penthouse of the Conrad Hotel for eight months when I was refurbishing my home. I loved it.' Even with a parking place for his Aston Martin thrown in at the Conrad, accommodation alone must have run to a high five-figure bill every month.

'I've always been a car fanatic. I used to have seven or eight cars – Ferrais, Porsches, Lamborghinis. I still have the Ferrari, two Porsches, a Lamborghini and a Range Rover jeep. One of the biggest kicks I got was taking my sisters and girlfriend shopping. You'd get a buzz off that. When Louise and I were going out, we would have been away five weekends out of six. Now I've happily swapped the weekends away for walking the Weimaraner dogs in the park with Louise. I'm saturated with the travel and shopping, although I can say that I never went into the drink or drugs. I was too into health and fitness.

'I'm a country guy and I've managed to keep my friends from 15 to 20 years ago. I don't talk about money and that's why I don't spend a huge amount of time with other developers. I don't go to race meetings or balls – I think that whole scene is not real. What's real to me are my friends and family.' But surely all that spending and extravagance simply confirms suspicions that developers were making obscene profits on the backs of struggling homebuyers? 'They deserve every single euro they make – though the exception I'd make are the ones who were doing poor design, defacing the public landscape. That particular type of 10-year boom will never happen again because, for most of it, the rewards were in no way proportionate to the efforts or brilliance of many developers. You could be the worst builder/developer with no sense of design or landscaping yet everything they built, they sold. So many poor builders made so much money that they didn't deserve.

'But most of them are honourable, good, solid people. And the point is that if you put your balls on the table, you get the reward or you get the kick. It can go one way or the other. Guys are now feeling the squeeze and if it goes on, a lot of them are in trouble. I was lucky. If you'd asked me a year and a half ago, I'd have said the market would still be flying now.' Of course, he would not have been the only one. In the words of Warren Buffett, investors should 'be fearful when others are greedy and greedy when others are fearful'. The trouble was that those who were fearful – or urging caution – were apt to be accused of 'talking' the country into a recession.

In 2005, at the annual Society of Chartered Surveyors' dinner in the Burlington Hotel, 1,200 members and guests from central and local government assembled as usual for the biggest bash on the construction and property calendar. That year, the prestigious platform of keynote speaker was handed to Colm McCarthy, the mordant, straight-talking founder of DKM Economics Consultants, who now lectures in the dismal science at UCD. McCarthy cast something of a dampener on proceedings by predicting a slowdown in housing output from the extraordinary 2004 levels. This was not what his audience wanted to hear. So for 2006, the society brought in a more upbeat sort of chap for the keynote speech: the Ballsbridge Baron himself, Seán Dunne, always bullish beyond the call of duty and with a particularly pressing personal interest in keeping the market buoyant.

His speech to a record attendance of 1,400 took aim at the old reliables such as stamp duty and the universally loathed M50 toll bridge. It was only when he took a particularly aggressive swipe at stockbrokers and bank economists, likening them to 'laughing hyenas . . . harbingers of doom and gloom', that some of the several 'hyenas' present began to studiously examine the contents of their wine glasses. For the previous six years, Dunne asserted, 'every economist associated with every stockbroker in Ireland mistakenly forecast the end of the housing and property boom in Ireland'. They had been 'vociferous and repetitive', in the process encouraging outside commentators, including the *Economist*, the IMF and the OECD, to issue warnings about Irish house prices being overvalued. Well, 'The hyenas have stopped laughing . . . Each and every one of them was wrong. Instead, the price and supply of housing units has continued to break records.'

When the slowdown began, it was accompanied by faintly reassuring talk from vested interests and estate agents – some of whom were quietly laying off staff already – that the market was heading for a 'soft landing'. Economists had been noting for some time that the boom in Irish exports which had fuelled spectacular growth in the 1990s had been supplanted by a boom in construction. Between 2000 and 2006, house prices had doubled relative to income and rents, and some 15 per cent of our GNP (nearly a fifth, if sales of second-hand houses were included) was being generated from the construction of new houses and apartments – three times as much as in other developed countries. 'We have spent the last five years learning to believe that exports and competitiveness do not matter, and that we can get rich by selling houses to each other,' wrote Morgan Kelly, Professor of Economics at UCD, in the *Irish Times* in December 2006, when house prices were still skyrocketing. 'We are likely to spend a painful few years as we unlearn that lesson.'

In April 2007, a documentary called *Future Shock: Property Crash*, made by Animo Television for RTÉ, asked whether Ireland's property bubble was about to burst – and suggested, with a soundtrack of ominous music, that it was. 'We have allowed building construction to grow too rapidly and take up too big a share of the ecomony,' the Economic and Social Research Institute's Professor John FitzGerald (son of Garret and elder brother of Mark, chairman of estate agents Sherry FitzGerald) told the presenter, business journalist Richard Curran. 'We are out on a limb at this stage; getting down off it is going to be delicate without hurting ourselves.' The programme pointed out that the construction industry now accounted for 25 per cent of the economy, employing 280,000 people, 30 per cent of whom were foreign nationals staying in rented accommodation, and asked what would happen to that market as they drifted off to jobs elsewhere. What's more, multinational companies such as Pfizer were laying off staff because they could no longer compete, what with the US dollar weakening month by month against the euro. We were also building far more new homes – 20 units per 1,000 in population, compared to just 5 units per 1,000 in Britain – and the government had failed to implement most of the recommendations made by economist Peter Bacon in his four reports on how to deal with house price inflation. Not only that: by continually extending the deadlines for tax incentives such as Section 23, the government itself was fuelling an already overheated market.

Meanwhile, a global financial crisis was brewing. In the spring of 2007, we started hearing about jitters in the US over 'subprime' mortgages: loans given to people with low credit ratings who couldn't get money from the mainstream banks. Through the alchemy of 'securitization', these inherently risky loans were bundled together and sold on to investors, including some of the world's largest financial institutions. The make-up of the bundles was often so opaque that even the bankers themselves couldn't tell what they were really worth, especially in a falling market; the credit rating agencies often gave these products implausibly strong ratings. And who was required to bail out the banks when these phantoms came back to haunt them? Joe and Mary Public, of course.

According to the IMF, there had been a 'collective failure' to appreciate the scale of risky borrowing indulged in by the financial institutions. The cancer at the heart of the western world's financial system caused turmoil on the stock markets and accelerated the steep fall in the value of the US dollar, already weakened by the spectacular levels of government debt run up by George W. Bush's war in Iraq and huge tax cuts for the rich. It also triggered a sudden shortage in the credit available to banks, causing the Bank of England to bail out Northern Rock – which had unusually low cash reserves – and to make available tens of billions of pounds in 'emergency liquidity' to the banking sector. Similarly, Bear Stearns had to be bailed out by the US Federal Reserve. As banks concentrated on rebuilding their balance sheets by raising additional funds and limiting future lending, homebuyers were finding it more and more difficult to get loans. The once-plentiful supply of mortgage credit was drying up, with knock-on effects on the construction industry and the property sector in general.

House prices started falling in Ireland several months before the global credit crunch hit in autumn 2007; the end of the days of 110 per cent mortgages accentuated a trend that was already well established, and the writing was on the wall. In October 2007, Morgan Kelly argued in another *Irish Times* opinion piece that 'we can expect prices here to halve in real terms over the next few years'. He noted that 'Ten per cent of housing units in Irish cities are vacant, and almost none of the 70,000 or so new units built this year have been sold.' By that time, some of the developers had begun slashing prices, and there were urgent calls for the government to shore up the faltering market by, for example, cutting the rates of stamp duty on the acquisition of second-hand homes.

The following month, the big builders got their annual opportunity to speak to the Minister for Finance in the run-up to the Budget. During the boom years, this exclusive dinner, organized by Ken MacDonald, chairman and chief executive of estate agents Hooke and MacDonald, was used by the builders to bellyache to the minister about the tortuous nature of the planning process and what objections and refusals were costing the development community in lost time and money.

This time, with Joe Cosgrave playing host in the Radisson SAS (owned by himself and his two brothers), the customary spread was laid on for about 25 big builders and developers. Building sites were idle, new schemes stood empty, and some builders were growing a trifle mutinous about the incessantly negative publicity about the property market and the inactivity of the government. They wanted to hear some positive stuff about stamp duty cuts and other proactive ways of getting the market moving again. Plus, being flint-eyed businessmen, they knew they would be paying through the nose for dinner, although some may not have been aware of quite how much at that stage.

Brian Cowen, then Minister for Finance and guest of honour, was unavoidably detained elsewhere and turned up three hours late, by which time several of the builders had grown somewhat 'tired and emotional', as *Private Eye* would say, or 'langers', as one of those present reported. The question-and-answer session that followed was shambolic, the more unruly multimillionaires in attendance making long rambling speeches about the state of the market and what needed to be done by the minister, who even then was a safe bet to become Taoiseach. It hardly helped that Cowen was adamant that there would be no change in the stamp duty regime. Nonetheless, a few weeks later, although it went against the grain with the then minister and even more so with senior Department of Finance officials, for whom stamp duty had become a huge cash cow, the Budget did indeed provide a modicum of relief.

Was dinner worth it, then? One bemused guest who could recall paying 'only' €500 the year before, later found himself meekly responding to a subsequent demand for €5,000, payable to Fianna Fáil. A splendid result for the party, at least, since a quick calculation suggests that a few hours' discreet dalliance with the minister raked in an amount equal to half the take for the week-long PR fiasco that was the Galway Races tent. As for the builders, the bit of relief on stamp duty hardly began to address their difficulties.

Around the same time, in the *Irish Times* property supplement of 22 November, a front-page story suggested that over 10,000 new apartments in Dublin were empty, because they had either failed to sell or hadn't been put on the market. 'In some cases developers are holding off launching entire schemes until conditions improve rather than risk a failed sales launch. Others are opting to retain the stock themselves and rent them out,' Fiona Tyrell reported. 'Construction in Dublin has come to a veritable standstill as builders respond to the changed environment. The larger developers can afford to hold the line and wait for pent-up demand rather than panic and cut prices.' It came as a bolt from the blue to read such grim news in the property market's leading organ, especially as the *Irish Times* has a vested interest in the sale of houses and apartments through its ownership of the website myhome.ie.

There were more wigs on the green in January 2008 when the Irish Auctioneers and Valuers Institute (IAVI) published a survey claiming that 40,000 apartments in Dublin were vacant, that prices had fallen by 10 per cent on average and that the value of second-hand apartments had taken the biggest hit (down 17 per cent in 2007). While forecasting a less steep fall in 2008, the institute said the market had 'some way to correct before activity is restored and prices are stabilised'. The survey provoked outrage among heavy hitters in the business, forcing the IAVI to withdraw the '40,000 empty flats' figure, saying it was a mistake. Coincidentally, the institute had protested to the Broadcasting Complaints Commission, claiming that *Future Shock: Property Crash* was not impartial and had had a detrimental effect on the property market. The complaint was not upheld.

In the same month, Ken MacDonald called a meeting of new homes agents in the St Stephen's Green Club to discuss strategy for the year ahead, suggesting that they hit back at the media by buying less advertising. However, rival agent Savills HOK took the opposite tack and forged ahead, widely advertising a swathe of new homes schemes with big price cuts; MacDonald's line on this was that, since HOK was being driven from Savills in London, the Brits were now dictating the underpricing of Irish property. And when Capel Developments decided to drop prices by €100,000 for their scheme in Ashtown, Ballymore's Seán Mulryan offered to buy up all of the apartments to stop them advertising the discount, since he had plenty to sell next door.

Denis Finn Buildings Ltd was one of the firms that got into serious difficulties around this time. A quantity surveyor by profession, Finn was one of myriad small builder/developers who prospered in the boom. His modus operandi was to buy desirable sites in Howth and develop small clusters of €1 million-plus houses. In 25 years, Denis Finn Buildings had worked its way up to an annual turnover of €9 million, with 32 direct and 100 indirect employees. The banks funded the sites and Finn pushed through the planning permissions – 'always the hardest part', he told the *Sunday Independent* in June 2008. But at the beginning of 2008, cash flow problems began to bite. Alleged bad debts of over €1 million had gone to litigation and there were no buyers for the houses; property values had dropped by 30–40 per cent at the 'high end' of the market, said Finn.

The company took advice from Deloitte and, in February 2008, called meetings with its six bankers. They agreed to roll over his interest payments until October, when Finn hoped to have recouped some cash to complete a number of developments. But on 22 May, ACC appointed a receiver to two sites, swiftly followed by NIB. By then, his firms owned more than €20 million, although he still had €25 million worth of property on his website, he said. It was a classic squeeze. His major concern was that the bankers would 'unload houses at a "give-away" price just to get some cash for themselves' instead of waiting for a recovery in the market. Further on in the same edition of the *Sunday Independent* that told Finn's story, a small ad summed up the plight of an anonymous builder/developer: 'Bargain of the year – seven houses near completion, County Leitrim. Being sold in one lot. Price €1,050,000, no offers.'

By then, as a consequence of the prevalence of high loan-to-value mortgages and dropping prices, negative equity had arrived in Ireland, just as it had in London after the end of the Thatcher boom; the number of High Court applications for repossession by lending agencies had gone up by nearly 50 per cent to 465 in 2007, while the number of repossession orders more than doubled in the first six months of 2008 compared with the equivalent period in 2007, and the likelihood is that this trend will intensify over time. Employment in the construction industry fell by 10.3 per cent in the 12 months to January 2008 and has been falling precipitately since, sparking a return to the old pattern of net emigration. Bertie Ahern, who had railed against 'prophets of doom' just three months earlier, saying he remained 'absolutely confident that there are good times ahead for the economy', had to concede that Ireland was facing a 'hard year' and wouldn't escape the effects of a looming recession in the US. Neither would there be any 'bounce-back' in the residential property market, at least in the short term. The 'rule of thumb', as he put it, was that every 10,000 new homes not built would knock 1 per cent off economic growth: an astonishingly strong correlation between activity in one sector and the health of the overall economy. (By 2006, housebuilding accounted for fully 13 per cent of Irish GNP – up from 6 per cent in 1998.)

As things got worse, the estate agents for whom champagne grapes had been the only fruit for over a decade were becoming desperate. In the property department of the *Irish Times*, there was growing unease about skewed house price results being supplied by various auctioneers. Property Editor Orna Mulcahy became aware of it when readers' letters started to arrive, accusing the paper of hyping up the market. 'While we weren't getting these every day,' she said, 'there were enough of them between last autumn [2007] and this spring to be uneasy.' Agents clearly believed it was acceptable to add €10,000 or €20,000 – or in one case, €2 million – to a price, using the word 'around' to justify it. When challenged by the owners themselves – as the *Irish Times* subsequently discovered – they would blame the paper, saying the incorrect figure was a 'typo'. Remarkably, these 'around' figures or 'typos' never seemed to err on the low side.

On 31 March, Mulcahy circulated a letter to scores of agents, not intended for general consumption. 'The implication is that the *Irish Times* is colluding with agents to give a false impression of the market. This is obviously damaging to both of us . . . Should agents be unwilling to supply accurate information, or indeed should vendors be reluctant to disclose the true selling price, then we would prefer not to carry the result at all.' The IAVI argued that the latter course would make the property market less transparent as, under data protection legislation, the publication of actual sale prices rather than rough estimates would need the consent of sellers and buyers. But Ann Fitzgerald, chief executive of the National Consumer Agency, accused estate agents of using data protection legislation to fudge the issue. 'The Data Protection Act is not new, and under it both parties have to agree to the prices being published,' she said. 'Either that has been happening or it hasn't, and if it has not been happening to date then estate agents have been in breach of that legislation for years.'

Of course, what lay at the root of it was pride, and not only on the agents' part. During the boom, vendors confidently – indeed, proudly – put a house to auction, and the price achieved was a matter of public record. They quaffed the bubbly, dined in Guilbaud's, bought a new SUV, and possibly a racehorse, confident that their scoop had added to the legend of the boom. Now, instead of ridiculously inflated auction guide prices, estate agents talked of 'asking prices' and discreet private treaties. And the eventual price might be a good bit lower than the asking price, achieved after weeks, or months, of wrangling and sometimes 'gazundering' (where a buyer offers a certain price to begin with, and then comes back with a lower offer prior to signing).

Come May, the numbers signing on the Live Register broke the 200,000 barrier for the first time since July 1999, showing an increase of 35,700 – on a seasonally adjusted basis – or 20.8 per cent since the start of the year, according to the CSO. Of those, 25,600 were men and 10,100 were women, reflecting the concentration of job losses in the construction sector. Later, the increasing numbers of women signing on suggested that the slowdown was spreading from construction into other sectors of the economy – or perhaps, as Damien Kiberd noted in the *Sunday Times* in June, it was the hitherto unheralded numbers of women in the industry, the 'thousands of women who are involved in legal conveyancing work, in processing mortgage applications for banks, in showing off houses at weekends, in surveying, in architecture and in valuing homes. It seems logical that some of these people will also lose their jobs as the building sector contracts from the high of 90,000 homes completed in 2006 to the 25,000 completions expected in 2009.'

A near-€1.2 billion shortfall in government tax receipts was announced for the five months to May. The clearest indication of the house sales slump was the stamp duty take on housing transactions: provisional figures from the Department of Finance showed they had fallen to €44.13 million in March, well under half the take in March 2006 and 2007. Registrations (an indication of the number of house starts) were down by 60 per cent, according to the Construction Industry Federation. Figures compiled by the accountancy firm Farrell Grant Sparks suggested that 53 construction and engineering companies had failed in the first three months of the year: this was by far the highest number of corporate failures in any sector and more than double the number for the same period in 2007. Ominously, the IMF singled out Ireland as one of the most vulnerable economies in Europe, in part because the economy was overly dependent on the building industry.

In June, the state employment agency, FÁS, hosted an international jobs fair for the construction sector. This time, it was foreign recruitment companies – from Poland, Britain and Slovakia – pitching for unemployed workers in Ireland, the primary purpose being to attract their own nationals back home. But a steady stream of Irish workers was included in the 500 who turned up in the first hour alone. And then, on 24 June, the nation woke to the news it had started to fear. 'We blew the boom: now it's recession,' read the *Irish Independent* headline, quoting an Economic and Social Research Institute report warning that Ireland was entering its first recession in 25 years. The review predicted that emigration would reach 20,000 in 2009, a level not seen since 1990, and that unemployment would increase by 60,000, or 60 per cent, between 2007 and 2009. 'The main culprit,' wrote Economics Editor Brendan Keenan, 'is still the collapse in house construction, which has plunged from 75,000 units last year to just 30,000 this year. This fall is so serious, it wipes out all the growth in the rest of the economy.' Consumption growth was predicted to slow to 1 per cent in 2008 – from 3 per cent only three months before – and recover to only 2 per cent in 2009. 'With personal consumption making up two-thirds of the economy,' said Keenan, 'and house-building having contributed more than a tenth, the effect of both is a fall in tax revenues and an "explosion" in government deficits.'

Also in June, the day after the country's newly appointed Minister for Finance Brian Lenihan noted at a European construction conference in Dublin Castle that he had had the misfortune to take up his position just as the building boom in

Ireland was coming 'to a shuddering end', the *Sunday Independent* ran a feature under the headline 'Construction Teeters on Brink of Disaster'. It said: 'Several of the country's leading banks said this weekend that they are now in daily contact with a number of their big clients, with many builders struggling to even pay the interest on their multimillion euro loans. The article also quoted one leading property developer as saying: 'If the banks came out and told the truth about what the situation is really like, there would be big trouble. It's the very, very big builders. Go to the very top guys and they're so borrowed that the banks can't do anything with them. There's three or four big ones who are so borrowed that there's just no way they could survive and the banks could go with them.' It was believed that the banks were taking equity stakes of up to 20 per cent on sites in order to protect their loans. Perhaps they had learned from the 1980s when they disdained the land banks offered by developers as debt collateral. As one experienced Irish company director ruefully observed, 'It's typical of the banks that they'd hold out an umbrella for you on a fine day, but when there's rain it's gone.'

Meanwhile, the relentless sell-off in Irish bank shares continued. In early July, the country's four leading banks saw a massive €1.8 billion wiped off their value in a single day. Since the peak in spring 2007, the Bank of Ireland had lost 75 per cent of its share value, Anglo Irish 72 per cent, AIB 66 per cent, and Irish Life and Permanent 80 per cent. (Even Seán Quinn suffered, taking a big paper loss when 'unwinding' his CFD positions in Anglo Irish and taking a 15 per cent stake in the bank.) For the bankers, in particular Anglo Irish – seen as the developers' main bank – these were delicate times, resounding with the distinctive cackle of chickens coming home to roost. As the *Sunday Tribune*'s Jon Ihle noted in June: 'Anglo's entire loan book is ultimately secured against property. And right now that means the value of its collateral is dropping all the time as the fizz continues to leak out of the property bubble. The bank's executives protest that it isn't property value *per se* that pays its loans back, but rather the rental income the property generates. This is true. However, a key feature of this recession is a decline in consumer sentiment, which means the retail tenants on whom Anglo depends are going to suffer. Some will surely fall. We've already seen Habitat, that exemplar of Celtic Tiger consumption, disappear from the retail landscape. It won't be the last.'

The bankers' travails were deepened by the continuing soap opera around solicitor and poster boy for the property boom, Michael Lynn, who had gone missing along with any proposals to repay an estimated €80 million in mortgages. Humiliatingly, at least 11 Irish banks and building societies had to confess that they had advanced multimillion-euro loans on what transpired to be double and triple undertakings from Lynn. A prime example was Lynn's own home in Howth. Although it cost him €5.5 million, he had convinced three lenders to advance loans totalling €11.7 million. As institutions armed with over 130 writs queued for a court hearing to secure what remained of their piece of the pie, the president of the High Court, Mr Justice Richard Johnson, piled on the agony by demanding details of bonuses paid to bank and building society officials who had approved the loans to Lynn. His curiosity, he said, was 'increasing day by day'. As David McWilliams remarked in the *Sunday Business Post* at the end of June: 'It is now dawning on the young stars of Dublin's banking community that there is more to finance than Ron Black's, a Prada suit, extra-firm hair gel and an Audi TT.'

Paul Tansey, Economics Editor of the *Irish Times*, got to the kernel of the crisis when he observed that 'the speed and scale of the decline in construction output is at the epicentre of the Irish recession'. Irish financial institutions had lent at least €106 billion to builders and developers, and this figure represented over half of all loans to businesses. At the end of June, the *Irish Mail on Sunday*, citing unpublished Companies Registration Office figures, reported that 134 construction companies had gone bust since January 2007, an increase of 46 per cent on the previous 18 months, with probable debts of €600 million. Kevin O'Brien, managing director of Construction Guarantee, which provided bond cover for €1 billion worth of building projects in 2007, reckoned that the €600 million figure was probably an underestimate.

An additional 19,000 people signed on the Live Register in June, prompting economists to suggest that the government's forecast of 210,000 unemployment benefit claimants at the end of the year might be conservative. And there were predictions of worse to come. Job losses in the construction industry were expected to add another 10,000 to the register in late August when the traditional builders' holiday ended, warned Tom Parlon, director-general of the Construction Industry Federation.

With pressure mounting from all sides, and rumours swirling that two mid-sized property developers were in danger of going to the wall, the sense was of an industry dying by a thousand cuts. The only way to begin the 'cleansing' of the property market would be for the banks 'to bite the bullet now and put the assets of one of its bankrupt property oligarchs on the market', wrote David McWilliams at the end of June. 'Yes, there would be huge falls in the price of sites, but that's the only way the market will clear – a child could understand this. Some of our senior bankers fail to grasp this idea, but maybe that's one of the problems with 10 years of cowboy capitalism; with all these nudges and winks, you forget how a real market works.'

In July, it was revealed that Ireland's commercial property market had suffered its worst performance for 35 years in the second quarter of 2008. According to Jones Lang Lasalle, which monitors its movement closely, returns from retail and office investments plummeted by 7.4 per cent, following a 2.5 per cent fall in the first quarter. Among once-cocky investors, the worst hit were syndicates that had sunk their money into office blocks or retail units at the height of the boom. An even more significant casualty was the government's National Pensions Reserve Fund, from which public service and social welfare pensions are due to be paid from 2025 onwards; it lost 12 per cent of its value in the first six months of 2008 as a result of continuing turmoil in the markets.

Was it possible to see this coming? John Gallagher would say yes. Gallagher, the husband of P. V. Doyle's daughter Bernie, oversaw the series of transactions whereby the Doyle family and the family of former Jurys Doyle chairman Walter Beatty took the group private in 2005, sold off its most valuable assets (notably in Ballsbridge) at what turned out to be the peak of the market and then sold the Jurys Inn chain to Quinlan Private in July 2007 – at a net profit just shy of €1 billion. Within weeks of the Jurys Inn sale, Gallagher offered a fat, public vote of no confidence in the Irish property sector. 'People don't understand that if you've got £1 million in a £10 million property and it drops by 10 per cent, your million is gone. The thing might be worth £9 million but yours is gone,' he told Arthur Beesley of the *Irish Times*. Asked about the prospects of a hard landing, Gallagher said: 'I think the reality is that sensible people ... will wait for froth to come out of this market.' And he made it clear that he would not be investing in Irish property because 'there is certainly no upside that I can see [in the market]. I cannot see the upside.'

To see a player of his magnitude gathering up the cash, then kicking the door behind him, should have been a major wake-up call for those left behind – but it wasn't. By the summer of 2008, 'interest roll-ups', a kind of benefit scheme for distressed developers, had been put in place by the banks. When developers run into cash-flow problems, the banks just let the interest payments ride indefinitely. As the *Sunday Tribune* put it in August: if your borrowings were big enough to sink your lender should you default, then you just might qualify for the programme.

'A whole sector of the economy is stuck,' wrote Cliff Taylor, editor of the *Sunday Business Post*, in August. 'It remains to be seen whether any financier – from Ireland or overseas – will move on a property developer in the months ahead; this is now the key topic of discussion in financial circles. If a fraction of the rumours around town are correct, then some significant developer liquidations are in prospect.' In the meantime, as one estate agent murmured, 'a lot of helicopters are going back'.

Acknowledgements

This book grew out of a series of articles in the *Irish Times* in October 2007 commissioned by the Editor, Geraldine Kennedy. We are indebted to her for the original idea and also for giving us time off to write the book.

We would also like to thank several colleagues from the paper who assisted us, including Property Editor Orna Mulcahy, Commercial Property Editor Jack Fagan, Deputy Property Editor Frances O'Rourke, News Editor Kevin O'Sullivan, Picture Editor Peter Thursfield, his deputies Frank Miller and Dave Sleator, Derek Scally in Berlin, and Esther Murnane and Irene Stevenson from the *Irish Times* Library. Also Brendan Barrington, our assiduous editor at Penguin Ireland.

There are many, many people in the property development and building sectors, including employees of major companies, whom we would dearly wish to acknowledge for the invaluable insights they so willingly provided, but none of them would thank us for mentioning their names. They know who they are, and all we can say is that we are deeply grateful to them.

Frank would particularly like to thank John Naughton for the opportunity of spending a term at Wolfson College, Cambridge, as a British Petroleum Press Fellow; Hilary Pennington, who administered the fellowship programme; Bill Kirkwood and Richard Synge from Wolfson; and all his friends in Cambridge, including Paul Brown, Claudia Fritz, Helena Lenihan, Anne Murray, Adam Peavoy, Steve and Dale Russell, Gagan Sood, Peter Wood, and especially Joe Smith, Renata and the boys for their marvellous hospitality in Bateman Street. He would also like to thank his parents, William and Maura McDonald, sister Edel and brothers Liam and Denis for their understanding of his long absences from family duties, as well as Eamon Slater, Brian Yore,

Paul Moley, Stephen O'Farrell, John Beattie, Eugene Downes, Graham Egan, Annie McCartney, Irial O'Sullivan, Javier Saez and David Watchorn for helping to keep him relatively sane.

Pep rallies around various dining tables were the secret of survival for Kathy, in particular those conducted by her sisters, Bridget Reilly and Mary T. Robinson, and her great friend Patsey Murphy. Her husband, Pat Geraghty, and daughters Sarah and Mary-Kate, had an eventful year of their own but, as always, were living proof that a home is not just another commodity.

Index